THE SINGING OF THE REAL WORLD

THE PHILOSOPHY OF VIRGINIA WOOLF'S FICTION

MARK HUSSEY

"To read *The Singing of the Real World* is to discover Virginia Woolf all over again. This is a long-needed study, the first to examine Woolf's writing in a fresh, philosophical context. It casts illumination on her entire work. Mark Hussey has caught the underlying philosophical pattern and deepened the understanding of her fiction. He shows how Woolf probes the deep questions of identity, life, and reality with fresh insights and discoveries. This is a splendid book. No future study of Woolf's work, no serious reader, can afford to neglect *The Singing of the Real World*." —HARVENA RICHTER, University of New Mexico

In a late memoir, Virginia Woolf wrote of the "philosophy" she felt had always stood behind her art. Mark Hussey explores that philosophy and makes it more accessible by examining the perennial themes of Woolf's fiction in the light of her own ideas on how we should read her work.

A central theme of Dr. Hussey's study is Woolf's idea of reality. Hussey shows that reality was something ineffable that Woolf felt was a pattern behind the randomness of everyday life. Woolf found that, when thinking, reality always doubles back on itself as the limits of language are reached. Perennial themes and events echo back and forth throughout her novels.

Mark Hussey provides a fresh look at the insights Woolf offers into the nature of human existence. He combines the insights of psychoanalysis, philosophy, and new feminist critical thought to produce a reading of Woolf that has implications beyond the field of fiction.

Mark Hussey is adjunct instructor of English at Pace University.

THE SINGING
OF THE REAL WORLD

If I could catch the feeling,
I would: the feeling of the
singing of the real world, as
one is driven by loneliness
and silence from the
habitable world.

—VIRGINIA WOOLF, *DIARY*

THE SINGING
OF THE REAL WORLD

THE PHILOSOPHY OF VIRGINIA WOOLF'S FICTION

MARK HUSSEY

OHIO STATE UNIVERSITY PRESS
Columbus

Copyright © 1986 by the Ohio State University Press

All Rights Reserved.

Library of Congress Cataloguing in Publication Data

Hussey, Mark, 1956–
    The singing of the real world.

    Bibliography: p.
    Includes index.
    1. Woolf, Virginia, 1882–1941—Criticism and interpretation.
2. Woolf, Virginia, 1882–1941—Philosophy.
I. Title.
PR6045.072Z728   1986   823'.912   86-12763
ISBN 0-8142-0414-7

To my mother and father

CONTENTS

ACKNOWLEDGMENTS

I WOULD LIKE TO THANK ROGER POOLE FOR HIS GUIDANCE IN THE EARLY stages of writing this book. My warm thanks also to Louise A. De Salvo for her continuing help and encouragement.

I would like to thank Mitchell A. Leaska for encouragement at a crucial stage.

The library staff at Pace University, New York, have helped as I made various revisions; my thanks especially to the ever-patient Kathy Clancy and Michelle Fanelli.

The following have helped in various ways, large and small, all indispensable: Margot Backas, Jeremy Barr, Jane Camp, Jane Holder, Ben Keane, Jan Kingdom, Evelyn Leong, Richard Lord, Pamela Musselman, Gerry Reedy, Anne, Alexandra, and Mary Truitt.

INTRODUCTION

ON READING THE MANUSCRIPT OF *JACOB'S ROOM*, VIRGINIA WOOLF'S
husband, Leonard, remarked that she had "no philosophy of life"
(*D*, 27 July 1922).[1] Certainly Woolf did not share Leonard's conviction of the "fresh air and pure light of plain common-sense"
he found in the ethics of G. E. Moore.[2] Furthermore, she found
no philosophical system from which she could derive satisfactory answers to the existential questions with which she was
constantly engaged. Some critics have traced a philosophy in
Woolf's writings to sources in, for example, Bergson, Moore, and
even McTaggart.[3] It is not my concern here to trace any such (real
or imagined) debts but rather to explore the deep concerns of
Woolf's art, which is implicitly philosophical. I would concur
with Harvena Richter that "one does not draw a particular philosophy or discipline from her work. One can only conclude that
her examination of her own encounter with lived experience
was transmuted into the novel's form: modes of life became
modes of fiction."[4]

What follows arose in part from a dissatisfaction with the
general trend of works on Woolf to devote a chapter to each of
her novels, from beginning to end. These books, though frequently offering useful insights, seem to me often to work
against the grain of Woolf's own procedures and aims, imposing
a linear development on her art that the novels themselves do
not support. A novel-by-novel approach invites "definitive" readings and a need for closure that leads to adapting the territory to
fit a particular map.

My starting point was to look at the persistent themes of
Woolf's fiction, taking account of the commentary on the act of
reading that can be gleaned from both her novels and her essays.
From such an approach it became apparent that the concerns of
Woolf's art remained constant throughout her life. Although her
angle of vision undoubtedly changed, the objects of that vision

remained the same. The constant echoing back and forth of perennial themes and events throughout the novels, and the many descriptive homologies (to which I frequently draw attention) lend credence to a view of Woolf's art as dynamic, in constant flux, rather than linear. She herself, as I will show, was explicit about the "circularity" of her own methods; indeed, the image of circle and circumference appears in myriad forms in everything she wrote.

The "philosophy" with which I am concerned is intended solely in the specific sense in which Woolf herself used the word in her late memoir, "A Sketch of the Past" (1939/40). There (MOB, 72) she wrote of her "philosophy" or "constant idea" as a conceptual rod that she felt stood always behind her art. It is the philosophy of her fiction in this restricted sense of what she felt was the background to her art that I wish to elucidate.

There are many contexts for inquiry, each of which privileges a particular set of concerns: such concerns might include the transactions between a writer and her times (the historical); the inscription of gender and the struggle of the body (the feminist); narrative technique and style (the literary); characterization and relationships (the psychoanalytic). Though all of these categories draw on all the others to a certain extent, and all certainly provide valuable readings of a writer's oeuvre, each must begin from a position outside the texts; each must seek, if only initially, to be objective.

The context of this study is in one sense extremely limited, yet I feel it might also be universal: the subjectivity of Virginia Woolf as embodied in her *writing* is the framework within which I have constructed an account of her worldview. The space dealt with here is essentially "inner space" in the sense that I have not taken the logical next step of formulating concepts and theories from what I see as offered in Woolf's art.

Simone de Beauvoir speaks of woman's need for ontological optimism. Recently, much women's writing has been concerned with the "wild zone," the "lacuna" (it is variously named) from which, some women feel, female experience and its expression must arise. There is a tension in Woolf's art, confirmed by her autobiographical writings, between the need for optimism and the real presence of absence, of nothingness. The "form of the sentence" that solicits her to fill it with meaning is charged with exhilaration and terror because in writing she simultaneously denies and affirms the emptiness at the heart of life.

It seems eloquent that as Woolf's status in the mind of the reading public undergoes revaluation much of the most innovative and challenging work is presented as collections of essays: Woolf seems to resist the summary and conclusiveness demanded of a book-length study. Those who have written books on Woolf have dealt with this by writing a chapter on each of her novels (in effect, nine essays). There are, of course, some very valuable readings obtained in this way, and some others have successfully written on Woolf without using this format.

Virginia Woolf's art tells us not about an external, objective Reality, but about our *experience* of the world. One of the most salient points she has to make is that the experience of being in the world is different for everyone and is endless, a process of constant creativity. "Every moment," she wrote in "The Narrow Bridge of Art," "is the center and meeting-place of an extraordinary number of perceptions which have not yet been expressed. Life is always and inevitably much richer than we who try to express it" (*GR*, 23). In her fiction Woolf seems always to be resisting definition and closure. It would, therefore, seem absurd to attempt to stand apart from her work and sum it up; to say it is, finally, *this* or *that.*

The "work" here refers to both her fiction and other writings—her diary, essays, autobiographical fragments, even (sometimes) her letters. More, perhaps, than any other person in literary history, Woolf *wrote* her life. Her day was a schedule of different writings: handwritten composing in the morning, typing up the draft in the afternoon, diary after tea, and perhaps some letters in the evening. Such a routine speaks of a certain socioeconomic circumstance, but the fact remains: writing *was* her life. Roger Poole has described Woolf's output—the novels and diary, specifically—as "an enormous, complex structure" that is a reservoir of "vast and complex subjectivity."[5] Apart from isolated insights such as this, it seems to me that the actual import of

Woolf's art is only just now beginning to be acknowledged and explored.

This study of her work hopes to light up a new field of inquiry: the philosophical implications of Woolf's art, and thus the implications for our lived experience of the world. The goal is not *conclusions*, but more searching *questions* than have yet been asked of that art. The form of the circle, then, might be said to organize this inquiry, as I hope to show it influenced Woolf's thinking. To be left with questions rather than answers seems to me indicative of a new and needed honesty, which might have appealed to the "restless searcher" in Woolf.

In an essay on "Montaigne" (1924), Woolf wrote of the "soul" that no one knows "how she works or what she is except that of all things she is the most mysterious, and one's self the greatest monster and miracle in the world" (*CRI*, 96). In the dominant tradition of Western thought, the *self* has constantly been the primary object of inquiry. Descartes, Locke, and Hume represent a tradition which held that human nature is, in Hume's words, the "capital or center" of knowledge. This tradition— which is predominantly Cartesian—is marked, up to Freud, by an objectivity that leads the honest philosopher into inescapable dilemmas. We thus find Descartes, in his *Meditations*, caught out by his intuition of the relationship between body and mind, which he cannot explain. Hume must eventually dismiss questions of personal identity from philosophy, saying that they are "grammatical" difficulties. In Freud's psychoanalysis his natural scientific bias leads to what Ludwig Binswanger termed "a one-sided, i.e. irreversible, relationship between doctor and patient, and an even more impersonal relationship between researcher and object of research."[6]

In contrast to this tradition stands the modern phenomenological movement, which sees human life as "being-in-the-world" (*Dasein*, in Heidegger's term). Phenomenology rejects the mechanistic/scientific conceptions of human being that have dominated (and to a large extent still do) philosophy and psychology. It is a mode of thought that sets out to recover our basic *experience* of the world. A leading exponent of phenomenology, M. Merleau-Ponty, articulates this in the Preface to *Phenomenology of Perception*:

> I am not the outcome or the meeting point of numerous causal agencies which determine my bodily or psychological make-up. I cannot conceive myself as nothing but a bit of the world, a mere object of biological, psychological or sociological investigation. I cannot shut myself up within the realm of science. All my knowledge of the world, even my scientific knowledge, is gained from my own particular point of view, or from some experience of the world without which the symbols of science would be meaningless. (P. viii)

Practical application of phenomenological theory can be seen in the existential psychoanalysis of, for example, Binswanger and R. D. Laing. There, the divisions and subdivisions of the dominant tradition (psyche and soma, mind and body, personality, self) are resolved into the idea of human life as being-in-the-world: an embodied self, in *relation* to others. As before, the question of the nature of self is primary, the center of all subsequent inquiry. Merleau-Ponty finds in the ambiguous self—as he believes Montaigne did—"the place of all obscurities, the mystery of mysteries, and something like an ultimate truth."[7]

Virginia Woolf's novels are concerned with knowledge: knowledge of others, and knowledge of the world. The question of the nature of self is at the heart of her thinking, and, I believe, is the dynamic of her fiction. Her novels uncover what Georges Poulet has called "the essentially religious nature of human centrality."[8] Beginning with Woolf's ideas of self and identity, we are led eventually to realize that her concept of the essential nature of human being was religious *in character.* Although an ardent atheist, Woolf gradually came to hold what can best be described as a faith, the essential element of which was belief in a "soul." Her point of departure is always a simple, but radical wonder in the face of being at all (what Heidegger called *Thaumazein*[9]). This is a style of thought that places her in the company of such thinkers as Pascal, Kierkegaard, and Heidegger, tempered though it is by an English dryness.[10]

The question of the nature of self seems always to underlie Woolf's thinking; however, it is rarely explicit. In the course of what follows, it will emerge that the problems of defining the self are, as Hume said, "grammatical": questioning the nature of self reveals a fundamental inadequacy in language. As a writer, Woolf was profoundly concerned with the scope of language and its ability to reflect human experience accurately, especially as her fictions explore what she quickly decided is beyond words—the self.

Fundamental to Woolf's thinking and art is a conflict between faith and despair: faith in the potential of human being to deny essential nothingness, and despair at the inadequacy of all human effort in the face of that nothingness. This conflict she felt was particularly acute for the artist, whose effort she sees as a continuous reaching after a certainty the artist knows better than anyone is an illusion. Throughout her writing, Woolf moves between the poles of faith and despair, sometimes extolling the power of art to overcome transience, at others denigrating its poverty. This tension between faith and despair is not explicitly linked to the question of the nature of self, but it should be understood that that question is the source of the tension.

The relationship between life and art is an important and constant concern of Woolf's that once more bears on the question of the nature of self. The tension in her work between faith in an autonomous self (or soul) that gives meaning to the world, and despair at the possibility that there is no such self anticipates an argument that is focused on in current critical thought (the roots of which, however, are found even well before Woolf's time). This argument is characterized by opposing views of the authenticity of literary art as an embodiment of "presence," and can be demonstrated by the juxtaposition of two representative passages:

> Lacan speaks of the ego as fictive. . . . What our analysis of Proust adds to this is a description of various forms of "art" as exemplary fictions which the (imaginary) self tells itself in order to defend its (illusory) sense of autonomy.[11]

> That object wholly object, that thing made of paper, as there are things made of metal or porcelain, that object is no more, or at least it is as if it no longer existed, as long as I read the book. For the book is no longer a material reality. It has become a series of words, of images, of ideas which in their turn begin to exist. And where is this new existence? Surely not in the

paper object. Nor, surely, in external space. There is only one place left for this new existence: my innermost self.[12]

In presenting this reading of Woolf I have generally confined myself to the terms of Woolf's own writing, drawing attention to the many points of contact between her fiction and autobiographical writings. I have tried as far as possible to read Woolf according to her own way of reading (which I will outline below). Where I have used theorists to expand and explain Woolf it should be understood that I have done so primarily for heuristic purposes only; because I find Georges Poulet, for example, illuminating should not require a complete devotion to the Geneva school of critical thought. Recent literary theory seems, as Wolfgang Iser remarks, to be "concerned primarily with approaches to literature and not with literature itself."[13] This study does not, therefore, follow dogmatically a particular, exclusive approach. It is hoped that whatever looseness is consequent on an eclectic rather than strictly selective method will be compensated for by the effort to read the works as they themselves suggest they should be read.

Throughout essays, diary, and letters, as well as in her novels, Woolf gives her version of the act of reading. She consistently emphasizes the importance of memory through repetition, and of suspending judgments and conclusions. It seems that the state to which a reader should aspire is one in which he or she could *write* the book. In "How Should One Read a Book?" (1926), she wrote:

> Wait for the dust of reading to settle, for the conflict and the questioning to die down; walk, talk, pull the dead petals from a rose, or fall asleep. Then suddenly without our willing it, for it is thus that Nature undertakes these transitions, the book will return, but differently. It will float to the top of the mind as a whole. And the book as a whole is different from the book received currently in separate phrases. (*CR*II, 266-67)

The actual process of reading, then, is linear; however, in the mind of the reader the book can assume a new shape that may overcome the linearity of language. The book "as a whole" can exist only virtually, an incommunicable synthesis of the reading mind and the text. Throughout her oeuvre Woolf stresses the *experience* of reading and the necessity of reading creatively. To read Woolf, it seems we should read from the inside out, recreating fictional experience. Richter notes this:

> Abstraction, reflection, metamorphosis, discontinuity—these and other modes are the means by which Mrs. Woolf brings the reader into the very center of the work. They are not artificial techniques, imposed from without, but the actual processes which, when rendered through the medium of language, tend to make the act of reading approximate the experience itself. (P. x)

Woolf appears to be an early reader-response critic, an amalgam, perhaps, of Wolfgang Iser and Georges Poulet!

> For both Iser and Poulet, the literary work is actualized only through a convergence of reader and text, but whereas for Poulet this means allowing one's consciousness to be invaded by the consciousness of another, to Iser it means that the reader must act as co-creator of the work by supplying that portion of it which is not written but only implied.[14]

Woolf asked for an alliance between reader and writer (e.g., in "Mr. Bennett and Mrs. Brown") for she felt that the truth of fiction was so many-sided that only a continuous permutation of perspectives could comprehend it. She stressed that words live in the mind, and so cannot be trusted to refer in isolation to just one thing: "It is the nature of words to mean many things. . . . one sentence of the simplest kind rouses the imagination, the memory, the eye and the ear—all combine in reading it" ("Craftsmanship," *DM*, 201-2). All these faculties must be brought into play in the "difficult and complex art" of reading: "You must be capable not only of great fineness of perception, but of great boldness of imagination if you are going to make use of all that the novelist—the great artist—gives you" ("How Should One Read a Book?" *CR*II, 260-61).

The thread of this commentary on the act of reading is that it is by circling backwards and forwards that the suggestive power of language can be realized, as opposed to the constricted image a linear progression produces. Taking as my sanction Woolf's statement in "Modern Fiction" that "any method is right, every method is right, that expresses what we wish to express, if we are writers; that brings us closer to the novelist's intention if we are readers" (*CR*I, 192), I have tried as far as possible to adopt an approach to reading she suggested in an essay of 1926 on De Quincey:

> Then it is not the actual sight or sound itself that matters, but the reverberations that it makes as it travels through our minds. These are often to be found far away, strangely transformed; but it is only by gathering up and putting together these echoes and fragments that we arrive at the true nature of our experience. ("Impassioned Prose," *GR*, 40)

This approach will allow, as Woolf suggested, "the sunken meanings to remain sunken, suggested, not stated" ("Craftsmanship," *DM*, 202). Apart from their usual function of reference, the notes to each chapter will provide a subtext of echoes from Woolf's writing that bear on what is being discussed. The philosophy of Virginia Woolf's fiction does not need to be transposed to critics' terms; it is implied in her work, which is above all a literature of rigorous honesty in its exploration of what it is to be.

The concept of identity that emerges from the novels allows for knowledge only of what Woolf termed (in *Mrs. Dalloway*) "apparitions." This concept has affinities with Hume's notion of imaginary identity in a constant flux.[15] What also emerges, however, is that Woolf was more interested in the gaps in being that such a concept revealed. Hume turned away from the soul as being beyond our comprehension; to Woolf it became the most significant aspect of being. "Soul" and "self," I will suggest, were synonymous for Woolf. The self, or soul, is an "essence" apart from all identities (apparitions) that cannot issue in the world but that may survive even death. By comparing passages and noting descriptive homologies it is seen that Woolf often writes about the soul without actually stating it; fish-like, the soul moves beneath the surface of her work, sometimes glimpsed, often hidden, but always there.

The primary focus of this study is Woolf's record of a 'reality' that she apprehended in the actual world, but that transcends it. Her sense of the numinous and her idea of the soul are seen to be intimately related. The inherent conflict between faith in 'reality' and the soul, and despair at the sense of futility in all human effort, is manifest in the various thematic concerns of Woolf's art.

What follows may be divided into two parts. The first part is primarily descriptive, seeking to provide an understanding of the actual context within which Woolf's exploration of human being takes place. The picture that emerges is of a world characterized by a lack, by a sense of an abstract "gap" in being that cannot be directly referred to in language, but which is certainly a potential of human experience. In the modes of art, this tension is formalized and in the fourth chapter Woolf's means of approaching fundamental existential questions by means of her aesthetic is demonstrated. At this point the problematic relationship between art and life is brought to the foreground of the discussion. The disjunction between language and reality is acute in *The Waves*. Usually regarded as her masterpiece, I find in *The Waves* a serious failure on the terms of her own aesthetic.

The sense of the numinous, Woolf's idea of 'reality', and its relation to art is the focus of the latter part of the study. Temporality, as particularly manifest by the fact of death, is isolated as the most important concern in her emergent "religion." Her ultimate resolution that literary art can embody the autonomous self, or soul, in the virtual space described by the act of reading is most confidently enshrined in her last novel, *Between the Acts*. There I find a circling back through the concerns of her entire lifework; indeed, there are startling similarities between passages from writings of her early twenties and from her last years. *Between the Acts* is at once a culmination and a new beginning, and discussion of it thus serves as a fitting conclusion to my reading. Woolf's suicide, and her belief that *Between the Acts* should not be published, might be taken as controverting that work's generally affirmative character: this is a final emblem of the profound polarity by which her life and art were riven.

THE SINGING
OF THE REAL WORLD

From this I reach what I might call a
philosophy; at any rate it is a constant
idea of mine; that behind the cotton
wool is hidden a pattern; that we—I
mean all human beings—are connected
with this; that the whole world is a
work of art; that we are parts of the
work of art. *Hamlet* or a Beethoven
quartet is the truth about this vast mass
that we call the world. But there is no
Shakespeare, there is no Beethoven;
certainly and emphatically there is no
God; we are the words; we are the
music; we are the thing itself.

—VIRGINIA WOOLF, "A SKETCH OF THE PAST"

CHAPTER ONE
THE BODY

IT SEEMS PROPER TO BEGIN BY EXAMINING BRIEFLY WOOLF'S AWARENESS of the body's role in human being. The tradition of empirical and rational inquiry into the self has had to face (or ignore) the question of the relation of body and "mind." The dominant tradition of Western philosophy is still Cartesian, treating body and mind as separate substances, one extended, the other not. Dualistic theories must assume the possibility of disembodied *existence*, but whenever such an idea is brought into contact with the world in which we actually live, its inadequacies are evident.[1] The self of Descartes, the individual "I" of his writings, is one that professes to need no body.[2]

Maurice Merleau-Ponty—whose phenomenology of perception has been influential in breaking down the Cartesian theory of the "ghost in the machine"—starts from a position very different to that of Descartes. Any apprehension of the world, and of our place in it, is from the situation of a body: the body is our general medium for having a world. The body is both that through which we experience the world immediately, and that by which we are experienced (initially) in the world by others; the body is the "vehicle of being in the world" (*Phenomenology of Perception*, 82).

Exponents of phenomenological theory have gone so far as to make the verb "to live" transitive, in so far as it implies a body. Thus, instead of the Cartesian formulation "I live in a body," Merleau-Ponty, Sartre, and, following them, R. D. Laing, would say "I *live* my body." The idea that to live is at once to "live" a body lies behind Laing's analyses of the *embodied* and *unembodied* self. In *The Divided Self*, Laing writes of the primary split in an ontologically secure person as being between mind and body: usually such a person feels most closely identified with mind. An *embodied* person feels he began when his body did and that he will die when it does; if a person is *unembodied*, has never quite become incarnate, he feels somewhat detached from life.

Laing's concepts can be used to identify the (phenomenological) way in which Woolf creates characters and conveys a sense of *lived* experience in her novels. He writes that "everyone, even the most unembodied person, experiences himself as inextricably bound up with or in his body" (*The Divided Self*, 66). Embodiment and unembodiment are not fixed, passive states but active tendencies, the possibilities of the way the body is lived giving rise to what Laing terms "a basic difference in the self's position in life" (*The Divided Self*, 66). Although the basic issues arise in the same way for the unembodied as for the embodied person, the contexts in which they are experienced are radically different, and thus the issues are lived differently. Although embodiment does not necessarily ensure ontological security, it is a starting point that is "the precondition for a different hierarchy of possibilities from those open to the person who experiences himself in terms of a self-body dualism" (*The Divided Self*, 68).

The body, therefore, is the correct starting-point in an account of self. Every person must "live" his or her body in some way, even if that way is to deny that it is "his" or "hers." As Laing suggests, the basic difference in ways of being lies in an individual's feeling of existing commensurately with the body or not: of being, in Laing's terms, embodied or unembodied.

Woolf's novels enquire into human being, and take account throughout of the effect on perception and action that ways of living the body have. Harvena Richter has noted that "before *The Voyage Out* was written, no novelist had ever tried to describe exactly how the eye-mind experiences the object, or how the body participates in this experience" (P. viii). From her first novel, Woolf was "aware of the effect of emotional and bodily states on the appearance of the external world" (Richter, 92). This early awareness of the lived body is well exemplified by her presentation of Rachel Vinrace, who becomes increasingly involved with her body as an object of thought; the way she lives her body is focused on as the novel progresses. *The Voyage Out* concentrates on the problems of engagement and marriage;

most significantly for our purpose here, the problems encoun-
tered by Rachel arise predominantly from her being forced to
live her body in a way she is totally unprepared for.

Richard Dalloway's kiss (*TVO*, 84-85) drives her to see her
body as an instrument of passion and temptation—one that she
cannot live. Her engagement with Terence Hewet compounds
the problem. Her body, to her, eventually becomes "the source
of all the life in the world" (*TVO*, 315). Rachel's escape from a
world she perceives as entirely threatening can be seen as an
existential "fading-out" which is conveyed in images of the
physical:

> Her body became a drift of melting snow, above which her knees rose in
> huge peaked mountains of bare bone. . . . [F]or long spaces of time she
> would merely lie conscious of her body floating on the top of the bed and her
> mind driven to some remote corner of her body, or escaped and gone flitting
> round the room. (*TVO*, 423-24)

The tendencies toward embodiment and unembodiment
can be taken as the opposing extremes of a scale of ways in
which the body is lived. In Woolf's novels the broad range of this
scale is well exemplified in the variety of ways characters are
more or less "at home" in their bodies. *The Waves* provides a
microcosm of this scale in the six different existential "settings"
of the characters in one actual world.

In the following examples, two of the characters from that
novel serve to demonstrate the opposing extremes of the scale
of ways in which the body can be lived: Jinny stands as the most
fully embodied of all Woolf's characters, whilst Rhoda lies at the
extreme of unembodiment. The examples given do not follow
the novels' chronology as they are intended to illustrate a spectrum against which all the characters of the novels may be
measured.

EMBODIMENT

Of all the novels' characters it is Jinny in *The Waves* who is
most "at home" in her body, most completely embodied. Jinny *is*
her body: she experiences no gap between consciousness and

body, but lives entirely through her body. Her life as a child adumbrates the fierce sensuality of her adulthood: "I see a crimson tassel . . . twisted with gold threads" (*TW*, 6). The words of her lessons—seen differently by each of the six children whose lives form the substance of the book—are bright and burning; they inspire in her a dream of the fiery, yellow, fulvous dress she will wear to parties, attracting attention to herself, to her body.

The other two girls with whom Jinny grows up (Rhoda and Susan) are her immediate rivals; even Rhoda's face—bestowed on her by Jinny, because to herself she has "no face"—is a threat, for it is "completed," whereas Jinny complains of eyes too close together, lips too far apart.

Jinny is complete to herself: "I see my body and my head in one now; for even in this serge frock they are one, my body and my head" (*TW*, 30). The implication is that she feels no difference at all between body and mind: she "lives" her body absolutely, with no mediation between thought and action. Jinny does not dream because her imagination is "the body's." Her mind is reduced to a mere breath in her body; her perceptions are vibrantly alive, but without mystery, without depth, for she sees only with her body: "Yet I cannot follow any word through its changes. I cannot follow any thought from present to past" (*TW*, 30). Memory can hardly exist for her, for the body does not remember: its experiences are all momentary.

That Jinny should try to banish night is understandable: it is the realm of dreams and solitude when, in sleep, the body falls away and the mental dominates. At night, Rhoda must stretch out to the hard rail at the foot of her bed to preserve some sense of embodiment; Jinny, however, longs "that the week should be all one day without divisions" (39), and attempts to make it so by turning night into day with bright lights in brilliant rooms, or by wearing a radiant white dress. Those experiences that terrify Rhoda delight Jinny: "The door is opening and shutting. People are arriving; they do not speak; they hasten in" (*TW*, 73). How strange it is, thinks Jinny, that people should go to sleep, putting out the light and losing consciousness of their bodies.

Her childhood aspirations are realized as she grows up to take her place in what she calls the "great society of bodies." In

Jinny's lived experience, consequent on her fully incarnate being, there is no need of a mind with any degree of detachment from the body, for life is carried on by instinct. Under an admiring gaze, her body "instantly of its own accord puts forth a frill" (45), communicating with others in a wordless society of bodies. Her body she describes as being "open" or "shut" at will (46), including or excluding another from that society, her world.

Jinny's life is a sexual adventure from the start, and it is at parties, where she makes her conquests, that she is seen at her most "at home" in the world: "Among the lustrous green, pink, pearl-grey women stand upright the bodies of men. They are black and white; they are grooved beneath their clothes with deep rills. I feel again the reflection in the window of the tunnel; it moves" (*TW*, 73). Dancing at a party is significantly described as a sea, and as a body; Jinny and her partner are swept in and out, round rocks, flowing but enclosed within a larger figure (*TW*, 74). The image of the sea emphasizes that Jinny's actual world is that shared world of all the others, existing in itself, beyond the individual world she experiences through the way she lives her body.

In the context of her full embodiment, the world for Jinny is a glittering party of bodies where names are unimportant. In this fulfilling of herself, she is supremely confident: "I look straight back at you, men and women. I am one of you. This is my world" (*TW*, 74). Only when the pact is firm between the bodies can she feel herself "admitted to the warmth and privacy of another soul" (*TW*, 75). The soul, though, has no interest for her because she constantly seeks moments of physical ecstasy; once passed, these moments give way to "slackness and indifference" and the search for a new partner—"beauty must be broken daily to remain beautiful" (*TW*, 124).

Jinny, I suggest, is at one extreme of that scale of ways in which the body can be lived; she can imagine nothing "beyond the circle cast by my body" (*TW*, 92). Her sense of unity projects itself through her body and affects others, as she is aware. Coming into the restaurant for Percival's farewell dinner, Jinny seems to Susan to center everything, to pull everything to her. She makes others conscious of *their* bodies: the men straighten their ties (clothes, which Jinny always notices, being in a sense an extension of the body), and Susan hides her hands beneath the table (*TW*, 86-87). Jinny proclaims herself wholly through her actions, and she perhaps makes others uncomfortable because she reminds them that they too have bodies, which they would rather forget: "My body goes before me, like a lantern down a dark lane, bringing one thing after another out of darkness into a ring of light. I dazzle you; I make you believe that this is all" (*TW*, 92). There is nothing interesting to Jinny in the stories one may read in people's faces, for there is no certainty about them. Body and mind to her are one: "We who live in the body see with the body's imagination things in outline" (*TW*, 125).

Most of the firmly embodied characters in the novels are in some degree threatening to those who fight a constant battle with their bodies. Those who tend to unembodiment are outcasts, outsiders, and visionaries. Jinny, though, is envied rather than feared, even if that envy is frequently manifested as a kind of fear. One of her friends, Bernard, remembers her in his summing-up, which concludes *The Waves*, as sterile, seeing only what was before her, on the surface; yet he admires her animal honesty. She relates to others solely through her body, as Bernard recalls: "It was a tree; there was the river; it was afternoon; here we were; I in my serge suit; she in green. There was no past, no future; merely the moment in its ring of light [cast by Jinny's body?], and our bodies; and the inevitable climax, the ecstasy" (*TW*, 179).

Jinny's embodiment is explicitly sexual. She cannot, like Neville, range in her memory back and forth in time, nor, like Susan, can she *be* a mother, for a relationship with children would not be physically sexual. When Jinny notices that she is ageing, this, to her, is not merely a case of more wrinkles on her face and less spring in her walk, but a real depletion of her very being. Her world begins to disappear as her charms fade: "But look—there is my body in that looking-glass. How solitary, how shrunk, how aged! I am no longer young. I am no longer part of the procession. . . . I still move. I still live. But who will come if I signal?" (*TW*, 137). To overcome this ontological depletion, she rouses herself to prepare a face to meet the faces that she meets; a face created by color, by the movement of the mechani-

cal world running smoothly and noisily about her (*TW*, 138).
Ultimately, Jinny is a machine; she thrives in the world of tech-
nology and manufacture, for it seems that "they" are, as she is,
engaged in prolonging the appearance of bodies, of erasing
mind and emotion in favor of the mechanistic physical: "Look
how they show off clothes here even underground in a perpetual
radiance. They will not let the earth even lie wormy and sodden"
(*TW*, 138).

Susan lives her body almost as completely embodied as
Jinny, but differs in that there is in her make-up a sense of distance between consciousness and body. She lives through her
senses (which are acute), accepting her body as the natural
home of her being, as she is at home in the larger world of nature. As a child she develops a hatred of anything foreign to her
native soil: the smells and regulations of school are anathema to
her, as are the firs and mountains of Switzerland, where she fin-
ishes her education; this radical autochthony characterizes her
throughout her life.

Jinny's kissing Louis, in the garden where the book opens
(*TW*, 9), is an event that affects all the children. The jealousy it
arouses in Susan makes her perceive acutely that her body is
"short and squat." This childhood trauma leads her to feel ex-
cluded from the sexual adventures of others; she feels low, near
the ground and the insects. This early body-image dictates the
subsequent development of the way she lives her body.

Susan is uninterested in the artificial, the meretricious: "I
do not want, as Jinny wants, to be admired. I do not want people,
when I come in, to look up with admiration. I want to give, to be
given, and solitude in which to unfold my possessions" (*TW*,
39). The idea of possession is central in Susan's character: by
possessing all that is around her, and that her senses bring her
evidence of, she can create her own world through her body. Her
identification with sensory experience is so intense that she can
believe herself to *be* what she experiences: "At this hour, this still
early hour, I think I am the field, I am the barn, I am the trees;
mine are the flocks of birds, and this young hare who leaps, at the
last moment when I step almost on him." (*TW*, 70). In this can
be seen the difference between the ways Susan and Jinny live

their bodies. Jinny is a sexual being; Susan is formed entirely from the experience of her senses and the feeling that her body is like the "body" of the earth: warm in summer, cold and cracked in winter. At times, indeed, her identification with the earth tends toward a sort of unembodiment. This can be observed in a moment, the description of which makes it sound strangely like Bernard's experience of the "world without a self": "I think sometimes (I am not twenty yet) I am not a woman, but the light that falls on this gate, on this ground. I am the seasons, I think sometimes, January, May, November; the mud, the mist, the dawn" (*TW*, 71). The moment is short-lived, as the weight of her body, leaning on the gate, recalls her from her reverie; it serves to illustrate the point that embodiment is not static, but a flux, conditioning the way an individual experiences the world. Susan's embodiment is more complex than Jinny's from the start.

Sometimes Susan envies Jinny and Rhoda living in London; it seems to her that they are able to control the inexorable pressures of life. To others, Susan presents someone who "despises the futility of London" (*TW*, 85), but there is in her some longing for variation, for an escape from the unchanging routine of the seasons. At the farewell dinner-party where the six friends gather to say goodbye to their hero, Percival (who is leaving for India), Susan feels out of place; it is Jinny's territory. She gathers her "possessions," her fields and damp grasses, to protect her "soul" (*TW*, 87). In the way they live their bodies, Jinny and Susan oppose against each other the lives of city and country. Although both are very fully embodied, they are so in different ways. Susan has accepted her body with what seems, compared to Jinny's positiveness, almost resignation. Being embodied so completely, Susan is similar to Jinny in disliking words and taking everything at face value, but distinct from her in the discomfort she feels about her body in the setting of a city restaurant.

The position of nature as the source of the way Susan lives her body is usurped by her newborn child. It is of her body, as a tree is of the earth. She cradles it with her body: ". . . all spun to a fine thread round the cradle, wrapping in a cocoon made of my own blood the delicate limbs of my baby . . . making of my own body a hollow, a warm shelter for my child to sleep in"

(*TW*, 122). Her body, to her, assumes the contours of the land. This child is more than just another possession; it is an extension of her body: " 'His eyes will see when mine are shut', I think, 'I shall go mixed with them beyond my body' " (*TW*, 122-23). Her idea here is of what could be called a "physical transcendence" rather than a transcendence of the physical.

There is always in Susan a sense that to have to live a body is regrettable but inevitable. "I shall never have anything but natural happiness," she says, somewhat ambiguously, with her friends in London, quietly hinting that she feels she misses something: "It will almost content me." From her early experience of herself as squat and ugly she comes to be embodied in a way that causes her none of the tension of the unembodied, but also prevents her from realizing aspects of herself that she is made acutely aware of by her visits to London, particularly in Jinny's company.

This sense of unfulfillment weighs on her when her children are grown. She feels that she has reached the summit of her desires; she has planted and nurtured and brought to maturity part of her own body. With this completion, she begins to tire of her life: "Yet sometimes I am sick of natural happiness, and fruit growing, and children scattering the house with oars, guns . . . and other trophies. I am sick of the body, I am sick of my own craft, industry and cunning" (*TW*, 136).

Susan has been constrained by her early experience of her body; she has lived in harmony with the nature she felt close to as a child, but has never overcome a sense of loss, of not being able to grasp the "air-ball's string" of words that Bernard and the other city-dwellers seem to grasp with such facility. She has resigned will to reaction, imagination to sensory experience, and as she grows old she thinks perhaps her life has not been "real," for she has made no effort to oppose nature: "Life stands round me like glass round the imprisoned reed" (*TW*, 137). A more adventurous, more "real" (to her) Susan looks out from her "rather squat, grey before my time" body, through "clear eyes, pear-shaped eyes,"[3] and it is this Susan who withdraws her square-tipped fingers from Jinny's sight in the restaurant. Susan begins to detach herself from her body as she grows older, filled with a sense of loss. For Jinny, the world of bodies is enough, but Susan sees beyond it.

At the final reunion of the six friends, at Hampton Court, Neville's self-confidence, bolstered by his qualifications, withers before Susan. In an effort to make her identity "crouch" beneath his, he tells her of the variety and vigor of his life, comparing it to Susan's seasonal routine. The difference in their lives is shown most clearly in the way they have lived their bodies. "I," says Neville,

> took the print of life not outwardly, but inwardly upon the raw, the white, the unprotected fibre. I am clouded and bruised with the print of minds and faces and things so subtle that they have smell, colour, texture, substance, but no name. I am merely "Neville" to you, who see the narrow limits of my life and the line [body] it cannot pass. But to myself I am immeasurable. (*TW*, 151-52)

Susan's life is emblematized in her body, with which she now challenges Neville: her life has been solid, in huge blocks, not flickering and evanescent like his, because she has lived through her senses, through her body, and the body does not refine, does not chop things small with words: "My body has been used daily, rightly, like a tool by a good workman, all over" (*TW*, 152). With her body she demolishes the world of phrases: "I sit among you abrading your softness with my hardness, quenching the silver-grey flickering moth-wing quiver of words with the green spurt of my clear eyes" (*TW*, 153). However, Susan has perceived the restriction her embodiment entails, and the last words she speaks in the book sum up her sense of loss: "Still I gape . . . like a young bird, unsatisfied, for something that has escaped me" (*TW*, 165).

For those, like Jinny and Susan, whose way of living the body tends very much to complete embodiment, the world is not usually a threatening place. They are marked by a sense of security, of "belonging." This is not to say that embodied being is immune to doubt, but at least such embodiment provides an initial firm foundation for being. When the way the body is lived tends more toward unembodiment, the self's position in the world is altogether more precarious. Again, by description of two examples, the other extreme of the scale of ways of living the body is illustrated.

UNEMBODIMENT

He had gone through the whole show, friendship, European War, death, had won promotion, was still under thirty and was bound to survive. He was right there. The last shells missed him. He watched them explode with indifference. (*MD*, 96)

Septimus Warren Smith, in *Mrs. Dalloway*, begins to tend toward unembodiment when he is urged by his employer, Mr. Brewer, to develop "manliness" (by playing football! [95]). When his friend Evans dies in battle, Septimus sees an opportunity to display his manliness to the world by showing no feelings. The Septimus that others experience is not at all identical with Septimus as he speaks to "himself." R. D. Laing is instructive in understanding the nature of the dissociation in Septimus: "The individual is developing a microcosmos within himself; but, of course, this autistic, private, intra-individual 'world' is not a feasible substitute for the only world there really is, the shared world" (*The Divided Self*, 74). Septimus believes that the world, not he, has altered, and he must hold on to this belief for the security of his own being: "It might be possible," he thinks, "that the world itself is without meaning" (*MD*, 98).

Septimus is not protected from the world by the defining line of his own body. His unembodiment leads him to experience his own being as terrifying and uncontrolled, for the medium by which the world can be kept at a distance seems not to be "there." He feels that his body has been soaked away, "macerated until only the nerve fibres were left" (*MD*, 76). From this way of living his body comes his sense of being freed from the earth, able to look down from "the back of the world" on all mankind (*MD*, 76).

Septimus's world initially depends, as each person's does, on how he lives his body. His unembodiment frees him from the constraints of a normal physical body in his own perception; this perception is in direct conflict with the world outside him, a world that makes no distinction between "him" and his body. Most of the time Septimus regards his body as an "other," as, for instance, when he melodramatically drops his head in his hands, making his wife, Rezia, send for help (*MD*, 100).

Throughout the novel, Septimus is largely unaware of his body as it appears to others in the actual world: "Happily Rezia put her hand with a tremendous weight on his knee so that he was weighted down, transfixed" (*MD*, 26). To him, his body is one more object in that world, bobbing up and down in the breeze along with the trees, feathers, and birds. Septimus's unembodiment causes a serious disjunction between his perceptions and those of others around him. In order to stave off the madness that Septimus feels this disjunction threatens him with, he translates his sensations into an inexpressible "religion" of which he is the prophet, and gives meaning to a world that he sees might well be meaningless.

If he was embodied he would have to feel, and thus have to face, primarily, Evans's death. Unembodied, he can create a solipsistic world in which "there is no death" (*MD*, 28). His body is in the world of death—"There was his hand; there the dead" (*MD*, 28)—and so he must abandon that body as far as he can. His sensations are given significance by his "self" (in Laing's sense of a "core" of being looking out of an alien body). Septimus must remain unembodied in order to live *for himself*; to live the body in this way, however, appears in the actual world as an aberration to be "cured."

In Septimus's world "there is no death," and so he reasons that he does not have to feel for Evans. The death of his friend and the demands on him to be "manly" have driven him to a state of extreme unembodiment. His omniscience ("He knew all their thoughts, he said; he knew everything. He knew the meaning of the world, he said" [*MD*, 74]) is necessary to him if he is to deny his body as a physical limit to himself. Again, the condition is described by Laing:

> The hidden shut-up self, in disowning participation . . . in the quasi-autonomous activities of the false-self system, is living only "mentally." Moreover, this shut-up self, being isolated, is unable to be enriched by outer experience, and so the whole inner world comes to be more and more

impoverished, until the individual may come to feel he is merely a vacuum. The sense of being able to do anything and the feeling of possessing everything then exist side by side with a feeling of impotence and emptiness. (*The Divided Self*, 75)

Woolf conveys the hopeless paradox of Septimus's position with telling psychological insight; he is trapped between the extremes of omnipotence and eternal suffering:

> Look, the unseen bade him, the voice which now communicated with him who was the greatest of mankind, Septimus, lately taken from life to death, the Lord who had come to renew society, who lay like a coverlet, a snow blanket smitten only by the sun, for ever unwasted, suffering for ever, the scapegoat, the eternal sufferer, but he did not want it, he moaned, putting from him with a wave of his hand that eternal suffering, that eternal loneliness. (*MD*, 29)

The world that Septimus tries to escape from is represented by the doctors, Holmes and Bradshaw, by Mr. Brewer, and even to some extent by his wife, Rezia. They try to make Septimus take notice of "real things." Such attention would necessitate embodiment for him, and thus feeling and recognizing death. The insistence of the actual world drives Septimus further into unembodiment. Holmes and Bradshaw treat the body, but Septimus, as *he lives* his body, cannot be touched by them. "But even Holmes himself could not touch this last relic straying on the edge of the world, this outcast, who gazed at the inhabited regions, who lay, like a drowned sailor, on the shore of the world" (*MD*, 103).

Just before his suicide, Septimus is alone with Rezia; he is calmed by the shimmering patterns of sunlight on the wall, but the peaceful atmosphere is shot through with intimations of his imminent death (*MD*, 153-54). Carefully, Septimus, drawing calm and courage both from the sights and sounds of nature, and from Rezia's stability, begins to take stock of his surroundings: "But real things—real things were too exciting. He must be cautious. He would not go mad" (*MD*, 156). He begins to move away from unembodiment, to "re-embody" himself through vision (primarily). When he closes his eyes, however, the world he has been carefully approaching, one item at a time, disappears. Alone, he feels that his world (that is, the world of his unembodied self) has gone forever—he is stuck with the sideboard and the bananas, which undermine his vision by their mundaneness, deny what he considers the truth. With what must be understood as a supreme effort, Septimus resolves to face "the screen, the coal-scuttle, and the sideboard" (*MD*, 160). He has begun to come back to his body, but the sound of Holmes—"human nature" (*MD*, 155)—on the stair, forcing his way in, reminds Septimus of that world that drove him to unembodiment and torment. Holmes and Bradshaw "mixed the vision and the sideboard" (*MD*, 163), his unembodied being and his appearance in the actual world; such people see with a single vision only, and yet have power over others. Septimus is now moving toward embodiment and sees vividly that he is subject to the doctors, and that what he thought was an omnipotent being has in fact no authority, no autonomy, in their world, the actual world.

Rationally, the only possibility for his embodied self is suicide, for it is the only way he can preserve his autonomy as embodied. Rezia understands why Septimus kills himself, having come to understand the way the world represented by Dr. Holmes tramples on those who do not fit in it. The union of Rezia and Septimus in opposing the single vision of Holmes (and thus Rezia's understanding of Septimus's act) is implied by an image both share. As Septimus begins to recover from his anguish, his torments are all "burnt out, for he had a sense, as he watched Rezia . . . of a coverlet of flowers" (*MD*, 157). After his death Rezia is calm, feeling like "flying flowers over some tomb" (*MD*, 165).

At the furthest extreme of unembodiment of all Woolf's characters is Rhoda, in *The Waves*. The gulf between what she calls "myself" and the body by which she is recognized in the world is wide and deep; her isolation is emphasized from the start of the book. She is more alone than her closest friend, Louis, who is also predominantly unembodied, but can at night "put off this unenviable body . . . and inhabit space" (*TW*, 38). Rhoda does not have the imagination that partly rescues Louis from his uncomfortable relationship with his body; she suffers in every situation. It is only near the end of the book, at the reunion at Hampton Court, that she has taught her body to "do a certain trick" so that she will appear to have overcome her terror of the leaping tiger of society.

Rhoda is thrown into the world by a body she hates and tries to avoid: " 'That is my face,' said Rhoda, 'in the looking-glass behind Susan's shoulder—that face is my face. But I will duck behind her to hide it, for I am not here. I have no face. Other people have faces; Susan and Jinny have faces; they are here. Their world is the real world' "(*TW*, 30-31). What makes Rhoda's position in life impossible, more painful than that of Septimus, is her understanding that the world of the embodied is, as she puts it, the "real" world, the world in which actions have effects, objects weight. The reflection of her "real" face shows her the actual world that has her in its grip, rather than her private fantasy of the swallow and the pool, which she can control. Always, though, Rhoda is trapped by her need for others, the need to replenish her dreams with figures from that world populated by those who are at home in their bodies. Louis, her ally in unembodiment, understands her position: "We wake her. We torture her. She dreads us, she despises us, yet comes cringing to our sides because for all our cruelty there is always some name, some face, which sheds a radiance, which lights up her pavements and makes it possible for her to replenish her dreams" (*TW*, 86). She longs for "lodgement" (*TW*, 94); that is, for a *home* in the world that her body does not provide. By copying others she hopes to share some of their ease, to "light my fire at the general blaze of you who live wholly, indivisibly and without caring" (*TW*, 94).

Rhoda does not deny her body entirely, as she knows that she *must* live it in some way as a living being: "Alone, I often fall down into nothingness. . . . I have to bang my hand against some hard door to call myself back to the body" (*TW*, 31). Her feeling of being "committed" to life, in the sense of being committed to prison, springs from the tension inherent in the way she lives her body. She does not want to die, but cannot be at home in her body, and so lives in a twilight between life and death. As the book progresses, Rhoda slips further into unembodiment; her increasing dissociation from her body is a strand of the book's overall movement as definite as the passage of the sun through the sky, or Jinny's ageing: "Month by month things are losing their hardness; even my body now lets the light through; my spine is like soft wax near the flame of the candle" (*TW*, 32-33).

The ambivalence in Rhoda's way of living her body is seen in her attitude to night and sleep. Going to bed, she must stretch her toes to touch the rail to assure herself of the world and her being in it. The night invites sleep, and Rhoda fears that if she sleeps she will lose the already slight hold she has on her body and never come back to it; yet to relinquish her body and enter the world of dreams is a solace for her: "Out of me now my mind can pour. I can think of my Armadas sailing on the high waves. I am relieved of hard contacts and collisions. I sail on alone under white cliffs" (*TW*, 19-20). As she falls asleep, however, the panic of losing identity overcomes her; she feels waters closing over her and struggles to emerge from them by recognizing the objects around her: "Oh, but I sink, I fall! That is the corner of the cupboard; that is the nursery looking-glass. But they stretch, they elongate. . . . Oh, to awaken from dreaming! Look, there is the chest of drawers" (*TW*, 20).

Rhoda does not want to give life up, and knows she must "live" her body, but because she can never feel "at home" in that body, her unembodiment is extreme and her tendency toward dissolution, against which she struggles less and less effectively, eventually overcomes her will to live. The "thin sheet" of her childhood bed can no longer save her. At the extreme pitch of her despair, Rhoda echoes Septimus Smith's fear of falling into the sea or into flames (*MD*, 155), and his bitter observation that "once you fall . . . human nature is upon you" (*MD*, 154): "After all these callings hither and thither, these pluckings and searchings, I shall fall alone through this thin sheet into gulfs of fire. And you will not help me. More cruel than the old torturers, you will let me fall, and will tear me to pieces when I am fallen" (*TW*, 158-59). Also like Septimus, Rhoda exhibits that feeling of omniscience and omnipotence that Laing notes as characteristic of the unembodied self in its retreat from the actual world: "Yet there are moments when the walls of the mind grow thin; when nothing is unabsorbed, and I could fancy that we might blow so vast a bubble that the sun might set and rise in it and we might take the blue of midday and the black of midnight and be cast off and escape from here and now" (*TW*, 159).

A crucial moment in Rhoda's life demonstrates her realization of the inevitability of living her body, a realization that is the source of constant anguish to her:

> Also, in the middle, cadaverous, awful, lay the grey puddle in the courtyard, when, holding an envelope in my hand, I carried a message. I came to the puddle. I could not cross it. Identity failed me. We are nothing, I said, and fell. I was blown like a feather, I was wafted down tunnels. Then very gingerly, I pushed my foot across. I laid my hand against a brick wall. I returned very painfully, drawing myself back into my body over the grey, cadaverous space of the puddle. This is life then to which I am committed. (*TW*, 46)[4]

Recalling this experience, Rhoda states, "Unless I can stretch and touch something hard, I shall be blown down the eternal corridors forever" (*TW*, 113). Rhoda is, in Laing's words, "guilty at daring to be, and doubly guilty at not being, at being too terrified to be" (*The Divided Self*, 157). She is saved from "chaotic nonentity" by the brief security her sense of being in a body provides. It is, however, the fact that she stretches unembodiment as far as possible that leads to her clutching at the experience of her bodily senses for a sense of being at all. Eventually—we must assume from Bernard's report—Rhoda no longer made the effort to draw herself "across the enormous gulf" into her body (*TW*, 113).

The four characters discussed—Jinny, Susan, Septimus, and Rhoda—are at either extreme of a scale of what I have called "at-homeness" in the body. All the other characters of the novels fall between these two extremes in terms of their embodiment or unembodiment, which is more or less emphasized. The question of the way the body is lived must precede any account of self precisely because human beings *live* their bodies as their foundation in the world. That Woolf saw the body as lived rather than merely as a given environment for a shadowy self is an indication of her intentions in the creation of character.

Having seen that the body is not taken for granted, the next step in describing the context of Woolf's inquiry into human being is to investigate what is meant by "I," the mark of a particular identity and that perspective from which even the most unembodied may speak.

CHAPTER TWO
IDENTITY AND SELF

"I" IS, AS MARTIN BUBER PUT IT, "THE TRUE SHIBBOLETH OF HUMANITY" (*I and Thou*, 115), but the word can be uttered in many different ways. Woolf's novels inquire into the status of "I" as it is spoken by various characters in various contexts, and from this we may draw her concepts of identity and self, the distinction between which will emerge as we proceed.

Frequently, there is a moment in the novels when, with a feeling either of exhilaration or anxiety, a character is suddenly overcome by a sense of being unique, of being "I." In *The Voyage Out*, that Rachel Vinrace has little sense of individual identity is emphasized from the start: she would "believe anything she was told, invent reasons for anything she said" (*TVO*, 31). Friendless, inexperienced, and sheltered, Rachel's ordinariness is the most striking thing about her. She has had no social intercourse, and any impulse toward an individual attitude has been quickly suppressed by her father or aunts; she thus believes that "to feel anything strongly was to create an abyss between oneself and others who feel strongly perhaps but differently" (*TVO*, 34).

For Rachel, what can be called the experience of self-discovery is fascinating; prompted by Helen Ambrose, there comes a moment when she sees herself for the first time standing out against a background composed of all other people:

> The vision of her own personality, of herself as a real everlasting thing, different from anything else, unmergeable, like the sea or the wind, flashed into Rachel's mind, and she became profoundly excited at the thought of living.
> "I can be m-m-myself," she stammered, "in spite of you, in spite of the Dalloways, and Mr. Pepper, and Father, and my Aunts, in spite of these?" She swept her hand across a whole page of statesmen and soldiers. (*TVO*, 94-95)

Similar moments of "self-discovery" occur throughout the novels, and provide what could be called a first signification of identity: the encountering of myself, called "I," distinct from all others in the world, as continuous and unmergeable.

Immediately, however, a problem is raised for which the novels after *Night and Day* successively seek and offer solutions. Rachel's "vision of . . . herself" raises the question of who has that vision. It is not enough to say simply that the individual divides into a reflected and reflecting part. "I" is, for the most part, spoken as a received cipher for one being among others. The experience of self-discovery distinguishes the individual "I" from the faceless crowd that moves through all the novels, obliterating "I," sweeping people along *en masse*. This crowd is the background against which the experience of self-discovery stands out. To emerge from that background requires an effort, for it is easier to flow with the crowd, as Katherine Hilbery, the heroine of *Night and Day*, finds:

> She stood fascinated at the corner. The deep roar filled her ears; the changing tumult had the inexpressible fascination of varied life pouring ceaselessly with a purpose which, as she looked, seemed to her, somehow, the normal purpose for which life was framed; its complete indifference to the individuals, whom it swallowed up and rolled onwards, filled her with at least a temporary exaltation. (*ND*, 465-66)

The problem I have referred to above is that of discovering what inspires the effort to rouse an individual's "I" to emerge from the crowd. The question is put simply in "An Unwritten Novel," a sketch written in 1920 as Woolf was planning *Jacob's Room*: "When the self speaks to the self, who is speaking?" (*AHH*, 21). There is a distinction between the voice of the "self speaking to the self" and the "I" that is uttered in the shared world of relationships between one identity and another. The status of "I" as the defining word of identity is thus complex rather than simple. In what follows I will describe the novels' inquiry into the nature and status of identity, and into the possibility of a unitary, autonomous self.

"There is," says the narrator of *Jacob's Room*, "something absolute in us that despises qualification" (143). In this novel that "it is no use trying to sum people up. One must follow hints, not exactly what is said, nor yet entirely what is done—" (29) becomes almost a refrain. The narrative tone in *Jacob's Room* is inquisitive, uncertain; in its hesitancy can be seen a determination to inquire honestly into the human situation, a refusal to assume control and dictate a system into which life will be made to fit. That "life is but a procession of shadows," that we cannot know others (except as what Clarissa Dalloway will call "apparitions"), that there is no way of defining an individual—all this is affirmed. *Jacob's Room* sketches out the frame within which Woolf's investigations into the strange nature of human being take place:

> In any case life is but a procession of shadows, and God knows why it is that we embrace them so eagerly, and see them depart with such anguish, being shadows. And why, if this and much more than this is true, why are we yet surprised in the window corner by a sudden vision that the young man in the chair is of all things in the world the most real, the most solid, the best known to us—why indeed?—For the moment after we know nothing about him.
>
>   Such is the manner of our seeing. Such the conditions of our love. (*JR*, 70-71)

Such, it might be said, the conditions of her inquiry.

"Human reality cannot be finally defined by patterns of conduct," writes Sartre in *Being and Nothingness*; cannot, *Jacob's Room* suggests, be finally defined at all. The novel undercuts its own purpose by trying to create a unique character while at the same time admitting the impossibility of the project:

>   But though all this may very well be true—so Jacob thought and spoke—so he crossed his legs—filled his pipe—sipped his whisky, and once looked at his pocket-book, rumpling his hair as he did so, there remains over something which can never be conveyed to a second person save by Jacob himself. Moreover, part of this is not Jacob but Richard Bonamy—the room; the market carts; the hour; the very moment of history. Then consider the effect of sex— . . . But something is always impelling one to hum vibrating, like the hawk moth, at the mouth of the cavern of mystery, endowing Jacob Flanders with all sorts of qualities he had not at all—(*JR*, 71-72)

The individual is enmeshed in the influences, relationships and possibilities of the world, caught up in the movement through time and space, and so cannot be realized as one absolute entity. If there is a unique self to be identified—a "summing-up" of the person—it must be separated from its intervolvement with the world. However, such an operation may well lead to nothing.

At the beginning of *Mrs. Dalloway*, Clarissa, recently recovered from an illness, delighting in a fresh day and the hustle and bustle of the West End, is undisturbed by the thought of her death. She will not say of herself "I am this, I am that" (11), preferring to see herself as a "mist" diffused among the familiar people and places of her life. "Did it matter then, she asked herself, walking towards Bond Street, did it matter that she must inevitably cease completely; all this must go on without her; did she resent it; or did it not become consoling to believe that death ended absolutely? but that somehow in the streets of London, on the ebb and flow of things, here, there, she survived" (*MD*, 11). In this mood Clarissa is particularly susceptible to the fading away of individual identity that engulfment by the crowd threatens. Content to be part of the "ebb and flow of things," her identity ("her life, herself" [12]) begins thinning away, spreading out further and further, until eventually no sense of "I" as an individual identity remains to her.

The crowd has absorbed Clarissa so completely that she can no longer say "I" and feel that she utters *her own* identity: "She had the oddest sense of being herself invisible; unseen; unknown; there being no more marrying, no more having of children now, but only this astonishing and rather solemn progress with the rest of them, up Bond Street, this being Mrs. Dalloway; not even Clarissa any more; this being Mrs. Richard Dalloway" (*MD*, 13). "I" is Mrs. Richard Dalloway, just one more fashionable woman shopping in the West End. The importance of names should be noted here as they will be seen to be significant in the question of identity. "Dalloway" is, of course, not "really" Clarissa's name but one imposed over her own by marriage; to be "not even Clarissa any more" means that the "I" she utters does not have, *to her*, the distinction of a unique individuality.

An interesting comment on the significance of names is provided by the scene in which Clarissa's old lover, Peter Walsh, just returned from India, is seen following a pretty young woman. Having just left Clarissa's house, where their meeting again after a long separation has aroused many painful memories for Peter, he fantasizes about this "ideal" girl he has glimpsed in the street:

> Straightening himself and stealthily fingering his pocket-knife he started after her to follow this woman, this excitement, which seemed even with its back turned to shed on him a light which connected them, which singled him out, as if the random uproar of the traffic had whispered through hollowed hands his name, *not Peter, but his private name which he called himself in his own thoughts.* (*MD*, 59, my italics)

This unnamed name seems suggestive of an essence transcending mere identity; but here we are anticipating what must be more clearly explained. As a comment on this passage I will cite the following from Geoffrey Hartman's *Saving the Text*: " . . . for those who have a name may also seek a more authentic and defining one. The *other* name is usually kept secret precisely because it is sacred to the individual, or numinous (*nomen numen*): as if the concentrated soul of the person lodged in it" (125). There will be more to say about names later, but for now it is enough to note their function of providing one of the bases for identity. Names may serve to fix an identity, but they may not reflect what a person feels is his or her "true" self.

In *Mrs. Dalloway* the simple "I," with which Rachel Vinrace was seen to lay claim to an individual identity, gives way to more complex notions. Clarissa is engaged in what may be seen as a search for her ownmost identity: her recollections of childhood and an unresolved early love affair often prevent her from having a sense of continuity in her being. Memories dislocate her sense of a single identity by irrupting into her present life, so that she "would not say of Peter, she would not say of herself, I am this, I am that" (*MD*, 11).

When she returns home to discover that her husband, Richard, has been invited to lunch without her, Clarissa feels empty and lost: identity once more drains away, because she has not been included. To regain her sense of identity she detaches herself from the present and dips into the past, into her memories. As the sense of a rich relationship (with Sally Seton) and a moment of vision returns to her, the emptiness occasioned by her exclusion fills. She abruptly returns to the present, and "plunged into the very heart of the moment, transfixed it, there—the moment of this June morning on which was the pressure of all the other mornings" (*MD*, 41-42). This circling of the moment with all the other moments of life gives her identity point and continuity. Memory thus plays a double role, both disturbing and restoring the individual's sense of identity; Clarissa is able to fill the moment and regain her sense of identity, of being someone in the world to whom things have happened; to whom people have spoken; someone who has caused both happiness and sadness. Her physical being also has a part to play in this gathering together of herself. To see her own body gives her some security; when she cannot see herself, the fading of identity that she experienced in Bond Street is quickened; she feels "invisible." On returning home, her image in a mirror joins with memory as she reassumes (what is here specifically called) her self:

> That was her self—pointed; dart-like; definite. That was her self when some effort, some call on her to be her self, drew the parts together, she alone knew how different, how incompatible and composed so for the world only into one centre, one diamond, one woman who sat in her drawing-room and made a meeting-point, a radiancy no doubt in some dull lives, a refuge for the lonely to come to, perhaps. (*MD*, 42)

There is another "self," the "she" who "alone knew" that this assembly of elements is "composed so for the world only," and so "self" here is not unique, but a momentary resolution of scattered attributes that saves Clarissa from a moment of despair.

The constitution of identity here takes place under the form of a circle: the "I" at the center, named and founded in part on an image of the body, holds in tension a circumference of memories that pertain to that center; furthermore, memories involve relations with others.

Identity, then, is not a "thing," as Rachel Vinrace put it, but a flux of sensations and attributes that can be drawn together by an effort based on such a security-ensuring stimulus as the sight of one's own body in a mirror. Identity is made up of what Clarissa later in the novel calls "apparitions." In this instance it appears to be an accumulation of reflections unified by a name. When there are no acute stimuli, nor an available "base" for identity, it can slip, as it does for Clarissa in the crowded street and for Peter Walsh walking through London after his reunion with Clarissa, which arouses a welter of memories: "The strangeness of standing alone, alive, unknown, at half-past eleven in Trafalgar Square overcame him. What is it? Where am I? And why, after all, does one do it? he thought" (*MD*, 58).

Thus far it is suggested that if identity is not to be the undifferentiated identity of the crowd, an effort must be made.[1] Individual identity is, however, formed in a nexus of relationships and influences without which it cannot emerge from the background of the crowd. What initially stimulates the necessary effort is not clear, but we may say that there is a tension between the desire for autonomy, and the necessity, in forming identity, of both interrelationships with others, and the boundaries of space and time.

The party is a foundation on which Clarissa can rely for identity, but, we now know, it is possible for identity to be "composed so for the world only." Because "anybody could do it" (*MD*, 187), and because she feels she must *act* a part as a hostess, Clarissa once again feels that a "true" or "real" identity, her *own* "I," eludes her:

> Every time she gave a party she had this feeling of being something not herself, and that every one was unreal in one way; much more real in another. It was, she thought, partly their clothes, partly being taken out of their ordinary ways, partly the background; it was possible to say things you couldn't say anyhow else, things that needed an effort; possible to go much deeper. But not for her; not yet anyhow. (*MD*, 187-88)

Even this late in the novel the sense of incompleteness in Clarissa's identity is still very strong; the "I" that she speaks in welcoming her guests does not satisfy her. She is still uncertain of what, or who, "herself" is; she still will not say of herself that she is one thing or another, a virgin in a narrow bed, or a smart London hostess.

Clarissa cannot feel herself as a single identity because she feels herself "everywhere; not 'here, here, here': . . . but everywhere" (*MD*, 168). Her "youthful theory" states what we have already seen to be the situation of identity: to know anyone "one must seek out the people who completed them; even the places" (*MD*, 168). All that appear in the world are "apparitions," but there is another "unseen" part of us that can survive even death, by attaching to other people, haunting other places.

> It ended in a transcendental theory which, with her horror of death, allowed her to believe, or say that she believed (for all her scepticism), that since our apparitions, the part of us which appears, are so momentary compared with the other, the unseen part of us, which spreads wide, the unseen might survive, be recovered somehow attached to this person or that, or even haunting certain places, after death. Perhaps—perhaps. (*MD*, 168)

The problem of identity is intricately bound up with that of knowing others, and because relationships form such a constantly shifting and widening web of interconnections there is no way of isolating one identity. Clarissa suggests an "essence" that is somehow "truer" than the "apparitions" of it which are identities in the shared world. The novel does not attempt to analyze what this essence might be, but clearly the fact of death is significant in the experience that allows for its perception.

The double aspect of death as a completion and cutting off of being dominates Clarissa Dalloway's thoughts. On one level *Mrs. Dalloway* can be read as her coming to terms with her death. During the day of the novel Clarissa moves from the crowd's understanding of death (the supreme expression of which is war) to a grasping of the fact of her own death for herself. Death is the prime manifestation of the horizon of time in human being, and it is important in Woolf's thinking, as will become increasingly clear; eventually we must be concerned with her idea of temporality.

The news of a young man's suicide disturbs that identity "composed so for the world only" that Clarissa had assumed for her party. It is through others' deaths that our "experience" of death comes. The first time Clarissa thinks about her death (*MD*, 11) she feels it does not really matter, as she is fixed on the present moment. "Everyone remembered," she thinks, and to set herself apart she plunges into "this, here, now, in front of her." Against the thought of death as absolute, ending her delight in the present moment, she sets her belief that she will survive on the "ebb and flow" of things, persist in the memories of those who know her. Later in the book, her "theory of life" recalls this belief, but for now her meditation springs from the loss of identity she suffers as she walks in the crowd up Bond Street.

That Clarissa is trying to recover an "image of white dawn in the country" reveals her more particular concern: the loss of time. Her quasi-mystical idea of death as transcending the limits of time is a turning away from the fact of death itself. The quotation from *Cymbeline*, that gently beats in Clarissa's mind throughout the book, and forms one of the links between her and Septimus, puts her thoughts under suspicion for the dirge operates under a double delusion: Guiderius and Arviragus not only believe wrongly that Imogen is dead, but also that she is the boy, Fidele.

Clarissa is further allied with Septimus by imagining herself as a mist. His death leads her to think of death itself; the finery of her party is stripped away; "one was alone" (*MD*, 202). For the first time in the novel, there is a sense that Clarissa has reached some sort of plateau; the death seems to have led her to a transcendence of identities; she becomes simply "Clarissa." The final lines of the novel—"It is Clarissa, he said./For there she was" (*MD*, 213)—endorse this sense (not *stated*) of completion, of unity.

That identity depends to a great extent on relationship, and that relationships are inevitably flawed (see next chapter), as Clarissa Dalloway feels, is an idea that we find in *To the Lighthouse*. The novel is pervaded by a bewilderment in the face of human relations and a longing for knowledge and intimacy. The question of *how* we can trust any of our feelings when each person presents to the world innumerable apparitions is still much in the writer's mind, particularly expressed in the character of the artist, Lily Briscoe: "How then did it work out, all this? How did one judge people, think of them? How did one add up this and that and conclude that it was liking one felt, or disliking? And to those words, what meaning attached, after all" (*TTL*, 42). The failed relationships of *To the Lighthouse* are testimony to that unsatisfactoriness of our knowledge of others that Clarissa Dalloway complains of.

Lily Briscoe's relationship with Mrs. Ramsay (presented

only from Lily's point of view) makes explicit the implications of the characteristic yearning for intimacy: in effect, Lily wants to *be* Mrs. Ramsay, to know her in a way that would dissolve all difference between them:

> What art was there, known to love or cunning, by which one pressed through into those secret chambers? What device for becoming, like waters poured into one jar, inextricably the same, one with the object one adored? Could the body achieve it, or the mind, subtly mingling in the intricate passages of the brain? or the heart? Could loving, as people called it, make her and Mrs. Ramsay one? (*TTL*, 82-83)

Knowing that she cannot "know one thing or another about people, sealed as they were," Lily Briscoe might be seen as a development from the hawk moth of *Jacob's Room* that hovered at the entrance to the cavern of mystery (*JR*, 72). Lily is a bee, haunting "the hives that were people" (*TTL*, 83). This ghostly bee accepts the inevitability of ignorance, giving the novel its affirming character. Apparitions are all that we know, and they are endless: "One wanted fifty pairs of eyes to see with, she reflected. Fifty pairs of eyes were not enough to get round that one woman, she thought. Among them, must be one that was stone blind to her beauty. . . . What did the hedge mean to her, what did the garden mean to her, what did it mean to her when a wave broke?" (*TTL*, 303-4). Even seen from everywhere, every experience understood, there remains missing that elusive "something absolute in us that despises qualification" (*JR*, 143): what I suggest might be the unnameable self, "the" Mrs. Ramsay, transcending all apparitions.

The "unseen part of us" that Clarissa Dalloway thought might survive death is given greater significance in *To the Lighthouse*. The "wedge-shaped core of darkness" of Mrs. Ramsay's solitary reverie (*TTL*, 99) is a development of what Clarissa called "the unseen part of us, which spreads wide" (*MD*, 168), a suggestion that is supported by a close similarity of description:

> . . . that since our apparitions, the part of us which appears, are so momentary compared with the other, the unseen part of us, which spreads wide, . . . (*MD*, 168)

> Our apparitions, the things you know us by, are simply childish. Beneath it is all dark, it is all spreading, it is unfathomably deep; but now and again we rise to the surface and that is what you see us by. (*TTL*, 100)

Just as in the previous novel, an invisible, spreading inner essence is posited which, it seems, is Mrs. Ramsay "herself."

This "wedge-shaped core of darkness" overcomes the boundaries of space and time ("Her horizons seemed to her limitless" [*TTL*, 100]) by not issuing in *action*. During this reverie it is emphasized that Mrs. Ramsay remains sitting upright in her chair, knitting. The being of this "core of darkness" is therefore put in question: to be is to live a body, subject to the passage of time and taking up so much space. If there is something that might be called self that does not share the modes of being so far established for identity, it will perhaps be impossible to *actually* describe.

I have spoken already of the need, expressed in *Mrs. Dalloway*, for a foundation for individual identity, and of the yearning for unity that is felt in the character of Clarissa. In *To the Lighthouse*, Mrs. Ramsay achieves a foundation and a unity by detaching herself from identity (as Clarissa seemed to when she withdrew from her party to the little room on hearing of Septimus Smith's suicide): "There was freedom, there was peace, there was, most welcome of all, a summoning together, a resting on a platform of stability. Not as oneself did one find rest ever, in her experience . . . but as a wedge of darkness. Losing personality, one lost the fret, the hurry, the stir" (*TTL*, 100). The question remains: what is left of an individual if she is abstracted from all involvements in the shared world of human relationships? Mrs. Ramsay's moment of solitude has about it an air of tending toward death; she seems to "triumph over life when things came together in this peace, this rest, this eternity" (*TTL*, 100). However, Woolf was certainly no mystic escaping the world through contemplation; once again, her understanding of the fact of death is centrally important.

Mrs. Ramsay is not only looking inward; she looks at the beam of the lighthouse, concentrating on it until she "became the thing she looked at" (*TTL*, 101). In this reverie, in which "personality" is lost, control is relinquished and the identity of the crowd can creep back in, as it does in the religious platitude that so annoys Mrs. Ramsay when she utters it:

It will come, it will come, when suddenly she added, We are in the hands of the Lord.

But instantly she was annoyed with herself for saying that. Who had said it? not she; she had been trapped into saying something she did not mean. (*TTL,* 101)

She is trying to reach a level of security that is not provided by the world in which she lives as mother, wife, and protector. A deity is no comfort in a world in which "there is no reason, order, justice; but suffering, death, the poor" (*TTL,* 102). In what is, in effect, her search for faith, Mrs. Ramsay looks to a world of beauty, to be found in nature and "oneself": "It was odd, she thought, how if one was alone, one leant to things, inanimate things; trees, streams, flowers; felt they expressed one; felt they became one; felt they knew one, in a sense were one; felt an irrational tenderness thus (she looked at that long steady light) as for oneself" (*TTL,* 101). To glance back at Clarissa Dalloway's moment of solitude (*MD,* 204), it may be that her looking out at the sky (which "held something of her own in it") is an adumbration of Mrs. Ramsay's act of faith here. What emerges from these two novels is a deep distrust of human identity and relationships, and a yearning for something "secure" that is not found by escaping from the world, but that inheres in it. Those bases of identity—body, name, memory, relationships—are double-edged: they can not only help form identity, but can also disperse it.

It may be that the realization of the self in the sense of a person purged of all apparitions (identities) is not a general human possibility, but the potential is certainly described again and again in Woolf's novels in characters from Mrs. Dalloway to Lucy Swithin. Before continuing with this investigation of the question of identity and self, I wish to draw attention to Woolf's experience over the years from the inception of *To the Lighthouse* to the beginning of *The Waves.* Judith Kegan Gardiner has written that "because of the continual crossing of self and other, women's writing may blur the public and private and defy completion. . . . The implied relationship between the self and what one reads and writes is personal and intense."[2] Many of the apparent obscurities of Woolf's fiction are illuminated by reference to her direct records of lived experience, primarily her diary. Certainly much more than a record of events, Woolf worked at her diary, sometimes rewriting parts of it, practicing and playing with ideas that often reappear transformed in her fiction. The discussion of identity and self has led now to a sense of "something more to life" that might compensate for the inadequacies of "apparitions" and their relationships; the diary may help us find out more about this yearning.

Virginia Woolf began to make up *To the Lighthouse* early in 1925 (see *D*, e.g., 6 January, 14 May). Toward the end of that year her relationship with Vita Sackville-West became closer and more intense and was to continue so for at least three years. I wish in particular to draw attention to the experiences of two summers at Monk's House, in Rodmell, Sussex, where Woolf lived from 1919. Both were recorded in her diary.

The first, in 1926, soon after writing the last pages of *To the Lighthouse*, echoes that experience of Mrs. Ramsay's just discussed:

> These 9 weeks give one a plunge into deep waters; which is a little alarming, but full of interest. All the rest of year one's (I daresay rightly) curbing & controlling this odd immeasurable soul. When it expands, though one is frightened & bored & gloomy, it is as I say to myself, awfully queer. There is an edge to it which I feel of great importance, once in a way. One goes down into the well & nothing protects one from the assault of truth. Down there I cant write or read; I exist however. I am. Then I ask myself what I am? & get a closer though less flattering answer than I should get on the surface— where, to tell the truth, I get more praise than is right. (*D*, 28 September 1926)

The invisible, spreading something is given a name here: the *soul.* Two days later she comments on the experience, wishing to "add some remarks to this, on the mystical side of this solitude." It is interesting that she is no clearer in her diary (where she might perhaps be expected to be more direct) than in the novel (assuming—as I do—that the diary and novel passages concern similar experiences). The "soul" still "despises qualification":

> . . . how it is not oneself but something in the universe that one's left with. It is this that is frightening & exciting in the midst of my profound gloom, depression, boredom, whatever it is: One sees a fin passing far out. What image can I reach to convey what I mean? Really there is none I think. The interesting thing is that in all my feeling & thinking I have never come up against this before. Life is, soberly and accurately, the oddest affair; has in it the essence of reality. I used to feel this as a child—

couldn't step across a puddle once I remember, for think-   *Perhaps The
ing, how strange—what am I? &c. But by writing I dont   Waves or moths
reach anything. All I mean to make is a note of a curious   (Oct. 1929)
state of mind. I hazard the guess that it may be the impulse behind another
book. At present my mind is totally blank & virgin of books.* (*D*, 30
September 1926)

The note she has written three years later encourages looking at
the diary to help understand the novels' provenance and indi-
cates the falsity of an approach to Woolf that proceeds along a
line of logical development. Her thought circles backwards and
forwards, creating webs of ideas, matrices of images.

It seems strange that she writes "life . . . has in it the essence of reality"; we might expect "life" and "reality" to be synonymous. However, 'reality' is a very special term in Woolf's lex-
icon and will be seen to be crucial in understanding her view of
self and its place in the world. To bring 'reality' into sharper
focus, let us turn once again to the diary.

Toward the end of the summer of 1928 Woolf wrote that
she had had a busy time; it had been "a summer lived almost too
much in public." She recalls previous summers spent at Monk's
House in which she had had a "religious retreat." It seems very
likely from what follows that she is remembering in particular
the summer of 1926:

> Often down here I have entered into a sanctuary; a nunnery; had a religious
> retreat; of great agony once; & always some terror: so afraid one is of
> loneliness: of seeing to the bottom of the vessel. That is one of the experi-
> ences I have had here in some Augusts; & got then to a consciousness of what
> I call 'reality': a thing I see before me; something abstract; but residing in
> the downs or sky; beside which nothing matters; in which I shall rest and
> continue to exist. Reality I call it. And I fancy sometimes this is the most
> necessary thing to me: that which I seek. But who knows—once one takes a
> pen & writes? How difficult not to go making 'reality' this & that, whereas it
> is one thing. Now perhaps this is my gift; this perhaps is what distinguishes
> me from other people; I think it may be rare to have so acute a sense of
> something like that—but again, who knows? I would like to express it too.
> (*D*, 10 September 1928)

With this entry the "something abstract" is clearer: it is 'not-
world,' 'not people,' suggestive almost of an *absence*. The "thing
I see before me" that resides in the downs or the sky at once

recalls the experiences of Clarissa Dalloway and Mrs. Ramsay. In this abstract 'reality,' Woolf says she will *rest*—as Mrs. Ramsay wishes to *rest* (*TTL*, 100)—and continue to exist, as perhaps Clarissa means when she says of the "unseen part" that it "might survive" (*MD*, 168).

Woolf feels privileged to have this consciousness of 'reality' and is explicit about wanting to express it. Near the end of her life she wrote that the "shock-receiving capacity" to perceive 'reality' was what made her a writer.[3] A little over a month after writing that passage in her diary, Woolf delivered two papers on "Women and Fiction" in Cambridge. These were expanded and published in 1929 as *A Room of One's Own*, where we find Woolf once more trying to explain 'reality':

> What is meant by "reality"? It would seem to be something very erratic, very undependable—now to be found in a dusty road, now in a scrap of news-paper in the street, now a daffodil in the sun. It lights up a group in a room and stamps some casual saying. *It overwhelms one walking home beneath the stars and makes the silent world more real than the world of speech*—and then there it is again in an omnibus in the uproar of Piccadilly. Some-times, too, it seems to dwell in shapes too far away for us to discern what their nature is. *But whatever it touches, it fixes and makes permanent.* That is what remains over when the skin of the day has been cast into the hedge; that is what is left of past time and of our loves and hates. *Now the writer*, as I think, *has the chance to live more than other people in the presence of this reality. It is his business to find it and collect it and communicate it to the rest of us* (165-66, my italics)

The question of whether there is an autonomous self apart from identity has led to the potential expressed in some of the characters of the novels and by Woolf herself in her diary, for apprehending a 'reality' that has no form or name in the world and that can only be experienced in solitude; a 'reality' that over-comes the horizons of space and time. This 'reality'—in Woolf's own words, "that which I seek"—will be the general focus of this study as it is the object of Woolf's faith, gradually conceived and expressed in her novels.

To the Lighthouse was published in May 1927, but even be-fore then Woolf conceived *Orlando*, a book she wrote at high speed while *The Waves* simmered in her mind. Indeed, the two books seem to have shared, in a sense, one creative impulse (see, e.g., a note made in 1933 against the diary entry for 14 March 1927). John Graham, writing on "The 'Caricature Value' of Parody and Fantasy in *Orlando*," puts well what I believe to be true of *Orlando*'s development of Woolf's thoughts on self and identity: "Caricature can explore because it ignores the complexity of the total object and isolates only its relevant features, thereby allowing a sharper focus of attention than is possible in a full treatment. In many ways it can function for the artist as a refined sort of doodling, in which he 'feels out' the forms and designs of his more serious work."[4] It is, nevertheless, generally agreed that *Orlando* gets increasingly serious; indeed, Woolf herself felt that what had begun as a "joke" did not end as one. The last chapter is greatly concerned with the heroine's identity and begins by musing on the difficulty of saying what "life" is. *The Waves* is prefigured at several points—e.g., 257: "Life? Literature? One to be made into the other? But how monstrously difficult!"

The tone of *Orlando* allows Woolf a directness that would be awkward in her other works. It should always be remembered in reading the book that it was an offering to Vita Sackville-West, and that it is "about" Knole and the Sackvilles in a much plainer sense than *To the Lighthouse* is about the Stephens. John Graham seems to have forgotten this when he complains, "By the time Orlando sits down in the long gallery of her home, she has become a distinctly credible aristocrat of the present age, down to the lavender bags, ropes, and name-cards which mark the passing of her private heritage into the public domain" (362). Orlando has *become* Vita, a metamorphosis that led to what Vita herself called "a new form of Narcissism." "I confess," she wrote, "I am in love with Orlando—this is a complication I had not foreseen."[5] That the "joke" was for Vita above all is demonstrated by the fact that it ends emphatically on the twelfth stroke of midnight, Thursday, 11 October 1928—the day *Orlando* was published and, as Vita's letter records, "the day I was to have it." This is perhaps a way of solving that problem of "Life? Literature? One to be made into the other?" that a work like *The Waves* could not achieve.

Having gone up to London to shop, Orlando is beset by memories that dislocate her sense of identity in the present. Getting into her car, Orlando, who has "gone a little too far from the present moment" (274), is vulnerable to a loss of identity caused by her failure to synchronize the different times that beat within her. To have an identity, it is suggested, there must be a sense of being in a present; also, identity appears to depend on coordinates of space. Motoring fast out of London, these coordinates of time and space are fragmented, and a "chopping up small" of identity occurs that, it is said, is like that which "precedes unconsciousness and perhaps death itself" (*O*, 276). As when Mrs. Ramsay slips into unconsciousness, there is a question as to the status of the person's existence: if identity is "chopped up small" where is the person to be located? The passage suggests that such unconsciousness is a different mode of existence altogether from identity in the actual world; the approach to death *might* reveal that mode also.

Once in the country, the continuity of the visual impressions Orlando receives gives her a "base" on which to reestablish identity. Identity is, as we have already learned, a series of apparitions, and it is apparitions that Woolf refers to by "selves" in this context. Orlando is composed of many different "selves," each having "attachments elsewhere, sympathies, little constitutions and rights of their own" (277): "How many different people are there not—Heaven help us—all having lodgement at one time or another in the human spirit?" (*O*, 277). There is nothing innovative about this view of human identity and, as the narrator says, "Everybody can multiply from his own experience the different terms which his different selves have made with him" (*O*, 277).

Orlando, however, seeks a particular identity, but this will not "come"; as she drives, her identities change. The problem of who it is that calls "Orlando?" and receives no answer is resolved by the introduction of the "conscious self, which is uppermost, and has the power to desire" (*O*, 279). Orlando is calling her "true self" which "some people" ("they") say is made up of "all the selves we have it in us to be; commanded and locked up by the Captain self, the Key self" (*O*, 279). The "true self" of Orlando, then, is an amalgam of all her identities (according to "some people"). This at once introduces the problem of how unity can be achieved while the person lives through time; *Orlando* escapes the problem by being a fantasy.

It is only when Orlando ceases to call for her "true self" that she becomes it, and it is in this that I believe the "joke's" serious underthought is glimpsed. In the paragraph describing Orlando's coalescence into a "true self" can be detected tenuous similarities with those "key" moments in both Clarissa Dalloway's and Mrs. Ramsay's life, that have been described above:

> The whole of her darkened and settled, as when some foil whose addition makes the round and solidity of a surface is added to it, and the shallow becomes deep and the near distant; and all is contained as water is contained by the sides of a well. So she was now darkened, stilled, and become, with the addition of this Orlando, what is called, rightly or wrongly, a single self, a real self. And she fell silent. For it is probable that when people talk aloud, the selves (of which there may be more than two thousand) are conscious of disseverment, and are trying to communicate, but when communication is established they fall silent. (*O,* 282)

There is a similarity of *mood* between this moment and (particularly) Mrs. Ramsay's moment of sinking down to "being oneself." Probably the experiences are quite distinct, but it must be admitted that the moment of "being oneself" is characterized by solemnity, darkness, and peace. In *Orlando* the "true self" comes in silence, which suggests that it cannot be named. Communication (voices, naming) is the mark of apparitions; but in what sense can something exist without a name, an actual being in the shared world? "Nothing should be named lest by doing so we change it," says Neville in *The Waves* (59). It is only by naming, however, that anything can be known. The problem of knowing what the "real self" 'is' in *Orlando* is explicitly founded in the problem of language. If the "real self" that Orlando sought comes only in silence, it is presumably outside language, outside naming.[6]

That there is "an emptiness about the heart of life" (*MD,* 35) is a recurring point in Woolf's fiction; for Lily Briscoe, for example, the scene she is trying to paint suddenly becomes "like curves and arabesques flourishing round a centre of complete emptiness" (*TTL,* 275). If "self" exists, its mode of existence is not that of a named thing in the actual world. The transcendent nature of 'reality' has already been implied. What I wish to elaborate is the idea in Woolf's fiction of a preverbal space from which human being arises (see *TTL*, 100). The "nothingness" it was earlier suggested the "self" might be (p. 24 above) will eventually be seen to be related to the modes of art in Woolf's aesthetic. In an essay of 1934, "Walter Sickert," Woolf wrote that maybe "there is a zone of silence in the middle of every art. The artists themselves live in it" (*CDB*, 191). Fundamental to Woolf's aesthetic is that these ideas must come to be felt in the reader's mind by "gathering fragments"; there can be no direct communication of self, of 'reality,' of nothingness. What we will eventually be led to is the strange notion of an absent presence, communicated in the act of reading.

Recent feminist criticism and speculative writing, in its discovery of women's experience, adds a further dimension to this issue, making Woolf's project, perhaps, seem less abstruse:

> I know that when I write there is something inside me that stops functioning, something that becomes silent. I let something take over inside me that probably flows from femininity. But everything shuts off—the analytic way of thinking, thinking inculcated by college, studies, reading, experience. I'm absolutely sure of what I'm telling you now. It's as if I were returning to a wild country. Nothing is concerted. Perhaps, before everything else, before being Duras, I am—simply—a woman.[7]

> And then, blank pages, gaps, borders, spaces and silence, holes in discourse: these women emphasize the aspect of feminine writing which is the most difficult to verbalize because it becomes compromised, rationalized, masculinized as it explains itself. . . . If the reader feels a bit disoriented in this new space, one which is obscure and silent, it proves perhaps, that it is women's space.[8] [dots in original]

> For some feminist critics, the wild zone, or "female space," must be the address of a genuinely woman-centered criticism, theory, and art, whose shared project is to bring into being the symbolic weight of female consciousness, to make the invisible visible, to make the silent speak.[9]

The "wild zone" that many women speak of (giving it various names) corresponds, I believe, to the empty center of Woolf's aesthetic. As will emerge, the apprehension of 'reality' is exclusive to women in the novels. This is not to say that it is only possible for women, but that women experience the world differently than men and experience it in such a way that silence and emptiness characterize their inward discourse.

This somewhat Shandean progression by digression is, I feel, valid in writing about Woolf as her art consistently defeats linear, discursive moves. The questions raised by the novels, that as readers we must attempt to answer for ourselves, stand in opposition to such thought as that of the early Wittgenstein, for whom "*the limits of my language* mean the limits of my world" (*Tractatus*, 5.6). The *Tractatus* (1908) concludes: "What we cannot speak about we must pass over in silence" (7). In her novels Woolf realizes that although what is outside life is outside language, what is outside language is not necessarily outside life. There is a silence at the heart of life in her works, but it is not Wittgenstein's silence. The fundamental question addressed by the novels is whether there can *be* anything *for us* outside language; can the self *be* if its mode of discourse is silence?

Woolf could not pass over in silence that whereof we cannot speak, but hovered over it incessantly. The idea of silence and emptiness at the heart of life seems to me the constant field of her inquiry, but it is not until her last work, *Between the Acts*, that this concern is brought into the foreground. She may well have taken courage from a writer who, as Allen McLaurin has noted, "was so deeply implanted in her thought that his ideas seemed to be her own" (*Virginia Woolf*, 3). In his notebook Samuel Butler wrote:

> The highest thought is ineffable; it must be felt from one person to another but cannot be articulated. All the most essential and thinking part of thought is done without words or consciousness. It is not till doubt and consciousness enter that words become possible.
>
> The moment a thing is written, or even can be written, and reasoned about, it has changed its nature by becoming tangible, and hence finite, and hence it will have an end in disintegration. It has entered into death. And yet till it can be thought about and realised more or less definitely it has not entered into life. Both life and death are necessary factors of each other. But our profoundest and most important convictions are unspeakable.[10]

Writing novels is, we might say, naming, however sophisticated,[11] and this might go some way to explaining the sense of longing common in Woolf's fiction. In a way she writes against herself all the time by adopting a position in which she says her task is hopeless, her goal impossible, but her effort inevitable. It should not be thought that this is a Beckettian pose[12]: Woolf's work is, on the whole, strongly affirmative; yet it may be that she affirms through the recognition of nothingness.

Having arrived at this somewhat Humean view of identity, we will do well to look briefly at some of the issues it raises, as the deeper concerns of the novels have emerged. In *The Waves* Bernard is a sort of spokesman for this view of human being, feeling that his life is a series of acts (apparitions): "They do not understand that I have to effect different transitions; have to cover the entrances and exits of several different men who alternately act their parts as Bernard" (*TW*, 55). When he invites "poor Simes" to dinner, he thinks he will have attributed to him "an admiration which is not mine" (55). Bernard says that the admiration inferred is not *really* his, and yet by inviting Simes to dinner one apparition makes contact with another. Bernard knows only apparitions of Simes; life indeed seems to be a mere procession of shadows, as was suggested in *Jacob's Room*.

Bernard is fascinated by the different apparitions he presents to the world, forever turning them around in his mind. The private Bernard—when "he" speaks to "himself"—is in a sense an internal apparition: "Underneath, and, at the moment when I am most disparate, I am most integrated" (55). "Bernard" to Bernard is merely the voice that speaks in him when he talks (as we all do) to himself. To conceive of oneself in this way is immediately to suggest duality—a "self" regarding a "self." We can say, then, that this (Bernard to himself) is not the "real self" because once communication is established, language has always already taken the "self" into its system of apparitions. If named, the "true self" would become an element of the novel, given a status, a being among others. It seems that there can be no such self in the light of what has already been said, because if it *is* to be absolute it escapes the limitations of time and space on anything in the world. Only nothing (no-thing) escapes those limitations (horizons).

Yet again and again, the novels enshrine privileged moments in which a self (or now, to be direct, a *soul*) is posited. What Woolf only very rarely called "soul" (e.g., in her diary, as referred to above, p. 33), and what I (and sometimes she) call "self" are both terms for that invisible "something" that is apart from all apparitions, that can transcend the horizons of space and time, and that has its "being" in silence. Also, it has appeared so far, the self or soul has a special and uncommunicable relationship with an abstract 'reality' residing in the actual world.

The self cannot be constructed from identities; to Neville's (paradigmatic) question "Who am I?" (60), there can be no single answer: "As he approaches I become not myself but Neville mixed . . . with Bernard" (*TW*, 60). Likewise, Bernard is "mixed" with Neville: "Now that we look at the tree together, it has a combed look, each branch distinct, and I will tell you what I feel, under the compulsion of your clarity" (*TW*, 60). Others cannot tell us who we are because they see themselves in us, who see ourselves in them, and so on; there is such a mingling together of different identities that another can only give a version of us. Bernard knew this as a child: "But when we sit together, close, . . . we melt into each other with phrases. We are edged with mist. We make an unsubstantial territory" (*TW*, 11). We can only think *about* ourselves through the medium of language; if there is a "real self" it cannot, as *Orlando* stated, be thought *about*.

As Bernard grows up, and the novel progresses, more and more fragments that have "Bernard" as their signature emerge: he is most himself to himself composed of many different parts, and so there is no one Bernard (no "what is called, rightly or wrongly" in *Orlando* "real self"). Bringing together his "shabby inmates," Bernard feels whole, but this wholeness is merely aggregation, not a divisionless synthesis. In Bernard is found an attitude to identity unlike any that has so far been described, because he welcomes his diversity; unity seems to repel him because he sees that wholes are illusions: "What am I? There is no stability in this world. Who is to say what meaning there is in anything? Who is to foretell the flight of a word? It is a balloon that sails over tree-tops. To speak of knowledge is futile. All is experiment and adventure" (*TW*, 84). Bernard, the writer, sees through the "veil of words," but rejoices in their capacity for giving at least a sense of wholeness to a world in which only apparitions can act: "I feel at once, as I sit down at a table, the delicious jostle of confusion, of uncertainty, of possibility, of speculation. Images breed instantly. I am embarrassed by my own fertility. I could describe every chair, table, luncher here copiously, freely. My mind hums hither and thither with its veil of words for everything" (*TW*, 84). Words fix as immutable a reality that is constantly changing, and by this naming provide a foundation for identity.

In the character of Bernard it is realized that identity cannot be fixed by the "I"; he does not *know* his identity as a unity, but never tires of describing its perpetual changes: "For there is nothing to lay hold of. I am made and remade continually. Different people draw different words from me" (*TW*, 96). As life continues Bernard becomes increasingly aware of how identity depends almost entirely upon circumstances. There are moments when a single identity dominates, under the influence of a particular event, such as when his proposal of marriage is accepted: "I, who have been since Monday, when she accepted me, charged in every nerve with a sense of identity" (*TW*, 80). In the street, in the crowd, he tries to shake off this enclosing singularity and let identity sink down, to become "like everybody else," but this is impossible for one who so persistently reflects on his own identity: "One cannot extinguish that persistent smell. It steals in through some crack in the structure—one's identity. I am not part of the street—no, I observe the street. One splits off, therefore" (*TW*, 82).

Identity closes off things as they are, for everything is experienced by a particular identity. Thus the world appears as an enormously complicated assembly of reflections, in which "I" exist only as the result of influences colored by other "I's," which in their turn are formed by reflection. Identity as a single, firmly grasped unity called "I" no longer exists: "To be myself (I note) I need the illumination of other people's eyes, and therefore cannot be entirely sure what is my self" (*TW*, 83). From this fascinating doubt Bernard becomes yet another "I," the "I" of his soliloquies, observing all the others. The world for Bernard becomes so familiar that eventually he no longer questions it, seeming to accept that "I" is never fixed: "We are all swept on by the torrent of things grown so familiar that they cast no shade; we make no comparisons; think scarcely ever of I or of you" (*TW*, 153).

To "explain to you the meaning of my life" (*TW*, 168), Bernard can only continue to tell stories, but "none of them are true" (*TW*, 169). Talking of his friends, Bernard tells his guest (who must listen for all of us) how they have contributed to him, made him what he is (*TW*, 196, 199). As he tells his story, he emphasizes that he is merely fabricating (as already noted, Woolf often seems to write against herself): "Let us again pretend that life is a solid substance, shaped like a globe, which we turn about in our fingers. Let us pretend that we can make out a plain and logical story, so that when one matter is despatched—love for instance—we go on, in an orderly manner, to the next" (*TW*, 178).

To do anything but merely exist (like a tree) we must make up stories; as soon as we dip into the great bran-pie we alter it forever, but we pretend we have left it just as it was. Again the nothingness of an absolute self is implied. Bernard echoes the others' soliloquies in the smallest details, showing that what is Bernard himself is indistinguishable from what is Louis, Jinny, Susan, Neville, or Rhoda—those others whose lives *The Waves* traces. Nevertheless, "if there are no stories, what end can there be, or what beginning?" (*TW*, 189). Bernard incessantly spins out words, because "it is the effort and the struggle, it is the perpetual warfare, it is the shattering and piecing together—this is the daily battle, defeat or victory, the absorbing pursuit" (*TW*, 191). Even as he says this, he sees through his "veil of words": "The true order of things—this is our perpetual illusion—is now apparent" (*TW*, 193).

Bernard's experience of the "world seen without a self" is an attempt to be in the world without any apparitions; to experience a moment of being from the position of the nothing that it has been implied "is" the self: "But how describe the world seen without a self? There are no words. Blue, red—even they distract, even they hide with thickness instead of letting the light through" (*TW*, 204). Again, it is language that comes between knowledge and experience: only an apparition can speak to us, and only words can tell the story of the "world seen without a self," which puts it among apparitions and so denies as it affirms.

The Waves exposes a gulf between language and reality, identity and self, that is rarely acknowledged in fiction. This, and the wider question it implies of the relationship between life and art, will be returned to below once the terms of Woolf's aesthetic have been established. Before that, however, the theme of relationship (upon which identity to a great extent depends) should be examined more closely. Identity is intricately bound up with embodiment, with perception, and with relationship.

CHAPTER THREE
OTHERS

TO BE IS TO BE WITH OTHERS, JUST AS IT IS TO BE IN TIME, AND TO "LIVE" A body. It is in relationships with others that the possibilities and limitations of human being are realized, and it is against the background of others that individual identity stands out. The most typical relationships of Virginia Woolf's novels are between two people only; there is, of course, interest in the "party consciousness," but the most frequent relationship is between two: husband and wife, parent and child, lovers, friends, meeting with a stranger, an old and a young person, male and female—these are the most common foci. All Woolf's work is concerned with knowledge, or the impossibility of knowledge; in relationships, knowledge can only be gained from communication, and it is this aspect of relating to others that is featured most prominently. "Communication is health; communication is happiness" (*MD*, 104), but it is also deeply unsatisfactory. The world that emerges from Woolf's first two novels is one in which any relationship that is not an illusion seems quite impossible: "In what can one trust? Not in men and women. Not in one's dreams about them. There's nothing—nothing, nothing left at all" (*ND*, 163).

There is not a broad spectrum or variety of types of relationship in Woolf's novels. The inward-looking tendency of most of the characters precludes any view of society at large, but to write of that would, in any case, be to write of the crowd. Relationships presented in the novels are often deeply flawed, marked by a strong sense of the inadequacy of communication and the hopelessness of love. Against this, as we might expect, is a countermovement: life is endlessly exciting, offering fresh possibilities at every moment: "Every time the door opened and fresh people came in, those already in the room shifted slightly; those who were standing looked over their shoulders; those who were sitting stopped in the middle of sentences. What with the light, the wine, the strumming of a guitar, something exciting happened each time the door opened. Who was coming in?" (*JR*, 109).

The characters of *Jacob's Room*, as Leonard Woolf noticed, are all ghosts; their contacts form "spiritual shapes" that shift and splinter, never enduring. A mood Woolf recorded in her diary seems to dominate the novel: "Why is life so tragic; so like a little strip of pavement over an abyss" (*D*, 25 October 1920). The diary mood is directly reflected in the novel: "What does one fear?— the human eye. At once the pavement narrows, the chasm deepens" (*JR*, 80).

Above it was said that apparitions are all that can be known in the actual world. In this novel the effect of this on human relations is pervasive: "Nobody sees anyone as he is . . . They see a whole—they see all sorts of things—they see themselves" (*JR*, 28-29). Life surrounds us as a network of "wires and tubes"; letters pass, telephones ring, visits are made—as they are throughout all the novels—but all this communication serves to cover the emptiness of being unable to know others as "I."[1] Language contaminates: for example, Jacob must not *say* that he loves Clara Durrant: "No, no, no . . . don't break—don't spoil'—what? Something infinitely wonderful" (*JR*, 70); and, we may add, unnameable.

Jacob's Room reflects the "blowing this way and that" of life; relationships are fleeting, observed obliquely by the shifting narrator. Relationship is marked by a longing for unspoken intimacy; not that silent understanding that grows up between a husband and wife from habit, that Woolf referred to as early as *The Voyage Out*, but a more perfect knowledge of others. Jacob's encounter in Greece with Sandra Wentworth Williams is an image of the nature of relationships: "For she could not stop until she had told him—or heard him say—or was it some action on his part that she required? Far away on the horizon she discerned it and could not rest" (*JR*, 158). The horizon moves perpetually as one moves toward it, and so it is in relationships: they are characterized by a yearning for an impossible communication. This part of *Jacob's Room*—his trip to Greece—is heavy with the sense of life's transience and a thought felt throughout Woolf's works that nothing remains of relationships. The "metaphysical" desire to escape the bounds of physical life is implied in Jacob's gift to Sandra of the poems of Donne:

> They had vanished. There was the Acropolis; but had they reached it? The columns and the Temple remain; the emotion of the living breaks fresh on them year after year; and of that what remains?
> As for reaching the Acropolis who shall say that we ever do it, or that when Jacob woke next morning he found anything hard and durable to keep forever? (160)

The failure of relationships, specifically of love, to "make of the moment something permanent" continues to be an important theme in *Mrs. Dalloway*. One of Clarissa's most vivid memories is of her youthful passion for her friend Sally Seton, and an occasion on which Sally kissed her. This special moment is significantly imaged by Clarissa as the receiving of something tangible: "And she felt that she had been given a present, wrapped up, and told just to keep it, not to look at it—a diamond, something infinitely precious, wrapped up, which, as they walked (up and down, up and down), she uncovered, or the radiance burnt through, the revelation, the religious feeling!" (*MD*, 40). This "religious feeling" is a *momentary* experience of that perfection of relationship that is longed for in the novels. It cannot persist in the actual world, but passes as all moments do. The feeling does, however, remain in Clarissa's memory, a mode of being that overcomes spatiotemporal horizons. The diamond is a symbol of unity (not just in this novel); it is recalled when Clarissa "points" herself at her mirror (42). The moment with Sally is destroyed when Peter Walsh intrudes (throughout the novels men—Mr. Ramsay, Bart Oliver—will intrude on moments of "wholeness" and harmony experienced by women, shattering them). The moment is, though, the source of Clarissa's longing for a perfect union. Possessed by that wonder at simply being at all that is a feature of all the novels, Clarissa wishes to combine people, in an effort to create a whole she can only imagine: "Here was So-and-so in South Kensington; some one up in Bayswater; and somebody else, say, in Mayfair. And she felt quite continuously a sense of their existence; and she felt what a waste; and she felt what a pity; and she felt if only they could be brought together; so she did it. And it was an offering; to combine, to create; but to whom?" (*MD*, 134-35). Her judgments remain "superficial . . . fragmentary," yet if she can put the fragments together she feels a *gestalt* may be formed.

The desire to combine with others is not confined to Clarissa; the provincial diners at Peter Walsh's hotel have a "desire, pulsing in them, tugging at them subterraneously, somehow to establish connections" (*MD*, 175). Peter Walsh, taken into the little world of the Morris family for a moment, feels contentment in the seeming wholeness of their relationships. The family is a system that sustains life over the "abyss." Similar to it is "that network of visiting, leaving cards, being kind to people" (*MD*, 86) that is Clarissa's way of sustaining life, of creating a complex over the emptiness she feels lies at the heart of things. Such complexes form, break, and reform perpetually: strangers glance at one another, or are united by perceptions (as in the episodes of the mysterious car and the skywriting aeroplane), but only momentarily. The horizon of time prevents wholes from forming, prevents the perfection of relationship because identity is always in flux. Wolfgang Iser has written interestingly on this in a chapter on "Self-reduction" in *The Implied Reader*:

> Past and present can never be completely synthesized. Every incipient systematization is refuted by time, which as a new present exposes the ephemeral nature of any such synthesis. But it is only through subjectivity itself that time takes on its form of past, present, and future; the self is not the passive object of this process, but actually conditions it. With which of its states, then, is the self to be identified? Is it that which existed in the circumstances of the past, is it that which it is at this moment in the present, or is it simply that force which constantly creates new connections and time relations but which, at the same time, constantly plunges every one of its visible manifestations into the maelstrom of change? The self is essentially incapable of completion, and this fact accounts both for its inadequacy and its richness. The knowledge that it can never be completely in possession of itself is the hallmark of its consciousness. (144-45)

The desire for *pattern* that is so strong in Woolf's fiction is a desire to overcome the disruption of time; circling backwards and forwards in memory is the form of her art, a mental challenge to the linear progress of time.

To Rezia Warren Smith love "makes one solitary" (*MD*, 27), and to Clarissa love is a "monster"; and yet love combines, and in the first flush of passion seems to transcend the reflecting apparitions of everyday life. Clarissa scoffs at Peter being "sucked under in his little bow-tie," but "in her heart she felt, all the same; he is in love. He has that, she felt; he is in love" (*MD*, 50). Whatever its status, love has the power of widening the pavement over the abyss, but only for a moment. Marriage weaves a cocoon round Clarissa in which she can "crouch like a bird and gradually revive" (*MD*, 203). She understands that Richard wishes to tell her that he loves her without his speaking (although his bunch of roses operates in the same way as words [130]), but in their silence Richard and Clarissa are closed to each other.

Whether we feel that we know nothing about others (as Sally Seton feels), or that we know everything (as Peter), relationships are characterized by a lack, by a pointing-up of our ultimate aloneness. *Mrs. Dalloway* is greatly concerned with communication and with relationships through time; memory affects present relationships and alters those of the past. As in *Jacob's Room*, there inheres in the book a longing to make a definite statement about a life that seems so amorphous.

Clarissa has an inherent desire to combine, in the hope of somehow discovering a revelatory order to the world. As this hope is perpetually defeated, the combinative instinct doubles on itself: her parties become "an offering for the sake of offering, perhaps." Peter wonders why he does as he does (*MD*, 58); there are no answers for him, only a drive to combine. Left too long in solitude, one's sense of individual identity begins to slip. The urge to combine, then, is in order to see one's "own" reflection, basing one's own identity on the fact that one is with others. At the close of the novel, Clarissa cannot bear solitude in the little room for long; "but she must go back. She must *assemble*" (*MD*, 205, my italics).

As a theme, relationship in *To the Lighthouse* is complex, although a sharply delineated pattern, with Mrs. Ramsay at the center, is discernible. The relationship between Mr. and Mrs. Ramsay is largely unarticulated, and yet it is in a way the source of the moods and rhythms of the novel. Mrs. Ramsay is the prime exemplar of the female's combining powers and influence; more, even, than Clarissa, she has "that woman's gift, of making a world of her own wherever she happened to be" (*MD*, 84-85).

Mrs. Ramsay, sitting in the window, is aware of a "scale of sounds pressing on top of her"; from the sounds of men talking, children playing, and waves breaking she weaves a fabric as she sits knitting her stocking. If one of these elements changes (e.g., the men stop talking), the pattern she perceives as life flowing on its natural course is disturbed; she suddenly perceives the beating of the waves as ominous. The sound of the sea is the base of the rhythmic pattern she perceives as she sits with James; it has a double aspect, therefore, of comfort and threat.

In the Ramsays' marriage is seen once more the impossibility of reaching another's solitude: Mr. Ramsay wants to protect his wife, but "he could not reach her, he could do nothing to help her" (*TTL*, 104). Men standing in a mysterious accord with "the laws of the universe," Mrs. Ramsay accepts that her husband's "great mind" must feed on hers, shadowing it as if his mind were a giant hand blotting out the sun: "So boasting of her capacity to surround and protect, there was scarcely a shell of herself left for her to know herself by" (*TTL*, 63).

The seventh section of "The Window" is almost entirely concerned with Mrs. Ramsay's sense of "the inadequacy of human relationships, that the most perfect was flawed." Her solitude is broken into by the effort of combining, leaving her depleted and dejected, uncertain of her own being. Aware of this, she must still create, combine, and offer, making matches because she sees potential in the union of two people for something whole and lasting.

Marriage still is an unsatisfactory compromise in which one person—invariably the woman—must sacrifice her own wishes to serve her partner's shortcomings. The remoteness of Mrs. Ramsay's reverie "pains" her husband because he feels she does not need him. He is mistaken, however, for she wishes upon herself his draining demands: "That was what she wanted—the asperity in his voice, reproving her." For anyone to see that *he* needed *her* would upset Mrs. Ramsay's idea of how the world is, a concept against which her children quietly rebel.

That love cannot overcome human separateness is emphasized by Lily's desire to "make her and Mrs. Ramsay one." Lily Briscoe unifies the Ramsays with a label: "So that is marriage, Lily thought, a man and a woman looking at a girl throwing a ball"

(*TTL*, 114). Near the end of the book, Lily thinks back on her previous visit (*TTL*, 305) and realizes that there can be no way of simplifying their relationship. It is in her memory of Mrs. Ramsay's silence that Lily comes to understand the imperfection of human relationships. Silence is not passive in Woolf's work; it questions language; silence "communicates" in its own mode.

> Mrs. Ramsay sat silent. She was glad, Lily thought, to rest in silence, uncommunicative; to rest in the extreme obscurity of human relationships. Who knows what we are, what we feel? Who knows even at the moment of intimacy, This is knowledge? Aren't things spoilt then, Mrs. Ramsay may have asked (it seemed to have happened so often, this silence by her side) by saying them? Aren't we more expressive thus? (*TTL*, 264-65)

It is worth noting that in the holograph draft of the novel, Lily relates this silence specifically to relationships between women: "Aren't we at any rate women <better> more expressive silently gliding high together, side by side, in the curious dumbness, which is so much to <their> ones taste than speech"[2].

Families, as is seen in the earlier novels, produce tensions of loyalty in their members. Ralph Denham, in *Night and Day*, has to wrest every moment of his privacy from the grasp of the family system; a desire to be alone is regarded with suspicion. Mr. Ramsay arouses extremes of passion in his children; their loyalties are divided not only between their mother and father but between each other and their parents. Though Cam, sailing to the lighthouse with James and their father, loves him for his eccentricity, she also hates his tyranny, which "poisoned her childhood." Her affection finds no voice because her detestation of his insouciance always rises up to counter it. Cam is in a position similar to that Lily experienced with regard to William Bankes: how can one ever say it is liking or disliking one feels if opinions about a single person so conflict? James, too, hates "the twang and twitter of his father's emotion" for it "disturbs the perfect simplicity and good sense of his relations with his mother" (*TTL*, 61).

Despite this, Mr. Ramsay is a heroic figure, even for James. On the journey to the lighthouse, James sees him as a personification of "that loneliness which was for both of them the truth about things" (311). The ultimate solitude of individual being is once again realized in silence. There is a constant yearning for communication—when James is praised by his father, Cam sees immediately that his indifference is only feigned—but when contact is made, nothing endures; the moment passes to reassert essential loneliness: "What do you want? they both wanted to ask. They both wanted to say, Ask us anything and we will give it you. But he did not ask them anything" (*TTL*, 318).

Lily's opinion of marriage is familiar from the preceding novels: "She need not marry, thank Heaven: she need not undergo that degradation. She was saved from that dilution" (*TTL*, 159). And yet, despite this feeling that "there is nothing more tedious, puerile, and inhumane than love," and that women are worse off for it than men, most people, especially, thinks Lily, most women, see love as "beautiful and necessary." This tension characterizes the attitude to love in the novels. Without love "life will run upon the rocks," but with it "she would never know him. He would never know her." Combination and creation wreathe an illusion around the emptiness at the heart of people, but without that there would be no life. Only the mind speaking the novel sees the emptiness within: "All of them bending themselves to listen thought 'Pray heaven that the inside of my mind may not be exposed,' for each thought, 'The others are feeling this. They are outraged and indignant with the government about the fishermen. Whereas, I feel nothing at all' " (*TTL*, 146).

As before, Woolf's diary can help to relate the fictional world to that of lived experience, filled as it is with her musings on relationships. There are two passages that I wish to examine, both of which can be related convincingly to the mood of *Mrs. Dalloway*, although they were written some years later. That sense of something tangible that Clarissa felt she received in Sally Seton's kiss is yearned for throughout the fiction. Lily Briscoe, in *To the Lighthouse*, longs for Mrs. Ramsay after her death, feeling that perhaps if she could demand it with enough force, "beauty would roll itself up; the space would fill; those empty flourishes would form into shape" (*TTL*, 277).

Human relationships in Woolf's fiction are characterized by a lack, a sense that the longed-for knowledge of another can never be achieved. Woolf records this feeling in her diary: "Eddy has just gone, leaving me the usual feeling: why is not human intercourse more definite, tangible: why aren't I left holding a small round substance, say of the size of a pea, in my hand; something I can put in a box & look at? There is so little left" (*D*, 8 August 1928). The sense of life's transience so prevalent in the fiction I would suggest stems from Woolf's own experience. This long reflection in her diary, for example, expounds thoughts that are familiar from as early as *The Voyage Out* (where Rachel Vinrace feels people may be patches of light crossing the surface of the world [*TVO*, 358]), and which become more and more central from *Jacob's Room* onwards.

> Yet these people one sees are fabric only made once in the world; these contacts we have are unique; & if E. were, say killed tonight, nothing definite would happen to me; yet his substance is never again to be repeated. Our meeting is—but the thread of this idea slips perpetually; constantly though it recurs, with sadness, to my mind: how little our relationships matter; & yet they are so important: in him, in me, something to him, to me, infinitely sentient, of the highest vividness, reality. But if I died tonight, he too would continue. Something illusory then enters into all that part of life. I am so important to myself: yet of no importance to other people: like the shadow passing over the downs. (*D*, 8 August 1928)

The image of human relationships as a series of apparitions, each reflecting others, is familiar in the fiction. It is the fact of living through time, being thrown into a life that tends only toward death, that gives Woolf her sense that other people are ephemeral and unknown, and yet that they are the only hope of covering over the emptiness at the heart of life. To survive through time, a relationship must live in the memory, but there it will be altered, given a shape other than that which it has in the actual world because the modes of being in memory cannot be bound by time in the same way as those of life in the "present." This, too, Woolf records: "And what remains of Eddy is now in some ways more vivid, though more transparent, all of him composing itself in my mind, all I could get of him, & making itself a landscape appropriate to it; making a work of art for itself" (*D*, 8 August 1928). A work of art—especially a novel—is the creation of a world within the actual world, a revelation of the possibility of a mode of existence not bound by the spatiotemporal horizons of actual life.

Lily Briscoe creates with the fragments of her memory:

"Going to the Lighthouse. But what does one send to the Light-house? Perished. Alone. The grey-green light on the wall oppo-site. The empty places. Such were some of the parts, but how bring them together?" (*TTL*, 228). Lily likens her memories to works of art, trying to recreate her past in the present. In the modes of art it may be that the curves and arabesques of memory can coalesce to "make of the moment something permanent"; certainly the life of the actual, shared world of human relation-ships alone does not offer this possibility.

Almost a year later, Woolf again wrote in her diary of life's empty center, seen in moments when the illusion of relationship fails. There is an exact homology between the entry in the diary and a passage in *Mrs. Dalloway* where Peter Walsh suddenly feels that his life is unreal. Standing alone in London (54 f.) he is overcome by a sense that because Clarissa refused him, his life has been meaningless, merely a habit forced on him by the flow of time.

> As a cloud crosses the sun, silence falls on London; and falls on the mind. Effort ceases. Time flaps on the mast. There we stop; there we stand. Rigid, the skeleton of habit alone upholds the human frame. Where there is nothing, Peter Walsh said to himself; feeling hollowed out, utterly empty within. Clarissa refused me, he thought. He stood there thinking, Clarissa refused me. (*MD*, 55)

Peter's "looking rather drearily into the glassy depths" (55) is exactly recalled in Woolf's diary in an entry made on returning from a trip to France in 1929:

> And a sense of nothingness rolls about the house; what I call the sense of "Where there is nothing." This is due to the fact that we came back from France last night & are not going round in the mill yet. Time flaps on the mast—my own phrase I think. . . . Time flaps on the mast. And then I see through everything. Perhaps the image ought to have been one that gives an idea of a stream becoming thin: of seeing to the bottom.[3] (*D*, 15 June 1929)

To *live* (in a positive, transitive sense) is a matter of *effort* in Woolf's eyes. Identity is formed partly by relating with others, and thereby a sense of purpose is bestowed on life; relationship widens the strip of pavement over the abyss. However, the shad-ows that we grasp at are known to be illusory, in the sense that they are impermanent and cannot share in the individual "I" of each human being:

> Now time must not flap on the mast any more. Now I must somehow brew another decoction of illusion. Well, if the human interest flags—if its that that worries me, I must not sit thinking about it here. I must make human illusion—ask someone in tomorrow after dinner; & begin that astonishing adventure with the souls of others again—about which I know so little. (*D*, 15 June 1929)

If identity in solitude fails so abruptly, something must be found to "anchor" oneself in the world. It is from the ambivalence of her attitude to human relationships that the need arises in Woolf to find a faith in something apart from those apparitions. This faith, though, is not always available, and at such times despair at the ultimate nothingness of existence, unrelieved by philosophical or religious comforts, takes over.

As in all the novels, in *The Years* the door keeps opening and people keep coming in. If we stop to wonder why we bother to combine and create, to talk and to smile with strangers or loved ones, to feel jealousy or hatred, it seems it is to deny the loneliness and intensity of solitude, to diminish the forces of life: "But one wants somebody to laugh with, she thought. Pleasure is increased by sharing it. Does the same hold good of pain? she mused. Is that the reason why we all talk so much of ill-health—because sharing things lessens things? Give pain, give pleasure an outer body, and by increasing the surface diminish them" (*TY*, 379). Such sharing, though, is "a bit of a farce," as Peggy Pargiter realizes when she talks with a young stranger at the family party that concludes the novel:

> She had heard it all before. I, I, I—he went on. . . . But why let him? she thought, as he went on talking. For what do I care about his "I, I, I"? Or his poetry? Let me shake him off then, she said to herself . . . She paused. He noted her lack of sympathy. He thought her stupid, she supposed.
> "I'm tired," she apologised. "I've been up all night," she explained. "I'm a doctor—"
> The fire went out of his face when she said "I." That's done it—now he'll go, she thought. He can't be "you"—he must be "I." She smiled. For up he got and off he went. (*TY*, 389)

The fault of the failure does not lie entirely with the young man, nor with Peggy, but with the structures of convention within which their contact is made; these structures are enshrined in language. Silence is forbidden by convention, but silence can not become the covering over that language is. When silence gapes—"the immense vacancy of the primeval maw"—we must rush to fill the gap: "Somebody has to say something or human society would cease" (*TY*, 408). Communication is used not to reveal but to conceal the abyss, dispelling silence but preserving the illusion of relationships:

> It's no go, North thought. He can't say what he wants to say; he's afraid. They're all afraid; afraid of being laughed at; afraid of *giving themselves away*. . . . We're all afraid of each other, he thought; afraid of what? Of criticism; of laughter; of people who think differently. . . . [in original] . . . That's what separates us; fear, he thought. (*TY*, 447, my italics)

Thus far, this account of Woolf's view of identity and relationship has revealed the horizons within which human beings must inevitably proceed: the limitations of embodiment; of living through time; the constant dispersing of unity; the lack of a tangible center. From a deep dissatisfaction with relationship and communication arises a drive to find meaning in solitude. Solitude, however, is repeatedly seen to reveal the nothingness of the ultimate possibility of non-being. To find a secure meaning seems an insoluble problem, at least in the context of the actual world of time and death. If there is any possibility of transcendence, it will be realized in a mode of being totally other than that of the actual world.

Again and again, the movement toward such transcendence in Woolf's fiction begins with a radical questioning of actual life:

> She was alone with Eleanor in the cab. And they were passing houses. Where does she begin, and where do I end? she thought. . . . [in original] On they drove. They were two living people, driving across London; two sparks of life enclosed in two separate bodies; and those sparks of life enclosed in two separate bodies are at this moment, she thought, driving past a picture palace. But what is this moment; and what are we? The puzzle was too difficult for her to solve it. She sighed. (*TY*, 360)

With the conditions of her inquiry into human being outlined as they have been, it would appear that Woolf's work is profoundly pessimistic. However, her fiction *does* offer the opportunity for transcendence. We should now gather some of the hints that have appeared in discussing identity and relationship and focus on the development of Woolf's aesthetic. Her idea of 'reality' cannot be grasped without an understanding of the transformative modes of her art, in which the paradigm of the "empty center" forms a link between the worlds of lived experience and of art in the formal structuring it receives in her fiction.

CHAPTER FOUR
ART

VIRGINIA WOOLF HAD A COLERIDGEAN ABILITY TO SEE HER MIND AS A thinking instrument and frequently pondered on the creative process and the artistic realignments of her lifetime, as well as her relation to her contemporaries and to tradition. She seems to me, however, to have stood apart from the vehemence and passionate concern with the actual, physical world that was frequently the characteristic of the work of her contemporaries in England and, more markedly, Europe. Although she certainly was concerned with politics—sexual politics in particular—there is a notable absence in her work of the sensual, tactile world that is so much a part of, say, Joyce or Lawrence, and the technological world that inspired Marinetti and the Futurists, the Dynamists, and to some extent the Expressionists. Some might construe this as Bloomsbury élitism, but I would prefer to see in it evidence of a political stance that contradicts art such as that, for example, of the Futurists.[1] The actual world, of course, takes a large part in her work, but she seems always to be seeking to express a perception of the numinous. There exists throughout Woolf's fiction a tension between Kantian "transcendental" knowledge, which shapes the world, and the sense of something beneath or beyond the shapes.

In her essays and fiction, Woolf's concern with art *per se* was primarily with writing, but she had much to say of music and painting also, and drew careful analogies between different artistic modes. As her writing career progressed, her deep and perpetual concern shifted in its focus from art to the artist (*To the Lighthouse* marking a definite change in perspective).

The ontological importance of writing to Woolf cannot be overestimated: she believed writing to *be* her life. In "Reading" she wrote, "somewhere, everywhere, now hidden, now apparent in whatever is written down is the form of a human being"

(*CDB*, 175). The human being in Woolf's writing is elusive, but never more apparent than when she writes about creating.

Having had no formal education in her youth and a fairly wide-ranging literary experience, Woolf was acutely aware of tradition. Her novels are laced throughout with quotations and allusions that are never merely decorative, but always apposite and enriching, often applying one more light touch, one more angle of vision, to the picture she is composing. Sometimes such a reference is used as a motif, gathering associations to itself as the novel progresses, recognition of which induces many links and memories. An example is the "fear no more the heat o' the sun" of *Mrs. Dalloway*, that gently beats in Clarissa's mind from the time she actually reads the line in Hatchard's window, to its absorption by her toward the end of the book; that the same words come to Septimus is a mirroring effect that should not go unnoticed. Apart from forming one bridge between Septimus and Clarissa, the lines from *Cymbeline* broaden that Shelleyan idea in the novel of death as a gentle release from the awful difficulties of life; the dirge is calming, an image of death not unlike Terence Hewet's representation in *The Voyage Out* of death as being just like sleep (170). Such careful choice of allusion has been noted operating very subtly:

> At the height of one of Mr. Ramsay's panics . . . Mrs. Ramsay is disclosed reading a fairy story to her son James. It is the Grimms' tale of "The Fisherman and his Wife," and through twenty-odd pages of the novel Virginia Woolf marvellously counterpoints their story with hers: the coastline setting, the clash of temperaments, the lessons of acceptance, and the ominous undertow of insatiable demands.[2]

Woolf wrote no lengthy manifesto of her artistic principles, nor would she have claimed to be a theoretician, but she lived at a time of great upheaval in art, and was herself influenced by and a major force in the shift in the way we perceive the world that became apparent in Europe from about the 1880s onward. Even had she not been born a writer she could not have avoided thinking about the nature and purpose of art, surrounded as she was by "great men" of the nineteenth and many iconoclasts of the twentieth centuries. Ideas have a way of influencing even those who have no direct contact with them; new thoughts seep into language, spreading far beyond those who experience their first formulations. An example in Woolf's work is her concern with the relations between different artistic media, and with the possibilities of synaesthesia, which were explored by many of her contemporaries on the Continent.

Although England was perhaps rather isolated from the modernist movements of Europe by its relatively poor tradition of visual art, these movements did have some effect. In the widespread experimentation with color and shape to express sensations and perceptions can be seen a movement toward a synaesthetic art. One (arbitrarily chosen) point of origin for the general shift in vision might be found in Richard Wagner's dream of a *Gessamkunstwerke*, an idea that found expression in varying forms among artists from the late nineteenth century onward.[3] In the early part of this century, Wassily Kandinsky and other artists of the *Blaue Reiter* group in Munich were engaged in the search for a common spiritual basis in the arts. Kandinsky, in "The Effect of Color" (1911), wrote of the psychological effect of color:

> Generally speaking, color directly influences the soul. Color is the keyboard, the eyes are the hammers, the soul is the piano with many strings. The artist is the hand that plays, touching one key or another purposively, to cause vibrations in the soul.
> *It is evident therefore that color harmony must rest ultimately on purposive playing upon the human soul: this is one of the guiding principles of internal necessity.*[4]

Nearly thirty years later, Kandinsky was still thinking of a unity of all the arts:

> All the arts derive from the same and unique root.
> Consequently, all the arts are identical.
> But the mysterious and precious fact is that the "fruits" produced by the same trunk are different.[5]

Even had Woolf never heard the names of, say, Cézanne, Kandinsky, Matisse, Debussy, Scriabin, or Mallarmé, their influence would have touched her deeply. In fact, she was in an excellent position from which to view the sweeping changes wrought by the European modernist movements; there were many routes by which she could receive the traffic of ideas. In 1904 her brother-in-law, Clive Bell, was in touch with the Nabis, and with Gauguin and Cézanne in Paris; in 1919 he met Derain,

Braque, Cocteau, and others. Although hampered by a rather formal, classical training and the general English reaction against German symbolist painting and music (and, indeed, against almost anything new, from Europe), Duncan Grant and Vanessa Bell were much in sympathy with their European counterparts. The influence of Fauvism and Cubism is evident in the products of the Omega workshop, begun in 1913 by Roger Fry with Bell and Grant as codirectors.[6] Fauvism might also be discerned in the tropical setting of *The Voyage Out* (though it perhaps owes much to Conrad's *Heart of Darkness* also).

The composer Skryabin's visit to London before the first War was well-publicized. Duncan Grant was partly inspired by the announcement of a concert of Skryabin's music (to be accompanied by changing colored lights) to paint a roll,

> nearly fifteen feet in length, eleven inches high and composed of seventeen sections of pasted paper shapes with paint sometimes overlapping the papers, sometimes simply surrounding them. It was intended to be seen through the aperture of a box as the roll passed through slots at the back at a pace dictated by a slow movement from a work by Bach. There was also to be lighting inside the box.[7]

Saxon Sydney-Turner, an early influence on Woolf's musical tastes, praised *Prometheus*, Skryabin's 1910 "Poem of Fire" in which he used a color organ. Again, the possibilities of synaesthesia were explored in Skryabin's project:

> In 1908 Skryabin began to compose what he believed to be part of the *Mystery* to which he had been making more than passing reference for a number of years, a large work which would unite the senses as Wagner had attempted to unite the arts. He spoke of "tactile symphonies", and of involving not just sound but sight, smell, feel, dance, décor, orchestra, piano, singers, light, sculpture, and colours. In the event light and colour were the only non-musical elements to be incorporated in this work.[8]

The current of ideas flowed widely and freely: Gertrude Stein's *Composition as Explanation*, for example, accepted for publication by the Woolfs' Hogarth Press in 1926, is comparable to the work of Cézanne, Matisse, or Picasso in terms of its attempt to maintain a "continuous present." Parallels can be drawn between developments in writing, painting, and music in the early part of this century: what Woolf did, for example, in the sketches of *Monday or Tuesday* (1921) could be compared to Monet's

Venice where the all-pervasive light seems to have eaten away the form; a parallel in music might be Debussy's "La Cathedrale Engloutie" where individual notes are indistinct and inseparable from the effect of the whole. To close what could become a very long list, I add a comment of Max Beckmann's *On My Painting* (1938), which seems pertinent to Woolf's work: "My aim is always to get hold of the magic of reality and to transfer this reality into painting—to make the invisible visible through reality. It may sound paradoxical, but it is, in fact, reality which forms the mystery of our existence."[9]

Music, for the tyro, seems best suited of all the arts to exemplify thoughts on the way art "works." It does not confine, does not dictate, and because it does not directly refer to anything, it is perhaps the least demanding of the arts for the uninformed perceiver. It is tempting to see music as the "substance" of art in its least altered state, bringing to mind Pater's dictum that "all art constantly aspires towards the condition of music." Because it is nonrepresentational and nonreferential, music comes closest to a "direct contemplation in thought and feeling, which could dispense with all symbolism and mediation."[10] The nature of the the structure of music was described "with remarkable foresight" by Rousseau in his *Essai sur l'origine des langues*:

> For us, each sound is a relative entity. No sound by itself possesses absolute attributes that allow us to identify it: it is high or low, loud or soft with respect to another sound only. By itself, it has none of these properties. In a harmonic system, a given sound is nothing by natural right. . . . It is neither tonic, nor dominant, harmonic or fundamental. All these properties exist as relationships only and since the entire system can vary from bass to treble, each sound changes in rank and place as the system changes in degree.[11]

The young Virginia Stephen was excited by music; on 23 April 1901, she wrote to Emma Vaughan: "The only thing in this world is music—music and books and one or two pictures. I am going to found a colony where there shall be no marrying—unless you happen to fall in love with a symphony of Beethoven—no human element at all, except what comes through Art—nothing but ideal peace and endless meditation" (*L*, 35). Happily, she soon moved away from this youthful Byzantium, but music continued to be an important factor in the development of her thoughts on art: "I have been having a debauch of music and hearing certain notes to which I could be wed—pure simple notes—smooth from all passion and frailty, and flawless as gems. That means so much to me and so little to you! Now do you know that sound has shape and colour and texture as well?" (*L*, 323. To Violet Dickinson, 16 December 1906). As already noted, the idea of synaesthesia was in the air; synaesthetic perception is sometimes displayed by characters in the novels, particularly in *The Waves*.[12] Clive Bell wrote of his appreciation of music as "pure form" and, as Woolf had met him six years prior to writing the letter quoted above, it is reasonable to suppose that such ideas were current in conversations among her friends.

This familiar strain is heard once more in 1909 when (probably under the influence of Sydney-Turner[13]) Woolf attended the great Wagner festival at Bayreuth. In an article written for the *Times*, she attempts some sort of music criticism,[14] admitting that she is only giving the impressions of an amateur. As with all her writing, the article is lively and interesting (despite its strained, almost euphuistic style), and her perceptions are noteworthy. She sees that music can express nonverbal feeling, and that it has a power over people that seems to stem from its lending form to people's emotions: "It may be that these exalted emotions which belong to the essence of our being, and are rarely expressed, are those that are best translated by music; so that a satisfaction, or whatever one may call that sense of answer which the finest art supplies to its own question, is constantly conveyed here" (*BP*, 19). This article anticipates her lifelong concern with the attempt at wording "those exalted emotions, which belong to the essence of our being." The idea of art supplying the answer to its own question is an early example of that form of the circle that is so often apparent in the structures of Woolf's own art. She was aware of the dangers of the literary judgment of music, but she trusted her ear, and with good reason as the following shows:

> Apart from the difficulty of changing a musical impression into a literary one, and the tendency to appeal to the literary sense because of the associations of words, there is the further difficulty in the case of music that its scope is much less clearly defined than the scope of the other arts. The more

beautiful a phrase of music is the richer its burden of suggestion, and if we understand the form but slightly, we are little restrained in our interpretation. We are led on to connect the beautiful sound with some experience of our own, or to make it symbolize some conception of a general nature. Perhaps music owes something of its astonishing power over us to this lack of definite articulation; its statements have all the majesty of a generalization, and yet contain our private emotions. (*BP,* 21)

In her sensuous, impressionistic article, Woolf comes at once to a conclusion similar to that reached methodically by the philosopher Susanne K. Langer in her theory of music: "Music is a tonal analogue of emotive life."[15] At the end of the article, Woolf again makes reference—in vague, romantic expression— to synaesthesia:

Here at Bayreuth, where the music fades into the open air . . . and sound melts into colour, and colour calls out for words, where, in short, we are lifted out of the ordinary world and allowed merely to breathe and see—it is here that we realise how thin are the walls between one emotion and another; and how fused our impressions are with the elements which we may not attempt to separate. (*BP,* 22)

When she wrote the *Times* article, Woolf had been working at "Melymbrosia" for about two years; it was another six before this was published as *The Voyage Out.*[16] In that novel the question of the value and nature of art is often raised, and music—a preoccupation of the book's protagonist, Rachel Vinrace—is the medium most frequently used in Woolf's explorations of this question. It is interesting to turn again to Langer: "A great many considerations and puzzles that one meets sooner or later in all the arts find their clearest expression, and therefore their most tangible form, in connection with music" (*Feeling,* 133).

The Bloomsbury atmosphere of discussion, of Thursday "evenings" and Cambridge friends, found its way into *The Voyage Out,* where Rachel is often seen perplexed by the relation between her music and the life she experiences. Early in the novel she frets over the great difficulty of adequate communication, and comes to the conclusion that "it was far better to play the piano and forget all the rest" (35). Music is seen here as an easy escape from the difficulties of relations with others and with the world, a view that finds repeated expression in the novel. Susan Warrington—not a character noted for intelligence—says to Rachel that music "just seems to say all the things one can't say oneself" (*TVO*, 197); she is perhaps the sort of person the worldly Clarissa Dalloway has earlier criticized for going "into attitudes" over Wagner (although she confesses to having been moved to tears the first time she saw *Parsifal* [*TVO*, 49]). This passive, thoughtless attitude is disparaged throughout *The Voyage Out*, for although a work of fiction, the novel does offer critical concepts. Again, we could turn to Langer for a formal articulation of what is implied in Woolf's writing: "The function of music is not stimulation of feeling, but expression of it" (*Feeling*, 28).

Another early question that receives attention in *The Voyage Out* is that of the nature of the structure of music and its power to express nonverbal states of mind. Woolf evidently believed in the possibility of such states early on; in the novels of her maturity the idea comes to be more and more important. The nonverbal imagination must be *felt* in the reader's mind; the books must be read actively to half-create from intimations their nonverbal origins. Rachel, thinking of the purpose of music, and depressed by her inability to communicate, thinks of music in terms that suggest a description similar to Rousseau's:

> It appeared that nobody ever said a thing they meant, or ever talked of a feeling they felt, but that was what music was for. Reality dwelling in what one saw and felt, but did not talk about, one could accept a system in which things went round and round quite satisfactorily to other people, without often troubling to think about it, except as something superficially strange. (35)

An art that expresses meaning and feeling without using referential signs would obviously appeal to a writer wishing to convey her sense of the numinous.[17]

Having thought about the system, Rachel falls asleep, and as the chapter ends, Woolf lightly reinforces the point when Helen Ambrose quietly withdraws from Rachel's room "lest the sleeper should waken and there should be the *awkwardness of speech* between them" (*TVO*, 36, my italics). Musical composition gives the "illusion of an indivisible whole" (*Feeling*, 126) and it is this wholeness of music that appeals to Rachel: music "goes straight for things. It says all there is to say at once" (*TVO*, 251). What Rachel does not go on to expound, but what implicitly underlies her thought, is that conception of music as a "system in which things went round and round quite satisfactorily," a system unhampered by external relations. Woolf's interest in music in *The Voyage Out* is clearly from the point of view of a writer; she has already begun her search for a suitable form through which to communicate her perception of the world that, as we have seen, had at its heart an empty, silent center that eludes communication in language.

Against music as the art of expressing the verbally inexpressible we should perhaps place Terence Hewet's projected novel "about Silence." Although many of Woolf's contemporaries conceived of a fundamental unity in the various modes of art, she was much concerned with ineffable areas of experience, and realized early in her career that words, for instance, could not have an effect always commensurable with that of music.

Toward the end of the novel, Terence reads to Rachel from *Comus*, and seems to wish Milton's poetry to act like music. He suggests that the words can be listened to for their sound alone, but of course the meaning obtrudes because words must relate to something other. The point is doubly made, as the lines Terence reads (*TVO*, 398-99) have a special significance for Rachel who is just beginning to experience the physical symptoms of the illness that culminates in her death. Music, then, does not have "meaning" but can express feelings that are beyond words. In *The Voyage Out* Woolf, through Rachel, acknowledges the great difficulty of creating music, and criticizes the passive attentiveness of those listeners who "go into attitudes." Music is seen in terms of its structure, usually by architectural analogy.

By the end of the book music is established as an individual art, dealing with aspects of experience that are not within the reach of words. Langer's formal articulations are useful in encapsulating the ideas that can be drawn from Woolf's first novel, and the basic concept of music that emerges from it is very similar to that expressed in Langer's special theory of music as an "articulate but non-discursive form having import without conventional reference . . . presenting itself . . . as a "significant form," in which the factor of significance is not logically discriminated, but is felt as a quality rather than recognized as a function" (*Feeling*, 32). It is the logical discrimination of symbols that prevents language from sharing this quality with music. Woolf recognizes this and I think her idea of the novel "about Silence" probably underwent a change as a result of her understanding. To have continued with the idea of language being able somehow to achieve the nonverbal communication of music would have resulted in actual silence. Her novels are *about* silence, an empty space at the heart of life, but they can only point to it, imply it, shape round it. The space is ineffable and impossible to construct, for construction or words would mean filling the space; the space must come to be apprehended in the act of reading.

In *Night and Day*, the emphasis of Woolf's interest in different media shifts from music to the literary canon: architectural metaphors now apply to structures composed of words rather than notes, and criticism of those who attitudinized over Wagner is now directed at those who do the same over Shakespeare. Woolf even feels confident enough for comment on her friends' aesthetic theories: Mary Datchet, looking at the Elgin Marbles, is "borne upon some wave of exaltation and emotion," but perhaps her emotions are "not purely aesthetic" (80), for she finds herself thinking of her love for Ralph. Mary is here guilty of that sentimentalism condemned in the previous novel. There is, perhaps, implicit questioning of the "aesthetic emotion" Clive Bell wrote of in *Art*, for this state of pure contemplation is an unrealistic aspiration: the personality of the perceiver cannot be evaded. In *Night and Day*, Woolf sets out a view of the established forms of literature that, in *Jacob's Room*, she says must be done away with. Literature is shown as the opiate of an intellectual élite who consider it their birthright, to guard and interpret. In *The Voyage Out*, and throughout her essays, Woolf emphasizes that life must be the source of art and art must be life-enhancing; in *Night and Day*, she shows the result of ignoring this dictum.

Katharine Hilbery tries to get her parents interested in modern novels, but even their appearance disturbs them; they prefer their reading to look as it is: portly and solid. Literature is viewed by the older generation as a vessel for private emotions that has enough generality to raise them to a plane above the individual. The works of literature do their thinking for them; they transfer their joys and sorrows to those of the heroes and heroines. This generation has made a religion of literature: their responses are dogma, the editor of an "esteemed review" is a "minister of literature" (369); they have a certain idea of what literature is and what it should not be. It was this dogmatism that Woolf saw as deadening and restrictive. Even Mrs. Hilbery, who is so passionate about "*my* William," seems to have things the wrong way around: the wonder is not that life continues as it does despite Shakespeare, but that Shakespeare continues despite life (an idea found in *Jacob's Room*, 108-9). Mr. Hilbery, in using the work of Scott as a pacifying homily to his daughter, typifies the smug attitude against which Woolf rebelled. At the end of the book is a telling description of this attitude: "The power of literature, which had temporarily deserted Mr. Hilbery, now came back to him, pouring over the raw ugliness of human affairs its soothing balm, and providing a form into which such passions as he had felt so painfully the night before could be moulded so that they fell roundly from the tongue in shapely phrases, hurting nobody" (*ND*, 528-29). This intellectual élite has stifled the spirit of literature and lost the ability to read creatively. The children of this côterie do not escape its influence: Cassandra mocks William with cliquish complacency for not having read Dostoevski (*ND*, 368), and Katharine assures her mother that clerks do not read poetry "as we read it" (99).

Woolf's dissatisfaction with the well-made Edwardian novel is expressed in "Modern Fiction," in which appears her famous image of life as "a luminous halo, a semi-transparent envelope surrounding us from the beginning of consciousness to the end" (*CRI*, 189). After the "traditional" *Night and Day*, Woolf searched for a form appropriate to the embodiment of her vision, one that would show her awareness of the profound change in "human character" she said had occurred "on or about December, 1910" ("Mr. Bennett and Mrs. Brown"). She wrote a number of "sketches" in which she made the transition from the perceptual world of *Night and Day* to that of *Jacob's Room* and the works for which she is best known.

It is to the world of the painter, specifically the post-impressionist, that Woolf turned in her search for a suitable form: perception, light, form, and color became her materials. Some of her early "sketches," as she called them, were published in *Monday or Tuesday*, a volume enhanced by four woodcuts by Vanessa Bell; most of the sketches were published posthumously in *A Haunted House* (1944). In "Solid Objects" (1920) Woolf gives a clue to the sort of perception she was trying to capture in words: "Looked at again and again half consciously by a mind thinking of something else, any object mixes itself so profoundly with the stuff of thought that it loses its actual form and recomposes itself a little differently in an ideal shape which haunts the brain when we least expect it" (*AHH*, 72). Throughout the sketches Woolf uses color to express mood, character, and communication. Her observation of the changing qualities of light is acute and, in a piece like "Kew Gardens," brings to mind Cézanne or Monet. She uses color in a plastic way, anticipating what Charles Mauron wrote in an article translated by Roger Fry and published by Woolf's Hogarth Press in 1926. In "The Nature of Beauty in Art and Literature," Mauron wrote of painters' use of color to establish "psychological volumes."[18] Woolf's close observation of color and light led her to experiment even with abstract color sketches: "Blue & Green," for example, records gradations of light moving over and through various objects, achieving painterly effects with words. Painters such as Gauguin and Van Gogh wrote letters recording the correspondences between color and sound harmonies[19]; Woolf experimented with color in her writing. It was not, perhaps, until *The Waves* that color and light achieved their most enriching effect in her work, but the groundwork for this aspect of her art was done in the transitional period between the publication of *Night and Day* and *Jacob's Room*.

Of "The Mark on the Wall" Roger Fry wrote to Woolf that she was the only contemporary writer "who uses language as a medium of art, who makes the very texture of the words have a meaning and quality really almost apart from what you are talking about."[20] Such astute criticism from Fry must have meant a great deal to Woolf as she sought to model into the space she felt was at the heart of life:

As we face each other in omnibuses and underground railways we are looking into the mirror; that accounts for the vagueness, the gleam of glassiness in our eyes. And the novelists in future will realize more and more the importance of these reflections, for of course there is not one reflection but an almost infinite number; those are the depths they will explore, those the phantoms they will pursue, leaving the description of reality more and more out of their stories, taking a knowledge of it for granted, as the Greeks did and Shakespeare perhaps—but these generalizations are very worthless. ("The Mark on the Wall," *AHH,* 38)

Jacob Flanders is caught at a period of transition, at the moment after the breaking of the old molds and before the formation of the new. He is thus full of youthful self-assertiveness, but fundamentally confused; this is a feeling Woolf herself exhibited in a letter to Roger Fry (16 September 1925): "For my own part I wish we could skip a generation—skip Edith and Gertrude and Tom and Joyce and Virginia and come out in the open again, when everything has been restarted, and runs full tilt, instead of trickling and teasing in this irritating way" (*L,* 1583).

Two months after the publication of *Jacob's Room,* Woolf wrote to Gerald Brenan of that sense of breaking and renewing, of being stuck in a period of transition that characterizes the novel, as very much her own feeling about herself as a writer. She felt, on Christmas Day 1922, that the "human soul" was undergoing one of its periodic reorientations. For those artists unfortunate enough to live at such a time, nothing is whole: "Nothing is going to be achieved by us. Fragments—paragraphs—a page perhaps: but no more. Joyce to me seems strewn with disaster" (*L,* 1337). She and her contemporaries are denied a sight of the whole human soul, but she feels the glimpses they *can* catch are more valuable than "to sit down with Hugh Walpole, Wells, etc. etc. and make large oil paintings of fabulous fleshy monsters complete from top to toe" (*L,* 1337). Having just published the first novel that speaks in her distinctive voice, Woolf is engrossed with her own creativity; indeed, she says to Brenan, "I am only scribbling, more to amuse myself than you, who may never read, or understand." She feels herself a microcosm of the world, suffering "every ten years" a reorientation of her own soul to match the larger one she sees occurring in the human race.

Looking back, she says when she first tried to write, she

found that she could not, for what she had to write about (life) was "too near, too vast." This is certainly borne out by the impression of being overwhelmed and the synaesthetic perception already noted in the young Woolf and in Rachel Vinrace. With *Jacob's Room* she begins to give form to the incoherent experience of being; to do this she must first recede from the object. The letter ends with a postscript in which she returns to the original matter, raised by Brenan, of renunciation. Woolf here fixes on a central paradox of her art when she says that beauty is achieved in the failure to achieve it; in other words, in the *effort*. In the virtual space of the act of reading, nonverbal thought is communicated. By "grinding all the flints together" (or "gathering fragments"), the whole that cannot be directly communicated is formed in the intersubjective relationship between literary art and the reader: "Are we not always hoping? and though we fail every time, surely we do not fail so completely as we should have failed if we were not in the beginning, prepared to attack the whole. One must renounce, when the book is finished; but not before it is begun" (*L*, 1337).

By the time she came to write *To the Lighthouse*, Woolf was an experienced writer with proven consummate control of the form she had worked out for herself. In this novel is seen a consideration of the artist at work that adheres closely to the problems posed by Lily Briscoe's painting. The novel is not an exploration of whether painting and literature are commensurable, as *The Voyage Out* tentatively explored that question with regard to music and language, but Woolf uses painting to shed a light on literary creation; significantly, to see *her* specific problems as a novelist in a fresh way. She knows well where the line comes between the two modes, and uses painting to distance herself from literature so that she will not be too close to her own difficulties to see them clearly.

Lily Briscoe finds William Bankes' scrutiny of her canvas an "awful trial," for her work is not representation, but contains the "residue of her thirty-three years, the deposit of each day's living, mixed with something more secret than she had ever spoken or shown in the course of all those days." (*TTL*, 84). Three years after the publication of *To the Lighthouse*, Woolf wrote in the introduction to a catalog of an exhibition of Vanessa Bell's paintings, "that they yield their full meaning only to those who can tunnel their way behind the canvas into masses and passages and relations and values of which we know nothing."[21] It seems to me that in these two instances—one fictional, one (f)actual— Woolf is making a definite statement to the effect that an artist's life must be inextricably mingled with his or her created work. She sees a novelist as even less able to conceal actual experience in a work of art: "One defies a novelist to keep his life through twenty-seven volumes of fiction safe from our scrutiny."[22] Here—and on many other occasions—she explicitly says that the writer's life is unavoidably intervolved with his or her fiction.

Lily Briscoe's painting stands for the art Woolf herself wished to achieve. Lily wants to realize on her canvas her perception of Mrs. Ramsay as "an august shape; the shape of a dome" (*TTL*, 83). She tries to explain to William Bankes that she is painting balance, harmony, and rhythm; at the heart of her perception, the true subject of her art, is Lily's love for Mrs. Ramsay and her urge to somehow bring that love into a shared world of art, out of the private world of memory. In this project, perhaps, the links between the modes of life and the modes of art in Woolf's aesthetic may become clearer.

Lily's struggle for unity, her attempt to realize her vision wholly, is an articulation of the basic problem for any artist. The passage from conception to realization imposes a change, for all visions must be mediated: "She could see it all so clearly, so commandingly, when she looked: it was when she took her brush in hand that the whole thing changed (*TTL*, 34). At the beginning of *To the Lighthouse,* Lily understands that her problem has to do mainly with relation: "If there, in that corner, it was bright, here, in this, she felt the need of darkness" (85). She cannot explain what she wishes to make of the scene before her; she only feels it within her, and here we have the problem: how to bring one's personal world into the shared world in such a way that others can understand it. This was Woolf's problem as it is Lily's:

I shall here write the first pages of the greatest book in the world. This is what the book would be that was made entirely solely & with integrity of one's thoughts. Suppose one could catch them before they became "works of art."? Catch them hot & sudden as they rise in the mind—walking up

Asheham hill for instance. Of course one cannot; for the process of language is slow & deluding. One must stop to find a word; then, there is the form of the sentence, soliciting one to fill it. (*D*, Rodmell, 1926)

Again, Woolf is explicit about the nonverbal origin of her art.

The problem remains with Lily; ten years pass, ten years of experience, of perceiving, of having visions; ten years in which Mrs. Ramsay dies; and she returns to the house. "The question was of some relation between those masses. She had borne it in her mind all these years" (*TTL*, 229). And it would seem that a decade has brought Lily new understanding: "It seemed as if the solution had come to her: she knew now what she wanted to do" (*TTL*, 229). However, the gap still exists between conception and realization, and although the struggle may be now more equal it is no less fierce,[23] as Lily discovers when she again approaches her easel: "But there was all the difference in the world between this planning airily away from the canvas, and actually taking her brush and making the first mark" (*TTL*, 243). Section 3 of "The Lighthouse" marks the beginning of a concentration on Lily's picture (concurrent with the voyage out to the lighthouse) which is, at this point, a framed space against the landscape that must be filled: "She saw her canvas as if it had floated up and placed itself white and uncompromising directly before her" (*TTL*, 242). If we glance back at the last diary entry referred to above, the correlation between the problems of Lily and Woolf is again made clear: "Then, there is the form of the sentence, soliciting one to fill it." Other writings of the period of *To the Lighthouse*'s composition are also concerned with the problems in verbal art that Lily has with painting. Writing in the *Times Literary Supplement* on De Quincey ("Impassioned Prose"), Woolf expressed those ideas that Lily found she could not put across to William Bankes (*TTL*, 84-87): "Then it is not the actual sight or sound itself that matters, but the reverberations that it makes as it travels through our minds. These are often to be found far away, strangely transformed; but it is only by gathering up and putting together these echoes and fragments that we arrive at the true nature of our experience" (*GR*, 40).

Again, as in the letter to Brenan, Woolf says that the only hope for wholeness is to put together the fragments of our experience, not to go directly for it. In 1925 she wrote in her diary that she had "an idea that I will invent a new name for my books to supplant "novel". A new—by Virginia Woolf. But what? Elegy?" (27 June 1925). In 1927, in "The Narrow Bridge of Art," Woolf described a new form of novel; it is a prophecy of *Between the Acts*:

> It will be written in prose, but in prose which has many of the characteristics of poetry. It will have something of the exaltation of poetry, but much of the ordinariness of prose. It will be dramatic, and yet not a play. It will be read, not acted. By what name we are to call it is not a matter of very great importance. What is important is that this book which we see on the horizon may serve to express some of those feelings which seem at the moment to be balked by poetry pure and simple and to find the drama equally inhospitable to them. Let us try, then, to come to closer terms with it and to imagine what may be its scope and nature.
>   In the first place, one may guess that it will differ from the novel as we know it now chiefly in that it will stand further back from life. It will give, as poetry does, the outline rather than the detail.
>
> .   .   .   .
>
>   So, then, this unnamed variety of the novel will be written standing back from life, because in that way a larger view is to be obtained of some important features of it. (*GR*, 18, 22)

In *To the Lighthouse*, this form can be seen applied to relation-ships: "But this was one way of knowing people, she thought: to know the outline, not the detail, to sit in one's garden and look at the slopes of a hill running purple down into the distant heather" (*TTL*, 299). The same conditions can be seen to apply to Lily's picture: before beginning she must draw back from life and subdue the "impertinences and irrelevances that plucked her attention and made her remember how she was such and such a person, had such and such relations to people" (*TTL*, 243). This is why she cannot communicate her vision directly to William Bankes:

> She could not show him what she wished to make of it [the scene in front of her], could not see it even herself, without a brush in her hand. She took up once more her old painting position with the dim eyes and the absent-minded manner, subduing all her impressions as a woman to something much more general; becoming once more under the power of that vision which she had seen clearly once and must now grope for among hedges and houses and mothers and children—her picture. (*TTL*, 86)

Overcoming the difficulty of beginning, Lily falls into a rhythm of marking the canvas and pausing ("The most character-istic principle of vital activity is rhythm." [Langer, *Feeling and Form*, 126]). A letter to Vita Sackville-West (16 March 1926) indi-cates Woolf's belief in this principle of rhythm, providing a further detail of the analogy between Lily's painting and the novel: "Style is a very simple matter; it is all rhythm. . . . Now this is very profound, what rhythm is, and goes far deeper than words. A sight, an emotion, creates this wave in the mind, long before it makes words to fit it" (*L*, 1624).[24]

The work of art begins with a *preverbal* rhythm; again and again Woolf comes back to this aspect of creation. Lily's rhythmic dabbing at the canvas presents a new problem, however, for her marks define a new space; "what could be more formidable than that space?" (*TTL*, 244). In the light of what Woolf has already said about creation, Lily's experience as she begins her picture can be taken confidently as analogous to the author's in writing her novel: "Here she was again, she thought, stepping back to look at it, drawn out of gossip, out of living, out of community with people into the presence of this formidable ancient enemy of hers—this other thing, this truth, this reality, which suddenly laid hands on her, emerged stark at the back of appearances and commanded her attention" (*TTL*, 244-45).

The arresting phrase "ancient enemy" emphasizes Woolf's conception of creation as a struggle. In the holograph manu-script of the novel, the stress of this moment for Lily, and the sense of artistic creation being beyond "human relations," is emphasized in a long monologue in which she speaks of art reaching "some more acute reality where it can rest." This de-scription recalls Woolf's idea of the soul or self: it was as a "wedge-shaped core of darkness" that Mrs. Ramsay found *rest* and a communion with a 'reality' apart from the actual. In writing of 'reality' in her diary, it should be noted, Woolf felt it was that in which she would "rest and continue to exist." There is also a remarkable similarity (the significance of which is fully realized in *Between the Acts*) between the *states* in which Mrs. Ramsay becomes a "wedge of darkness" and in which Lily paints to achieve her "vision"; the most salient feature common to both states is the loss of identity (see *TTL*, 100, 246). It may also be noteworthy that Mrs. Ramsay's "wedge" shape is endorsed by the purple triangle as which she is represented in Lily's painting.

In the published novel, Woolf seems to have realized that Lily's doctrine is unconvincing because it comes at the problem so directly; the hyperbole obstructs the active reader's imagination, and it is therefore excised. The draft is significant, nevertheless, because it explicitly connects artistic creation with transcendence of the actual and revelation of the soul. It is only by gathering together fragments and echoes in this way that the connection between experience of the self and artistic creation is brought to light.

Lily, in the draft, is seen as "extended & freed" while painting: "She enjoyed that intensity & freedom of life which, for a few seconds after the death of the body, one imagines the souls of the dead to enjoy: one imagines then that they have gathered themselves together . . . complete & forcible with the force of an organism which is now at last able to unite all its powers" (Dick, 280).[25] The holograph continues by describing Lily's experience of a transcendence of time and death through art:

> It was attended, too, with an emotion, which could be compared only with the gratification of <hum> bodily human love. So, unhesitatingly, without fear or reserve, at some moment of culminat<ing>ion, when all separation is over, except that <final> delight of separation—which is that it <can be> has consciousness of mixing—<the two people> bodies unite; the human love has its gratification. But that, even, was less complete than this; for who can deny it? Even while the arms are locked, or the sentence married in the air with complete understanding, a cloud moves across the sky & each lover knows, but cannot confess, his knowledge of the transcience of <all> love: the mutability of love: how tomorrow comes; <how> they words & other kisses. <but> & they are only tossed together & nothing survives.
> But here, since the lover was the <horrible> formidable enemy—space—their union, could it be achieved, was immortal. No cloud moved, in that landscape; no death came <nowhere> between them. It was an awful marriage; forever. (Dick, 280)

The space that Lily has created is more awful than the original space of the canvas for it is "truth . . . reality . . ."; it is the space at the heart of life so often felt in the novels; the emptiness that can only be felt and never directly communicated: nothingness. Another excised passage is a clue to the import of Lily's experience:

> There is something better than helping dying women. Something, heaven be praised, beyond human relations altogether, in all this talk of you & me, & me & you, & <for> one loving another, & one not loving another, all this little trivial baseness of about which we made so incessant a to do of marrying & giving in marriage, pales beside it is irrelevant beside it. Yet so terrible a doctrine could not be confessed. . . . Pictures are more important than people. (Dick, 279)

The "terrible doctrine" of art, perhaps, underlies that sense of the inadequacy of life that has been felt in Woolf's writing.

The overwhelming difficulty that the space Lily has created presents is that it demands to be filled, but can never be filled for then it would no longer be space: "But this form, were it only the shape of a white lamp-shade looming on a wicker table, roused one to perpetual combat, challenged one to a fight in which one was bound to be worsted" (*TTL*, 245). The space in the painting corresponds to one side of that tension between meaning and nothingness that is felt throughout Woolf's writing. To her thinking, the artist is closest to 'reality' and is constantly torn between the antinomies of emptiness at the center and the possibility of creation. This division in human being is acute for the artist because she perceives it more clearly than others. Art can "make of the moment something permanent" (*TTL*, 249); perhaps it can even fill the space, but only for an instant and not in the shared world of common reality. In her essays and diaries, Woolf often referred to the unconscious reverie in which artistic creation takes place, and in *To the Lighthouse* we find a definite statement of the basis in the unconscious of artistic creation that bears a strong resemblance to that state in which Mrs. Ramsay found "rest," seemingly in harmony with her self (*TTL*, 100). Lily feels part of

> some rhythm which was dictated to her (she kept looking at the hedge, at the canvas) by what she saw, so that while her hand quivered with life, this rhythm was strong enough to bear her along with it on its current. Certainly she was losing consciousness of outer things. And as she lost consciousness of outer things, and her name and her personality and her appearance . . . her mind kept throwing up from its depths, scenes, and names, and sayings,

and memories and ideas, like a fountain spurting over that glaring, hideously difficult white space, while she modelled it with greens and blues. (*TTL*, 247)

That "her name and her personality and her appearance" recede from Lily's consciousness is significant for these have been shown as "bases" of identity. Artistic creation and experience of the self/soul are linked by the loss of identity.

As Lily comes to grips with the difficulties of her painting, she solves problems of shape and mass by use of color. A painter's use of color is active, vital, Woolf knew; colors are alive in a painting, elements determined by their environment. Allen McLaurin devotes chapter 7 of his *Virginia Woolf: The Echoes Enslaved* to an excellent analysis and minute observation of Woolf's use of color, which I do not wish to repeat here. The essay "Walter Sickert" (1933), to which McLaurin refers, is extremely interesting with regard to Woolf's view of a basic unity in the arts, and again of the areas of experience that are beyond words: the "silent kingdom" of paint holds many lessons for the writer, but their ways must eventually part.

When we consider the atmosphere of discursive rationalism that Woolf lived in, it is surprising to see the consistency with which her work shapes nondiscursive, intuitive perceptions. Her essay on Sickert is typical in its intimate awareness of tradition; she sees that great writers are "great colorists, just as they are musicians into the bargain." McLaurin's attention to her use of color in *The Waves* makes clear that Woolf learnt all she could from the painters; the expressiveness of color and line, seized upon as of paramount importance by the Symbolist painters of the early twentieth century, is reflected in words by Woolf. Indeed, it might be noted, she used color in a "psychological" way as early as *The Voyage Out*: as the intimacy between Rachel and Terence deepens (and Helen's sense of danger grows), Rachel looks out to sea: "It was still very blue . . . but the light on it was yellower, and the clouds were turning flamingo red" (*TVO*, 261).

The limitations of language in the psychological use of color, enunciated by McLaurin, were completely understood by Woolf by the time she had finished *To the Lighthouse*. She uses colors in relational sequences, solving Lily's problems of relation, modeling into the hollows of experience by causing words to suggest shapes beyond themselves, as Roger Fry said she had done in "The Mark on the Wall." Lily, having mastered the skillful employment of color to establish "psychological volumes," comes to have a surer grasp of the form her work must take, and this conception we can take, again with confidence, as analogous to Woolf's literary work, noting especially its paradoxical nature:

> Heaven be praised for it, the problem of space remained, she thought, taking up her brush again. It glared at her. The whole mass of the picture was poised upon that weight. Beautiful and bright it should be on the surface, feathery and evanescent, one colour melting into another like the colours on a butterfly's wing; but beneath the fabric must be clamped together with bolts of iron. It was to be a thing you could ruffle with your breath; and a thing you could not dislodge with a team of horses. And she began to lay on a red, a grey, and she began to model her way into the hollow there. (*TTL*, 264)

Early in the novel it was made clear that the artist's life had an integral influence on her work. As the book and Lily's picture near completion, it is increasingly emphasized that Lily mixes memory and desire with her vision; the past and her wish to regain her experience of Mrs. Ramsay's influence become worked into her painting as a definite shaping element: "And as she dipped into the blue paint, she dipped too into the past there" (*TTL*, 265). Still something is lacking, for Lily's problem of balance, of relation, persists; and, as she shows in her diary, Woolf shares the difficulty of getting hold of "the thing itself before it has been made anything" (*TTL*, 297). In view of this, that the novel ends with Lily triumphant ("I have had my vision"; the tense is significant) may at first be confusing. If Lily has realized her vision on her canvas, it is not a static realization, but a moment of creation that must be *re*created by each perceiver. Lily's "vision" takes place within her: the moment at which she completes her painting is the closing of the circle of the journey to the lighthouse, and thus the vision is Woolf's as well. Once again, the moment of perceiving a harmonious pattern takes place under the form of the circle: from the center of her creative act, Lily holds the circumference of her vision, her past and her present, in synthesis. It is such a "moment of being" that Woolf strove to give the opportunity for in her novels; the moment is recreated in the act of reading. *To the Lighthouse* constitutes her most extensive statement on her understanding of art; that she managed to expound and exemplify her insights simultaneously is an adequate mark of her genius.

CHAPTER FIVE
AESTHETIC FAILURE

AT THE END OF CHAPTER 2 I ALLUDED TO THE GULF BETWEEN LANGUAGE and reality that *The Waves* exposes. Having seen in *To the Lighthouse* the successful expression of an aesthetic formulated to convey Woolf's particular vision of lived experience, I would like to turn again to *The Waves* where, I believe, that aesthetic breaks down. That question of the complex nature of the relationship between life and literature that *Orlando* flirts with is the focus of *The Waves*. This work is often regarded as a "classic text" of modernism; and indeed the work is useful as a storehouse of typical ideas, but not much more than this. It is a kind of warehouse in which are found the materials from which novels such as *To the Lighthouse* or *Between the Acts* may be created. Early on in the work's construction Woolf herself felt that "I am only accumulating notes for a book" (*D*, 30 November 1929). *The Waves* never gets beyond this state, and yet there are many who would disagree.

Critics have found *The Waves* a work in which form and content are "closely bound together to form one substance" (Fleishman, *Virginia Woolf*, 157); a work in which is displayed "the artist's ability to create unity" (van Buren Kelley, *The Novels of Virginia Woolf*, 198). More recently, Lyndall Gordon has written that "Virginia Woolf's main ambitions came together in *The Waves* and never fused so perfectly again" (*A Writer's Life*, 247). It is eloquent that for two chapters Gordon does little more than *describe* the work. The book's reputation as a classic text of modernism owes much to its abstruseness; its hostility to "common reading" seems to qualify it for a special prominence among notoriously "difficult" works of modern art. It is because of its peculiar position in critics' estimations that I choose, for a moment, to treat *The Waves* in isolation from the other works.

The Waves is an antinovel that yields very little to the processes of assimilation, memory, and comparison that constitute reading; it is not strong enough to forge its own conventions in the way that, say, *To the Lighthouse* is (see above, p. 72-81). It is particularly significant that in its conception and development, Woolf was far more concerned with the *shape* of the book than anything else. In the process of writing other novels, she had been interested in the characters, their movements and relations; but a reading of the entries that refer to *The Waves* in her diary shows very different prevalent concerns:

> Why not invent a new kind of play—(21 February 1927) . . . All the time I shall attack this angular shape in my mind. (28 March 1929) . . . Altogether the shape of the book wants considering—(16 September 1929) . . . Also, never, in my life, did I attack such a vague yet elaborate design; (11 October 1929) . . . anyhow no other form of fiction suggests itself except as a repetition at the moment. (26 January 1930) . . . felt the pressure of the form—the splendour & the greatness—as—perhaps, I have never felt them. (28 March 1930) . . . The abandonment of Orlando & Lighthouse is much checked by the extreme difficulty of the form—(9 April 1930) . . . this hideous shaping & moulding. (23 April 1930) . . . I suspect the structure is wrong. (29 April 1930)

Abstraction is the dominant note in entries about the new work.

As so often, Woolf recorded the genesis and development of her new fiction in her diary. The first stirrings of what would become *The Waves* are interesting in that Woolf is concerned with her own "process" of creation ("I want to watch & see how the idea at first occurs. I want to trace my own process." [*D*, 30 September 1926]). A month later she was still watching carefully: "At intervals, I begin to think (I note this, as I am going to watch for the advent of a book) of a solitary woman musing[?] a book of ideas about life. This has intruded only once or twice, & very vaguely: it is a dramatisation of my mood at Rodmell. It is to be an endeavour at something mystic, spiritual; the thing that exists when we aren't there" (30 October 1926). This was written during revision of *To the Lighthouse*. In the central "Time Passes" section, Woolf attempted to convey a sense of "something that exists when we aren't there." I have said that if the self exists it does not share the modes of being established for identity; it may be impossible *actually* to describe (see above, p. 31).

Bearing this in mind, and also that basic tenet of Woolf's aesthetic—that the way to achieve beauty or wholeness was not to come at it directly, but to communicate indirectly—it is strange that in *The Waves* she seems to abandon the lessons of earlier works and to approach directly that empty center of acute 'reality' that seems to be the soul's domain.

The "mood at Rodmell" (to which some attention has already been given; see above, p. 33-35) is given central importance by Woolf (J. W. Graham calls it "the seminal experience out of which the book grew" and notes that she refers to it, in a "ritualistic gesture," at the end of each draft over four and a half years[1]), and so, intensely private though it is, I repeat its description here as it might throw some light on her expectations for *The Waves*. The mood is described in two diary entries written just after Woolf had finished *To the Lighthouse*:

> Intense depression: I have to confess that this has overcome me several times since September 6th. . . . It is so strange to me that I cannot get it right—the depression, I mean, which does not come from something definite, but from nothing. "Where there is nothing" the phrase came <back> to me, as I sat at the table in the drawing room.
> ·
> All the rest of the year one's (I daresay rightly) curbing & controlling this odd immeasurable soul. When it expands, though one is frightened & bored & gloomy, it is as I say to myself, awfully queer. There is an edge to it which I feel of great importance, once in a way. One goes down into the well & nothing protects one from the assault of truth. Down there I cant write or read; I exist however. I am. (*D*, 28 September 1926)

> I wished to add some remarks to this, on the mystical side of this solitude; how it is not oneself but something in the universe that one's left with. It is this that is frightening & exciting in the midst of my profound gloom, depression, boredom, whatever it is: One sees a fin passing far out. What image can I reach to convey what I mean? Really there is none I think. The interesting thing is that in all my feeling & thinking I have never come up against this before. Life is, soberly & accurately, the oddest affair; has in it the essence of reality. I used to feel this as a child—couldn't step across a puddle once I remember, for thinking, how strange—what am I? &c. But by writing I dont reach anything. All I mean to make is a note of a curious state of mind. I hazard the guess that it may be the impulse behind another book. (30 September 1926)

It is revealing that Woolf treats this as a *new* experience, for it bears the characteristics of a fundamental experience of several characters in the preceding novels. Clarissa Dalloway, for example, is seen to undergo precisely this sense of wonder at simply being at all and to feel the "presence" of nothing, which at once fascinates and depresses her.

Perhaps it is because the creation of earlier novels was "unconscious"—in the sense that Woolf felt artistic creation to be predominantly unconscious—that she finds the experience one she has "never come up against" when she tries actually to write it out directly. It is this directness that flaws *The Waves*, and it is surprising that she even made the attempt in the light of that aesthetic seen to govern *To the Lighthouse*. As she began to work on the book, she wrote in her diary of the futility of such an endeavor: "But who knows—once one takes a pen and writes? How difficult not to go making 'reality' this & that, whereas it is one thing" (*D*, 10 September 1928).

Bernard seeks "the one true phrase" that will sum up life; he feels that all his stories are ancillary to the "true story" or "final statement" that will fix the elusive "reality" of life.[2] It is in a way ironic that the diary entry just quoted should explain why *The Waves* must fail: 'reality' is 'no-thing,' but writing is naming, an attempt to substantize, to give a form to that which has no form. This might seem to suggest that all the novels are equally failures as I have stressed that they are concerned to give a form to this formless 'reality.' Why they are *not* failures is that Woolf's aesthetic is fully cognizant of the nature of the act of reading. The novels—except *The Waves*—enter into a communion with the reader. Reading is a dynamic and dyadic experience, analogous to other events in human life, in which the reader creates a *virtual* form of actual life, and is enabled to enact experience (to re-create it) on the terms of the novel. In *The Act of Reading*, Iser describes the structural similarities of lived experience and reading:

> Reading has the same structure as experience, to the extent that our entanglement has the effect of pushing our various criteria of orientation back into the past, thus suspending their validity for the new present. This does not mean, however, that these criteria or our previous experiences disappear altogether. On the contrary, our past still remains our experience, but what happens now is that it begins to interact with the as yet unfamiliar presence of the text. This remains unfamiliar so long as our previous experiences are

precisely as they had been before we began our reading. But in the course of the reading, these experiences will also change, for the acquisition of experience is not a matter of adding on—it is a restructuring of what we already possess. (132)

The Waves is antireading in this respect: it does not allow for the participation of the reader, but continually dictates through a highly self-conscious structure. In an essay on "Jane Austen," Woolf wrote, "She stimulates us to supply what is not there. What she offers is, apparently, a trifle, yet is composed of something that expands in the reader's mind and endows with the most enduring form of life scenes which are outwardly trivial" (*CRI*, 174). This is but one of an enormous number of references in Woolf to a reader's participation in the constitution of a text. Iser refers to this passage: "The 'enduring form of life' which Virginia Woolf speaks of is not manifested on the printed page; it is a product arising out of the interaction between text and reader" (168). What I contend is the prime reason for *The Waves'* failure is the avoidance of what Iser calls "the structured blanks of the text," that "stimulate the process of ideation to be performed by the reader on terms set by the text" (*Act*, 169). Turning again to the diary, it is clear that Woolf herself was aware of the dangers that the form she was developing was open to:

> Who thinks it? And am I outside the thinker? One wants some device which is not a trick. (25 September 1929) . . . In particular is there some radical fault in my scheme? (11 October 1929) . . . Is there some falsity, of method, somewhere? Something tricky? (5 November 1929) . . . But how to pull it together, how to compost it—press it into one—I do not know; (26 January 1930) . . . it may miss fire somewhere. (9 April 1930) . . . I think this is the greatest opportunity I have yet been able to give myself: therefore I suppose the most complete failure. Yet I respect myself for writing this book. Yes—even though it exhibits my congenital faults. (20 August 1930) . . . I imagine that the hookedness may be so great that it will be a failure from a reader's point of view. (2 February 1931)

When published, the reviews were favorable, which of course pleased the author. Nevertheless, she wrote in her diary that the book had not been understood: the *Times* praised her characters "when I meant to have none"; the book was "an adventure which I go on alone" (*D*, 5 October 1931). *The Waves* is hostile to reading, and yet has nearly always been read as a com-

plete, harmonious work of art. It is, though, a product of crisis
and reflects this in its form.

In two insightful articles,[3] J. W. Graham documents Woolf's
growing distaste for "psychology" and her search for voiceless,
characterless expression. In the introduction to his edition of the
two holograph drafts of the book, Graham explores the background to its conception as seen in the diary and essays written
between 1927 and 1930. In contemporary modes of fiction,
Woolf saw an excessive concern with psychology. In "The Narrow Bridge of Art" she says that writers have been too much
taken up with personal relations:

> We have come to forget that a large and important part of life consists in our
> emotions toward such things as roses and nightingales, the dawn, the
> sunset, life, death, and fate; we forget that we spend much time sleeping,
> dreaming, thinking, reading, alone; we are not entirely occupied in per-
> sonal relations; all our energies are not absorbed in making our livings.
> (GR, 19)

In "Phases of Fiction," two years later, she wrote of just that aesthetic she had achieved in novels like *To the Lighthouse*, but
which is largely abandoned in *The Waves*:

> As the pages are turned, something is built up which is not the story itself.
> And this power, if it accentuates and concentrates and gives the fluidity of
> the novel endurance and strength, so that no novel can survive even a few
> years without it, is also a danger. For the most characteristic qualities of the
> novel—that it registers the slow growth and development of feeling, that it
> follows many lives and traces their unions and fortunes over a long stretch of
> time—are the very qualities that are most incompatible with design and
> order. (GR, 143)

Here she has stated exactly the danger to which *The Waves* falls
prey. The passage continues by saying that the "most complete
novelist" is the one who can achieve a balance of the powers so
that "the one enhances the other."

It is evident that *The Waves* was intended to give a sense of
"life itself going on" (*D*, 28 May 1929); among early working
titles were "the life of anybody" and "life in general." This universal scope is not new in the fiction: Rachel Vinrace wished to
be told "everything" and Lily Briscoe is overwhelmed by no less
a question than "What is the meaning of life?" *The Waves*—

explicitly in the final episode—attempts to answer this question directly, attempts to map life completely with art.

At this point we might make a useful excursus to examine a sketch of 1920 that adumbrates Bernard's project of summing up life in a story: "An Unwritten Novel." The narrator is on a train, sitting opposite a woman whom the narrator "reads," believing that she is trying to tell her something simply by the way she sits, moves, looks: "I read her message, deciphered her secret, reading it beneath her gaze" (*AHH*, 14). The unreliability of such "reading" is demonstrated when the unknown woman gets off at her destination and shows that her life has nothing in common with the narrator's interpretation; the narrator is bewildered: "Well, my world's done for! What do I stand on? What do I know? That's not Minnie. There never was Moggridge. Who am I? Life's bare as bone" (*AHH*, 23). That *life* is impoverished because it does not tally with a reading is a characteristic feeling of Bernard's: he makes up scenes (stories) and expects life to fit them. For example, he goes to visit Louis and Rhoda, imagining Rhoda murmuring poetry, Louis filling a saucer with milk for a cat, but neither of them are even there: he feels at once that life is a poor affair (*TW*, 195). In the sketch the similar sense of loss gives way almost immediately to a euphoric celebration of life's richness and variety:

> Oh, how it whirls and surges—floats me afresh! I start after them. People drive this way and that. The white light splutters and pours. . . . Wherever I go, mysterious figures, I see you, turning the corner, mothers and sons; you, you, you. . . . If I fall on my knees, If I go through the ritual, the ancient antics, it's you, unknown figures, you I adore; if I open my arms, it's you I embrace, you I draw to me—adorable world! (*AHH*, 23)

The Waves was intended to express "life itself," to "give the moment," and yet it is more about art than life. It is an intensely self-regarding work, and its failure is partly due to this inwardness. In *Beyond Egotism* Robert Kiely remarks that Neville's comment that "our friends are not able to finish their stories" "is not merely an idle criticism of Bernard's inability to hold an audience but a deeply serious and universally applicable expression of life's refusal to conform to narrative convention. Friends cannot finish their stories because their audiences and their subjects are forever dispersing" (173-74). Life will not conform to stories, a recalcitrance that prevents Bernard from ever realizing the integrated "selfhood" that some critics (e.g., Richter, van Buren Kelley) claim for him, and reduces his experience to mere phrases.

In *The Act of Reading* Iser writes, "events are a paradigm of reality in that they designate a process, and are not merely a 'discrete entity' " (68). He continues this theme with a theoretical formulation that could be taken as parallel in a way to that important image in *The Waves* (which also appears in Woolf's diary) of a fin turning in a waste of water:

> Each event represents the intersecting point of a variety of circumstances, but circumstances also change the event as soon as it has taken on a shape. As a shape, it marks off certain borderlines, so that these may then be transcended in the continuous process of realization that constitutes reality. In literature, where the reader is constantly feeding back reactions as he obtains new information, there is just such a continual process of realization, and so reading itself "happens" like an event, in the sense that what we read takes on the character of an open-ended situation, at one and the same time concrete and yet fluid. The concreteness arises out of each new attitude we are forced to adopt toward the text, and the fluidity out of the fact that each new attitude bears the seeds of its own modification. Reading, then, is experienced as something which is happening—and happening is the hallmark of reality. (68)

We may say, then, that literature paradoxically complements reality in that it provides a perspective on the world, through symbols, which is not available to the world of actual experience. "Symbols enable us to perceive the given world because they do not embody any of the qualities or properties of the existing reality; in Cassirer's terms, it is their very *difference* that makes the empirical world accessible" (*Act*, 64). Fiction is described by Iser as "the pragmatically conditioned gestalt of the imaginary"[4]: "It appears to be a halfway house between the imaginary and the real. It shares with the real the determinateness of its form, and with the imaginary its nature of an 'as if.' "[5] Crucial in the failure of *The Waves* as a work of literature that can be successfully and fruitfully read is Bernard's failure to distinguish between story-telling and life and Woolf's failure to harmonize design and content. In the summing-up—Bernard's ultimate story—the reasons for the book's failure are focused on.

The summing-up is distinguished from the eight preceding

episodes in a number of ways, most significantly by its narrative voice. The dominant tense (like that of the interludes) is not the pure present of the other episodes—a tense that J. W. Graham notes, necessitates repetition of "I," as there is no helpful copula like the "am" of the progressive present. The "phantom dinner party" mirrors the situation of text and reader. It is not a normal social situation: the silent, unnamed guest is a "reader" of Bernard's story.

In the second holograph draft (1930), the final episode begins: " 'There are times,' said Bernard, 'which seem to be no time: & places which are no particular place, just as you, if you will pardon me, are not <any particular> person. in particular' " (Graham, 656). This is the situation of a literary work as regards the reader. The impression of timelessness is also indicated by the possibility that the summing-up is largely a dream, something that is only very slightly hinted at in the published text. At the end of episode eight Bernard is sleeping on a train: "But what is odd is that I still clasp the return half of my ticket to Waterloo firmly between the fingers of my right hand, even now, even sleeping" (*TW*, 167). The draft—as is usual in Woolf's work—is more explicit about the dream state: a note written as a reminder of what has still to be composed reads:

> (he goes in to be shaved, & sees the wind in looking glasses—regularity of
> the man's hand like the gardeners broom—& the dream)
>
> (April 12th) 1930
>
> (Graham, 360)

Another plan for the section reads:

> The walk (after arriving at Waterloo)
> hairdresser [sc.?]
> Then the loss of identity.
> Then the return
> The wave falls.
> He wakes.
> Death
> O Solitude.
>
> (Graham, 766)

The status of draft material should not be taken for granted in reading a published text; however, it is of particular help in reading *The Waves* as revisions are nearly always contractions or deletions. One further plan reads:

> Then the phantom dinner party when <the> others
> are not present; but only Bernard, &
> he sums up all their lives; &
> becomes part of them.
> Then the general death.

> (Graham, 757)

The conception jotted down in drafts and notebooks, of Bernard summing up "all their lives," is not realized in the book itself, and indeed could not be realized. Bernard's summing-up is not a uniting of the characters; it does not create that single human being he says they saw laid out before them on the restaurant table at their reunion dinner (196). The conclusion is merely one more story in the repertoire of *The Waves*. The book is not an "*ars poetica* for fiction" (Fleishman, *Virginia Woolf*, 152), but a sketchpad for an unwritten novel.

The wish to put ourselves in an unmediated relation to whatever "really" is, to know something absolutely, means a desire to be defined totally: marked or named once and for all, fixed in or by a word, and so—paradoxically— made indifferent. (Hartman, *Saving the Text*, 97)

Bernard's intention to "explain to you the meaning of my life" (168) can be read as Woolf's intention to explain the "meaning" of *The Waves*. The summing-up is not just the conclusion to Bernard's life, it is the author's way—as she states in her notebooks and diaries—of drawing together the various elements of the book, rounding it off and making some "final statement" about all the characters. Bernard himself alternates between extolling the power of art to express life in this way, and denigrating its poverty. The real problem, however, lies in his inability to distinguish between life and art and, as we shall see, in his refusal of the distinctions of identity and difference.

The first difficulty he encounters is the politics of experience: "the globe full of figures" as which Bernard images his life, his companion can not see. "You see me . . . opposite you," says Bernard, but whose, or which, "me" is this? The problem of voice, that is never solved in *The Waves*, is most particu-

larly Bernard's, a confusion that leads to inextricably complicated identifications. In evidence of this, we might take Bernard's
recollection of his reaction to Percival's death: "I said, 'Give him
(myself) another moment's respite' as I went downstairs" (TW,
187). The three pronouns exemplify the confusion of voices in
the work, a confusion that stems from the attempt to fix what is
impossible to fix. A further note of Samuel Butler's is apposite
here: "Besides what is the self of which we say that we are self-
conscious? No one can say what it is that we are conscious of.
This is one of the things which lie altogether outside the sphere
of words."[6]

James Naremore (The World Without a Self) is one of very
few critics to have found The Waves a failure ("though a highly
interesting one"). He too finds a confusion of voices:

> It is as if Virginia Woolf were asking the reader to suppose that the six types
> she has arranged in the novel can at any given moment be represented by six
> detached spokesmen who are continually going through a process of self-
> revelation. These voices seem to inhabit a kind of spirit realm from which,
> in a sad, rather world-weary tone, they comment on their time-bound selves
> below. Even while the voices assert their personalities, they imply a knowl-
> edge of a life without personality, an undifferentiated world like the one
> described by the interchapters. (173)

Naremore feels that "the reader almost drowns in the language"
of The Waves (189). Yet, despite his feeling that the book is one
of those that "generate an aesthetic crisis and call into question
their very being" (175), Naremore surprisingly concludes that it
achieves "that ultimate synthesis which . . . [she] sought to
depict in her fiction" (160).

Bernard attempts to discover a grammar of life, to reduce
experience absolutely to language, but there is a disjunction between the two, felt even in the discrepancy experienced by Bernard between himself and his name. This discrepancy is explained by J. Hillis Miller:

> All proper names, as linguists and ethnologists have recognized, are meta-
> phors. They alienate the person named from his unspeakable individuality
> and assimilate him into a system of language. They label him in terms of
> something other than himself, in one form of the differentiating or stepping
> aside which is the essence of language. To name someone is to alienate him
> from himself by making him part of a family.[7]

As already noted (see above, p. 41), the self cannot be named; what Hartman calls the "*nomen numen*" is extralinguistic. Bernard's assertions of identity (e.g., "I rose and walked away—I, I, I; . . . I, Bernard") are repeatedly undercut by his uncertainty as to how much others have contributed to that identity. Ultimately, Bernard is trying to verbally reduce the "I" that is his identity, to "sum up" his life and *speak* his self (or soul) into being in the actual world. "In a sense that cuts much deeper than semantics," writes George Steiner, "our identity is a first-person pronoun."[8] Bernard wishes to go beyond this *semantically, verbally*. His desire (and Woolf's) to reduce life to art, to fix the movement of identity by speaking into the world his secret name, leads eventually to the strange concept of "a man without a self."

One day, Bernard tells his guest, he did not answer the call of "I"; he experienced a world drained of all color, devoid of all features. However, while he can still say "I am dead" (*TW*, 202), he is still living, voicing his identity, still in the world he *says* he has transcended. If Bernard is "a dead man," who speaks? As Bernard says that he has dissolved all difference, resolved all identities into one, the biblical allusions of his "Last Supper" take on a greater import. "Take it. This is my life." says Bernard at the beginning of the last episode, echoing 1 Corinthians 11:24. He believes he has "summed up" all the others in this communion, forming one body, one being:

> And now I ask, "Who am I?" I have been talking of Bernard, Neville, Jinny, Susan, Rhoda and Louis. Am I all of them? Am I one and distinct? I do not know. We sat here together. But now Percival is dead, and Rhoda is dead; we are divided; we are not here. Yet I cannot find any obstacle separating us. There is no division between me and them. As I talked I felt "I am you." This difference we make so much of, this identity we so feverishly cherish, was overcome. (*TW*, 205)

This dislocation of identity reflects the crisis the book generates. Throughout, Bernard has questioned the nature of his own being in an empirical fashion quite unlike any other of Woolf's characters. The limits of subjectivity (what Naremore calls the "ultimate refinement") are reached as Bernard tries to undo the tautological knot of identity, enshrined, as Steiner says, in monotheistic religion's "I am that I am" (*Extraterritorial*, 64).

Distinction between one and other is dissolved in this quasi-religious self-glorification of Bernard's. He is claiming universal knowledge (which denies death) by what he imagines is a summing-up in an instant of his entire being; he claims access to "the mystery of things" (*TW*, 207), to being one of God's spies.[9]

The illusion that Bernard expresses is shattered (as we will see below, chapter 7) in the "Time Passes" section of *To the Lighthouse*, and it is perhaps a mark of the rigor of the writer's mind that Bernard is returned to consciousness of his actual identity by the (Sartreian) look of his dinner companion: "You look, eat, smile, are bored, pleased, annoyed—that is all I know. Yet this shadow which has sat by me for an hour or two, this mask from which peep two eyes, has power to drive me back, to pinion me down among all those other faces, to shut me in a hot room; to send me dashing like a moth from candle to candle" (*TW*, 208). From his self-apotheosis Bernard is returned to simple identity—"I." Perhaps an echo of that tautological irreducibility is heard in his wish to be left alone, "myself being myself" (*TW*, 210). The failure of Bernard, and consequently of *The Waves*, to make the promised "final statement" is perhaps admitted a few pages earlier: "What does the central shadow hold? Something? Nothing? I do not know" (*TW*, 207). Indeed, the summing-up has acknowledged its own failure even before this, when Bernard says, "Life is not susceptible perhaps to the treatment we give it when we try to tell it" (*TW*, 189). Such an admission is irreconcilable with the sense of transcendence of all limits, the dissolution of identity and difference that Bernard professes, and is an example of those unresolved tensions that fragment *The Waves*. Language cannot go beyond the nominal pronoun in representing self. R. D. Laing (amongst others[10]) has expressed the catch succinctly in *The Bird of Paradise*: "The Life I am trying to grasp is the me that is trying to grasp it" (156). Bernard—and Woolf—try to transpose the problem into otherworldly terms, but the argument remains strictly earthbound.

Before the truly Victorian melodrama of the ending's memorial to Woolf's brother, Thoby Stephen, is perhaps an admission of defeat: "However beat and done with it all I am, I must haul myself up, . . . I, I, I . . . must take myself off and catch some last train" (*TW*, 210). The "I" here contains the triumph and humiliation of human being, what Buber termed "the sublime melancholy of our lot" (*I and Thou*, 68). Severely flawed though it is, *The Waves* must not be rejected; it continues to develop and expound the perennial themes of Woolf's fiction. It is also important as evidence of a conflict that points toward the last and in many ways most difficult novel, *Between the Acts*. In that work's fusion of design and substance, in its dazzling play of voices, is conveyed that sense of something there when we are not that *The Waves* attempted.

The contours of Woolf's art reveal the paradigmatic experience of "emptiness" at the heart of life. The idea of "absent presence" emerges from recognition of the disjunctive filiation of art and life. This strange concept is associated both with Woolf's idea of self, or soul, and with her consciousness of 'reality.' With this description as a context, we will turn now more specifically to 'reality' and Woolf's sense of the numinous, which at once disturbed and enthralled her.

CHAPTER SIX
'REALITY'

THUS FAR I HAVE BEEN MORE CONCERNED WITH THE ACTUAL CONTEXT within which Woolf's sense of a special 'reality' is felt than with the nature of that 'reality' itself. The apprehension of a numinous 'reality' has usually manifested itself as a yearning for transcendence of the world of time and death on the part of a particular character, or a suggestion in the narrative structure of an abstract "gap" in actual life that cannot be directly referred to in language, but is certainly a potential experience of human being. 'Reality' was something particular to Woolf that she felt she (and other writers) could better apprehend than most people. Her solitary experiences in Sussex were religious in character ("The country is like a convent. The soul swims to the top." [D, 2 August 1924]). In this and the following two chapters, the nature of Woolf's sense of "something more" to life will be elucidated.

In her fiction, and in numerous essays and sketches, Woolf vacillates between faith in a meaningful world and a sense of life's absurdity, of a world in which human beings are blown aimlessly about. This tension in the work has been noted already several times; it is mapped in great variety in all her writing, in imagery, thought, form, theme, and conception. There is a desire to be lyrical, to find and interpret meaning (in the sense of finding some base on which life can stand), to answer the questions repeated by many characters with an affirmation of purpose; against this works a profound pessimism that believes human effort to be a sham, a pretence that saves us from an abyss of nothingness, bottomlessness. Another of those summer diary entries, made at Rodmell, illuminates the two sides of the conflict in Woolf's thinking:

> And so I pitched into my great lake of melancholy. Lord how deep it is! What a born melancholiac I am! The only way I keep afloat is by working. . . .

Directly I stop working I feel that I am sinking down, down. And as usual, I feel that if I sink further I shall reach the truth. That is the only mitigation; a kind of nobility. Solemnity. I shall make myself face the fact that there is nothing—nothing for any of us. Work, reading, writing are all disguises; & relations with people. Yes, even having children would be useless.

.   .   .   .

Well all this [planning *The Waves*] is of course the "real" life; & nothingness only comes in the absence of this (*D*, 23 June 1929)

The struggle between faith and despair is the heart of Woolf's thought, the impulse behind her fiction: it arises from the question of the nature of "human centrality" which, Georges Poulet writes, is "essentially religious" (*Circle*, 95).

There is the sense in Woolf's work (the work of an avowed atheist) of an immanent beyond: "By conviction an atheist perhaps, he is taken by surprise with moments of extraordinary exaltation" (*MD*, 63). Pressing on the world of the novels is a mystery, glimpsed only in fleeting moments, in solitude. Although she describes the endless modalities of human being, it seems to me that Woolf's effort is at the same time to express her perception of a 'reality' that transcends all modalities and gives them their being. This abstract 'reality' is not bound by the spatiotemporal horizons of actual human life, but is distinguished from mysticism by its rootedness in lived experience.

Her ideas of 'reality' and the soul can, though, readily be construed as theological; indeed, it is difficult to speak of the import of the novels if words such as "spirit," "visionary," and "mystery" are not secularized (which requires a considerable mental effort). In those extracts from her diary kept at Rodmell that have already been quoted, a religious tone that is unavoidable when she writes of 'reality' and the soul is very evident.

There is an opposition in Woolf's thinking between the symbolical, inclusive, intuitive, and nondiscursive mode of thought that seems particularly female, and the masculine style of rationality and logic, which tends to exclude. It is this counterbalancing that prevents her thought from being merely mystical, rooting it firmly in actual experience. The roots of this fundamental opposition may be found in her early life. Leslie Stephen, who married into the heart of the Clapham Sect, was one of the leading agnostic thinkers of his time—a time when agnosticism was a widely-held position, supported by Darwin's theories. Woolf later wrote of her frustration at the lack of "imagination" in her father and his agnostic friends. This dryness was inherited by the young men of her own circle of friends; "the fourth generation of the Clapham Sect," as Noel Annan calls them did, though, reject the moral code of their forebears.[1]

In "Old Bloomsbury" (ca. 1922) Woolf wrote that "Moore's book had set us all discussing philosophy, art, religion" (*MOB*, 168). In *The Voyage Out*, Helen Ambrose takes *Principia Ethica* on the *Euphrosyne*, reading as she embroiders "a sentence about the Reality of Matter or the Nature of Good." Despite the mockery of Apostolic fervor in her first novel, the Cambridge friends of Woolf's youth were an influence hard to ignore. The significance of G. E. Moore to those who surrounded Woolf in the years following her father's death can be assessed from the following remarks:

> The tremendous influence of Moore and his book upon us came from the fact that they suddenly removed from our eyes an obscuring accumulation of scales, cobwebs, and curtains, revealing for the first time to us, so it seemed, the nature of truth and reality, of good and evil and character and conduct, substituting for the religions and philosophical nightmares, delusions, hallucinations in which Jehovah, Christ, and St. Paul, Plato, Kant, and Hegel had entangled us, the fresh air and pure light of plain common sense. (Leonard Woolf, *An Autobiography*, 93)

> It was exciting, exhilirating, the beginning of the renaissance, the opening of a new heaven on a new earth, we were the forerunners of a new dispensation, we were not afraid of anything. (Maynard Keynes, *My Early Beliefs* in Rosenbaum, ed., *The Bloomsbury Group*: 52)

Keynes also provides a clue as to why Woolf may have been repelled by Moore's ethics:

> Like any other branch of science, it was nothing more than the application of logic and rational analysis to the material presented as sense-data. Our apprehension of good was exactly the same as our apprehension of green . . .

> If it appeared under cross-examination that you did not mean *exactly* anything, you lay under a strong suspicion of meaning nothing whatever. (ibid., 54, 56)

Bishop Butler provides Moore's epigraph to *Principia*

Ethica: "Everything is what it is, and not another thing." As an epigraph to what I understand as Woolf's "philosophy," and against Moore's, we might set this:

> So that was the Lighthouse, was it?
>   No, the other was also the Lighthouse. For nothing was simply one thing. The other was the Lighthouse too. (*TTL*, 286)

The Moorean universe, endorsed by such as Russell and Keynes, is continually questioned by the novels. The actual world is the context in which apprehension of the numinous occurs, suggesting that reality—the nature of which was plain enough to Leonard Woolf—is to be questioned deeply. Moore's system, to Woolf, was one more attempt to cover over the emptiness at the heart of life. Philosophies and religions for the most part attempt to order life; they do not explore it as her art does, with recognition of the nothingness that human being opposes and yet ultimately succumbs to. From her perspective on human experience, Woolf quickly arrives at the paradoxical character of human being that inspires the invention of unifying systems. From *The Voyage Out* onward, she sees religion as a deadening restriction that cuts people off from the very "invisible presences" (*MD*, 138) it pretends to reach. In an early essay, "Reading," she lamented the enclosure of thought by faith in an external deity:

> What, one asks, as considerations accumulate, is ever to stop the course of such a mind, unroofed and open to the sky? Unfortunately, there was the Deity. His faith shut in his horizon. Sir Thomas himself resolutely drew that blind. His desire for knowledge, his eager ingenuity, his anticipations of truth, must submit, shut their eyes, and go to sleep. Doubts he calls them. "More of these no man hath known than myself; which I confess I conquered, not in a martial posture, but on my knees." So lively a curiosity deserved a better fate. (*CDB*, 173)

A God makes the world one and indivisible, but denies the curious antinomies of the actual experience of human being, falsely reconciling them, and providing a means of escape from the ultimate horizon of death through the consolation of eternal life.

Pascal wrote of the human situation as being like that of a man who wakes on a desert island, not knowing where or when he is (*Pensées*, 88). This man, Georges Poulet remarks, is "not without a tragic resemblance to the Heideggerian or Sartrian being," and the moment is mirrored also at the beginning of Proust's *À La Recherche du Temps Perdu* (*Circle*, 33). The fading away of the sense of individual identity is a familiar experience in the novels that has been noted several times. Wonder at simply being at all is the starting point of Woolf's exploration of the human situation: "She was next overcome by the unspeakable queerness of the fact that she should be sitting in an armchair, in the morning, in the middle of the world. Who were the people moving in the house—moving things from one place to another? And life, what was that? . . . She was overcome with awe that things should exist at all" (*TVO*, 145). Thrown into the world like dice (*MD*, 15), each individual must somehow come to terms with the fact of being: "Then (she had felt it only this morning) there was the terror; the overwhelming incapacity, one's parents giving it into one's hands, this life, to be lived to the end, to be walked with serenely; there was in the depths of her heart an awful fear" (*MD*, 203).

The radical astonishment at simply being that many of Woolf's characters display is also recorded in the author's diary at several points. It is in *Mrs. Dalloway* that the apprehension of an abstract 'reality' is first strongly felt. The entire day of the novel is circumscribed by an aura of mystery that promises a revelation that will console Clarissa (in particular) in her perception of the "emptiness about the heart of life" (35).[2] The "inner meaning" is only *almost* expressed,[3] but it is enough to sustain Clarissa's faith in life and renew her efforts to find a solid purpose in it. Woolf, as I have suggested (p. 97), is in the position of the "solitary traveller" of Peter Walsh's dream. Despite our inability to know anything absolutely or to reach any resting-place in our actual lives, we continue to hover at the entrance to the cavern of mystery, making up the stories that become religions and philosophies.

There is an entry in the diary—made early in the composition of *To the Lighthouse*—in which Woolf records her own wonder at being, and also writes very directly about her special sense of 'reality.' It is particularly interesting in the light of what was said in chapter 2 about Clarissa and Mrs. Ramsay's experiences of the soul, to note that 'reality' is apparently synonymous with "beauty":

As for the soul: why did I say I would leave it out? I forget. And the truth is, one can't write directly about the soul. Looked at, it vanishes: but look at the ceiling, at Grizzle, at the cheaper beasts in the Zoo which are exposed to walkers in Regents Park, & the soul slips in. It slipped in this afternoon. I will write that I said, staring at the bison: answering L. absentmindedly; but what was I going to write? . . .

. . . I enjoy almost everything. Yet I have some restless searcher in me. Why is there not a discovery in life? Something one can lay hands on & say "This is it?" My depression is a harassed feeling—I'm looking; but that's not it—thats not it. What is it? And shall I die before I find it? Then (as I was walking through Russell Sqre last night) I see the mountains in the sky: the great clouds; & the moon which is risen over Persia; I have a great & astonishing sense of something there, which is "it"—It is not exactly beauty that I mean. It is that the thing is in itself enough: satisfactory; achieved. A sense of my own strangeness, walking on the earth is there too: of the infinite oddity of the human position; trotting along Russell Sqre with the moon up there, & those mountain clouds. Who am I, what am I, & so on: these questions are always floating about in me; & then I bump against some exact fact—a letter, a person, & come to them again with a great sense of freshness. And so it goes on. But, on this showing which is true, I think, I do fairly frequently come upon "it"; & then feel quite at rest. (*D*, 27 February 1926)

This entry brings to mind both Clarissa's tending to the sky above her house (*MD*, 204) and Mrs. Ramsay's seeking a world of beauty in nature (*TTL*, 101); and, again, the state of *rest* is achieved.

There is also an echo here of an essay on "Montaigne" which was written during the composition of *Mrs. Dalloway* (in 1924). The mystery of life seems intimately bound up with the mystery of self as an absolute, conclusive center. In the essay Woolf writes of the soul, saying it is "all laced about with nerves and sympathies which affect her every action"; none, however, know "how she works or what she is except that of all things she is the most mysterious, and one's self the greatest monster and miracle in the world" (*CR* I, 96). Behind this rather playful essayist's tone can be detected the overriding concern of the novels, which surfaces at the essay's conclusion:

But, as we watch with absorbed interest the enthralling spectacle of a soul living openly beneath our eyes, the question frames itself, Is pleasure the end of all? Whence this overwhelming interest in the nature of the soul? Why this overmastering desire to communicate with others? Is the beauty of this world enough, or is there, elsewhere, some explanation of the mystery? To this what answer can there be? There is none. There is only one more question: "Que scais-je?" (*CR* I, 97)

"Movement and change are the essence of our being" she wrote in the same essay (*CR* I, 90); the circular movement of the conclusion is typical also of the novels. The circle, as Poulet amply demonstrates, is the form under which thinking about self (as absolute) or God inevitably takes place.

An unobtrusive moment in *To the Lighthouse* reveals the scope of Woolf's thought and exemplifies much of what has been discussed so far; it can be taken as a paradigm of the movement between center and circumference as which the tension between faith and despair might be imaged.

One of the Ramsay children, Nancy, broods alone over a rock-pool, then raises her eyes to look across the sea to the horizon (118-19). Her sense of vastness and littleness recalls an important fragment of Pascal's entitled *Disproportion of Man* (*Pensées*, 88).[4] The contrast between human being and nature has been given significance from *The Voyage Out* onward (especially noticeable in that first novel are the shifts of horizon and perspective occasioned by the setting). In that contrast Pascal finds the medium by which one can, in the words of his chapter's title, make the "transition from knowledge of man to knowledge of God" (*Pensées*, 87). To understand the human situation, says Pascal, is to despair: to escape from this despair we must pass to knowledge of God. "Nature is an infinite sphere whose centre is everywhere and circumference nowhere. In short it is the greatest perceptible mark of God's omnipotence that our imagination should lose itself in that thought." (89). Virginia Woolf does not roof in Nancy's thought with a similar recourse to a deity, but faces the conception of all human being reduced to nothingness when set against infinity. Nancy is "bound hand and foot" between the two extremes, and, as Pascal writes, trembles at being suspended between "these two abysses of infinity and nothingness" (*Pensées*, 90). Still following Pascal, Nancy contemplates these marvels in silence: "So listening to the waves, crouched over the pool, she brooded."

For, after all, what is man in nature? A nothing compared to the infinite, a whole compared to the nothing, a middle point between all and nothing, infinitely remote from an understanding of the extremes; the end of things and their principles are unattainably hidden from him in impenetrable secrecy.

Equally incapable of seeing the nothingness from which he emerges and the infinity in which he is engulfed. (*Pensées,* 90)

The ineffable meeting-point of the two extremes, of center and circumference, is for Pascal God: God, then, is a sign for the unattainable. Woolf cannot reconcile the opposites to a unity in this way; she acknowledges the tension, but does not seek the easy resting-place of a deity. "God," to her, is a convenient way of leaping over the limits of language and thought, an imagined transcendence that does away with the anguish and rapture of the search for 'reality.' She is at once close to and far away from a thinker like Pascal: the movement is identical but at the crucial moment she refuses to place her trust in a mystery, to leap out of human being into mystical faith; her thought explodes in tension, does not rest in faith in a supernatural agency. Pascal, again, voices the fundamental concerns of Woolf's art when he writes:

Such is our true state. That is what makes us incapable of certain knowledge or absolute ignorance. We are floating in a medium of vast extent, always drifting uncertainly, blown to and fro; whenever we think we have a fixed point to which we can cling and make fast, it shifts and leaves us behind; if we follow it, it eludes our grasp, slips away, and flees eternally before us. Nothing stands still for us. This is our natural state and yet the state most contrary to our inclinations. We burn with desire to find a firm footing, an ultimate, lasting base on which to build a tower rising up to infinity, but our whole foundation cracks and the earth opens up into the depth of the abyss. (*Pensées,* 92)

Pascalian anguish is countered in the novels by the thought that it is this very hopelessness that makes human being so exhilarating and unique; it is the journey over the abyss that gives life purpose, the restless seeking after 'reality.' While Pascal stays on the human plane, his thought and that of the novels exactly correspond; he is, as most are, lured away from the human by the "essentially religious" character of human centrality. The mind that speaks the novels allows itself no resting-place from which to view human being, and thus the basic question is restated by the very form of the art. The free-spinning mind can never conclude, can never create a whole because wholeness can arise only from a fixed point: there can be no center to infinity or nothingness and so all wholes are illusory. Pascal writes that man can never know the whole of which he is a part; he assumes there *is* a whole because he has faith in his God; Woolf is not so sure.

The moments of "rest" that Woolf records in her diary, and that such characters as Mrs. Ramsay experience, are but brief glimpses of the rich potential of human imagination that cannot be sustained in the actual world. The novels (and diary) display Pascalian dread in the face of an irresolvable problem, but they never give in entirely or permanently to that dread: their joy is in being able to achieve that state of dread or anxiety. In the movement to despair, hope is renewed; a wavelike rhythm that informs all the novels.

That "philosophy" with which Woolf is engaged in *Mrs. Dalloway* and *To the Lighthouse* is extremely abstruse. However, in *Orlando* its lineaments can be discerned with a clarity that, though lacking the poetic force of the other works, is helpful in unravelling their more complex moments. Orlando shares Clarissa Dalloway's feeling of surviving after death by absorption in the "ebb and flow of things" (*MD*, 11): "She, who believed in no immortality, could not help feeling that her soul would come and go forever with the reds on the panels and the greens on the sofa" (*O*, 285). This soul, then, bears no resemblance to the Christian idea of the immortal breath of God informing human life. It is what might be described as the "faculty" that apprehends beauty in the world (which, it was noted above, p. 100, seems almost synonymous with 'reality').[5]

Toward the end of the book, Orlando looks down the long tunnel of time that her life has been, but the shock of realizing herself in the present moment, as the clock strikes, instantly dissolves her memories. She is suddenly gripped by tension, for "whenever the gulf of time gaped and let a second through some unknown danger might come with it" (287-88). From that moment when "the whole of her darkened and settled" (282), we should understand that she is "one and entire" (288) and for the first time experiencing time as a passage toward death. It is clear from what follows that the abstract 'reality' Woolf records her experience of, that Clarissa senses in the sky, and that Mrs. Ramsay gleans from nature, is intimately related to the effort of overcoming the shock of the present experienced as a passage to inevitable death.

Blinking her eyes in a moment of faintness, Orlando shuts off the visible, and "in that moment's darkness . . . was relieved of the pressure of the present":

> There was something strange in the shadow that the flicker of her eyes cast, something which (as anyone can test for himself by *looking now at the sky*) is always *absent from the present*—whence its terror, its nondescript character—something one trembles to pin through the body with a name and call beauty, for it has no body, is as a shadow without substance or quality of its own, yet has the power to change whatever it adds itself to. (*O,* 289, my italics)

Here we have the familiar contours of that paradigmatic experience of Woolf's fiction: this abstract, insubstantial "shadow" (or *beauty,* or 'reality') is nameless; it is a quality absent from the present like that apprehended in the sky (see *MD,* 204) in which the soul finds *rest;* it is a transcendence of the passage of time. This "beauty" is an ordering quality, giving shape to experience, composing what Orlando has seen into "something tolerable, comprehensible" (*O,* 289), or, it might be said, into *pattern.* Throughout the oeuvre a state of rhythmic rest gives rise to the psychic perception of pattern: Clarissa sewing, Mrs. Ramsay knitting, Lily painting, Lucy Swithin "one-making"—these women perceive a pattern behind daily life, a harmony that contrasts with male methodolatry, theorizing, and system-making. Rhythm, rest, and loss of identity, silence, darkness, and namelessness are the common features of this primary experience in the fiction and are common to "self-awareness" and apprehension of 'reality.'

In the darkness of the mind in solitude is a pool "where things dwell in darkness so deep that what they are we scarcely know" (*O,* 290). The style of *Orlando* (see above, p. 36) enables Woolf to come directly at ideas in a way that would seem strained in another work. It is in this "part furthest from sight" where things are unnamed (*O,* 290) that the "shadow" of beauty is received, becoming a pool that reflects all that is seen. What she describes is a sort of psychic sight that apprehends not objects but their "beauty": the thing itself; the beauty of the world that cannot be fixed with a name. In this state, of the apprehension of the numinous, art and religion arise, those efforts to overcome life in time. The actual objects of the visible world remind Orlando of the present, and thus, a tension is introduced between the actual and the transcendent world of beauty. This tension is necessary if mysticism is to be avoided. The danger of the tendency to mysticism is described in *Mrs. Dalloway*, in that passage about the "solitary traveller": "Such are the visions which ceaselessly float up, pace beside, put their faces in front of, the actual thing; often overpowering the solitary traveller and taking away from him the sense of the earth, the wish to return, and giving him for substitute a general peace" (*MD*, 64). The complacent contemplation of nature and the dangerous mysticism it can lead to will be the focus of the next chapter. Orlando experiences brief moments in which she seems to live her memory, but she is constantly anchored in the actual world of time by the visible world around her (*O*, 291).

In darkness, when the myriad details of actual life are obscured, it is easier to "see" "where things shape themselves and to see in the pool of the mind now Shakespeare, now a girl in Russian trousers" (*O*, 294). 'Reality' is not bound by the particular, named world, and yet inheres in that world. The possibility of transcendence that Woolf offers is not an *actual* possibility, in the sense that it cannot share the modes of being established for identities in the actual world. The being of that abstract 'reality' that Orlando perceives in darkness, that Clarissa feels in the sky, and Mrs. Ramsay tends to in nature, is evidently intimately bound up with the question of the temporality of human being, to which we must now turn.

CHAPTER SEVEN
ACQUIESCENCE

BEFORE MOVING TO THE QUESTION OF TEMPORALITY IN THE NOVELS generally, it will be useful to look at what many readers have found to be a gratuitously obscure and eccentric piece of writing: the central "Time Passes" section of *To the Lighthouse*. Ostensibly, it is intended as a representation of the passage of time, and if this were its only function it might justifiably be said that Woolf has lost control of her pen here. However, "Time Passes" contributes significantly to the "philosophy" implicit in the novels. What are seen as its excesses can be explained as Woolf's efforts to find some means of communicating what (in several diary passages) she acknowledges is beyond language. Her method in "Time Passes" is to state what 'reality' is *not*.

"As an infinite circumference," writes Georges Poulet, "eternity . . . is the vastest possible circle of duration; as the center of this circumference it is the fixed point, and unique moment, which is simultaneously in harmony with all the circumferential points of this duration" (*Circle*, xii-xiii). *To the Lighthouse* (which Woolf felt had "fetched its circle pretty completely") partakes of such double infinity, embodying a movement at once toward center and circumference. Intimations of this movement occur early on: "Both of them looked at the dunes far away, and instead of merriment felt come over them some sadness—because the thing was completed partly, and partly because distant views seem to outlast by a million years (Lily thought) the gazer and to be communing already with a sky which beholds an earth entirely at rest" (*TTL*, 36-37).

In her diary on 5 September 1926, Woolf wrote: "The lyric portions of To the L. are collected in the 10 year lapse, & dont interfere with the text so much as usual." The "lyric portions" do, nevertheless, connect with the "text" as they reiterate Lily Briscoe's questions and raise matters already seen to be of paramount importance in the conception of the world of the novels in general. That theme discussed above of the "disproportion of man" returns in "Time Passes," but embedded less accessibly in a symbolic poetry that attempts a pure abstraction. In her diary and working notes, Woolf frequently emphasized the experimental nature of the middle section of the novel and felt at a loss as to how to approach it: "I cannot make it out—here is the most difficult abstract piece of writing—I have to give an empty house, no people's characters, the passage of time, all eyeless & featureless with nothing to cling to" (*D*, 18 April 1926). When she dashed off a couple of pages, however, she felt that "This is not made up: it is the literal fact" (*D*, 30 April 1926). Writing to Vita Sackville-West a week after *Lighthouse*'s publication, she admits that she once thought "Time Passes" "impossible as prose" (*L*, 1754)—an indication, perhaps, of how it should be approached.

The actual passage of time is fairly directly conveyed by the description of the house's decay, the encroachment of nature, and phrases telling the reader that time is indeed passing, e.g.: "Night, however, succeeds to night"; "Now, day after day"; "Night after night, summer and winter." This section of the novel has an import beyond its functional message of a ten year "lapse," however. In her working notes, Woolf seems to emphasize her deeper concerns. It is worth setting down her plan for the section, as from this it is clear that she intended to encompass and probe themes prevalent in all her fiction, not just interpolate a piece of "poetic prose":

> To the Lighthouse
> [<Tie?>] *Ten Chapters*
> Now the question of the ten years.
> [<Tie?>]
> The Seasons.
> The Skull
> The gradual dissolution of everything
> This is to be contrasted with the permanence
> of—what?
> Sun, moon, & stars.
> Hopeless gulfs of misery.
> Cruelty.

The War.
Change. Oblivion. Human vitality. Old woman
Cleaning up. The bobbed up, valorous, as of a
principle
of human life projected
We are handed on by our children?
Shawls & shooting caps. A green handled brush.
The devouringness of nature.
But all the time this passes, accumulates.
Darkness.
The welter of winds & waves
What then is the medium through wh. we regard human beings?
Tears. [di?]
<Sleep th> Slept through life.   (Dick, Appendix B)

I think it is important to focus on "Time Passes" to deflect any inference of mysticism from what is being discussed. My intention is to present a sort of palimpsest: Woolf's text should be imagined showing through what is in effect my commentary. As "Time Passes" begins, the horizon between sea and sky almost disappears: night falls. This night adumbrates the ten years of abandonment and yet is only an "ordinary" night. A quasi-religious note is sounded almost immediately, an indication of the broader import of this section: "divine goodness" responds to "human penitence" by giving a glimpse of *noumena*, the "thing beneath the semblance of the thing" (*TW*, 116): "It seemed now as if, touched by human penitence and all its toil, divine goodness had parted the curtain and displayed behind it, single, distinct, the hare erect; the wave falling; the boat rocking, which, did we deserve them, should be ours always" (*TTL*, 198).

Religious terms and ideal forms persist in "Time Passes": "divine promptitude," "light bent to its own image in adoration," "tokens of divine bounty," "dreamt holily"; "the shape of loveliness itself," "persistency itself," "some absolute good." The "deity" allows only a glimpse of perfection: the "drench of hail" that shrouds the world's treasures makes it seem impossible "that we should ever compose from their fragments a perfect whole or read in the littered pieces the clear words of truth" (199). Here, certainly, Lily's aspirations are recalled, and the idea of a whole (or the "true nature of our experience," as it is termed in the contemporaneous "Impassioned Prose"—see above, p. 74) arising from gathered fragments links "Time Passes" to the wider thought of the novels as I have elucidated it. There can also be seen a close association between religion and art. The momentary visions of a 'reality' apart from actual reality are the typical concerns of Woolf's artists, that which they seek to capture and convey. The tendency to a transcendental beyond in religious faith, it is suggested, shares the *form* of artistic perception and creation. The difference between the two yearnings lies in the willingness of art—at least Woolf's art—to accept defeat and negation as part of the experience, never to wish to be "blown to nothingness" (*MD*, 64) in a mystical transcendence of the actual.

In "Time Passes" the beach—which can certainly be taken in one sense as that beach upon which the Ramsay children walk and play—is the scene of many questionings of life's purpose. This, of course, anticipates Lily's longing to find "the meaning of life" in the third section of the novel ("The Lighthouse"). Before an answer can be approached, however, the questioners must learn the honesty Woolf's art propounds.

The first seeker after an answer is a solitary sleeper who seeks on the beach "what, and why, and wherefore" (199), a typical Romantic looking to nature—and particularly the sea— for an explanation of life and himself. His desire to make the world "reflect the compass of the soul" (199) is disappointed; Poulet is instructive here: "Here there is the place, the moment, there an indistinct immensity. How to link them, how to place them in rapport with one another? How to establish a *proportion?*" (*Circle*, 33). Once again, the text is following the path of Pascal's "unaided knowledge." Standing on the ambiguous beach (so because it is at once part of the land and part of the sea), the sleeper is mocked by the bellowing wind for his vain attempt. Mrs. Ramsay's death appears as an impassive fact, contrasted with the ethereal quest of the solitary sleeper: it is a fact of life the meaning of which is not to be found in nature.

The empty house is "seen" by the "nameless spirit" around which Woolf's thoughts were to revolve so incessantly as she wrote *Between the Acts*. As distance between perceiver and perceived is annihilated, in the vacancy arises pure form: "the shape of loveliness itself" (*TTL*, 201). Such form is not in the actual world, and so not in time; lifeless and solitary, the form "is" in eternity. Without the distancing, distorting, shaping, and *naming* of human being, there is nothing: "pure form" is one of the myriad (false) names of nothingness (N.B.: "a form from which life had parted" [*TTL*, 201]). Such form may, it is suggested, be glimpsed ("seen from a train window, vanishing so quickly"). It shares this characteristic with 'reality' and the notion of self or soul.[1] Stillness is the key to the ideal; movement is essential to life; stasis is death. This shape of loveliness is, then, a form of death (the jugs and chairs are suitably shrouded). Qualities (like the beauty of the Acropolis in *Jacob's Room*, 147-48) do not share the modes of being of actual human life; only by human perception are they brought into the actual world.[2] The sounds of the world are folded into silence; only with the return of human life do those sounds again become the fragments of a sought-after pattern (*TTL*, 218). As Woolf noted in her diary, her intentions in "Time Passes" were impossible to realize if come at directly. The meaning can only emerge as part of its overall context; by shaping round what is unsayable, it is "said" in the act of reading.[3]

Mrs. McNab—the "principle," "human vitality"—has moments of light in her darkness. Despite the quotidian rhythms of her existence, there is something in her that makes her smile and sing; a fundamental humanity, inarticulate, but sufficient to motivate life. The answer that is "vouchsafed" the beach-walking mystic and visionary (implying a resting in transcendence) is not to be shared. The sense here is that the inward-looking visionaries have little to offer human life. It is to the world of being with others, to the shared experience of actual human being that Woolf would direct our thoughts, illuminating the "incorrigible hope" that twines about even the most apparently desolate aspects of life.

The third walkers on the beach are "the wakeful, the hopeful" (*TTL*, 204): they see a commensurability between nature and man, a comforting assurance that "good triumphs, happiness prevails, order rules" (*TTL*, 205). The wakeful and hopeful assemble elements of nature in the belief that they thus bring together the fragments of an inner vision. Nature "declares" the truth of this vision, but if questioned, the vision at once evaporates. What seems to be implied here is that it is only the apparent order and unity of nature that impels man to seek a commensurate unity within himself. The passage is dotted with indications that such a project is to be rejected: the minds of men are *mirrors* in which clouds and shadows form; the season of the wakeful and hopeful is "acquiescent" spring, the significance of which is soon revealed.

The wakeful and hopeful seek universal knowledge that as Pascal knew, is hopeless: "If, as Descartes believes, the first question is to know oneself, the very act of the knowledge of self, contrary to what Descartes held, leads us at once, either to despair through the comprehension of our misery, or else to catastrophe by making obligatory the impossible, that is to say, universal knowledge" (*Circle*, 35-36). Death again starkly controverts all hope of security; the "diamond in the sand which would render the possessor secure" (*TTL*, 205) is unattainable. "Time Passes" is implicitly concerned with the urge to fix an absolute self, for it is time that proves always to be the downfall of the attempt to compose self. In this section of the novel, Woolf is not so much attempting to render the *experience* of time, as time "itself," the time of nature and eternity in which all human being appears as but a spark. This concern will loom larger in her last novel, but the notion is really impossible to grasp unless put in terms of human being. Poulet, writing about one of Woolf's favorite authors—Montaigne—draws attention to the inextricable relation of time and self, using an image familiar in Woolf's writing:

> The instant is the kingdom of the imperceptible. It is the home of what Leibnitz was later to call the infinitely small entities. It is an instant which is an instant of passage, and which therefore is less an instant than the passage from instant to instant; there is, so to speak, an infinity of the microscopic changes in all the shades of being. It is a wager to attempt to "choose and lay hold of so many nimble little motions" [Montaigne], to hope to disentangle "a thing so mixed, so slender, and so fortuitous." It is all the more so because the incommensurable volubility of tenuous elements, which makes up the mind, is volubility of the thinking act as well as of its thoughts. Thus the self is dissolved, not only from instant to instant but even in the middle of the instant-passage, in a *prismatic play like that of a spray of water*.[4]

War ultimately demonstrates the illusion that a commensurability between man and nature is. "Those" who go down to the beach to seek answers in sea and sky are finally shaken out of complacency by the evidence of war. How does the image of an ashen-colored ship reflect their benevolent deity? The tone is deeply mocking of that "scene calculated to stir the most sublime reflections and lead to the most comfortable conclusions" (*TTL*, 207), setting itself firmly against the visions of divine harmony the Romantics (in particular) found in the contemplation of nature.[5] This intrusion of an image of man-made death forces the beach-walker to a new honesty: nature is entirely indifferent to man.[6] "That dream, then, of sharing, completing, finding in solitude on the beach an answer, was but a reflection in a mirror, and the mirror itself was but the surface glassiness which forms in quiescence when the nobler powers sleep beneath?" (*TTL*, 208). The question-mark is surprising, but expressive of the movement toward the conclusion that "the mirror was broken" (*TTL*, 208). By only looking outward to nature, away from their own being, by making no *effort*, people simply reflect the nature they are thrown into, denying their actual being by losing it in the universal.[7]

In support of this idea we can turn to a most significant entry in Woolf's diary, made on 11 October 1929, in which the word "acquiescence" forms a direct link with the novel; the concerns of *Between the Acts*, it might also be noted, are once more adumbrated:

> . . . & for all this, there is vacancy & silence somewhere in the machine. On the whole, I do not much mind; because, what I like is to flash & dash from side to side, goaded on by what I call reality. If I never felt these extraordinarily pervasive strains—of unrest, or rest, or happiness, or discomfort—I should float down into acquiescence. Here is something to fight: & when I wake early I say to myself, Fight, fight. If I could catch the feeling, I would: the feeling of the singing of the real world, as one is driven by loneliness & silence from the habitable world; the sense that comes to me of being bound on an adventure; . . . But anything is possible. And this curious steed, life; is genuine—Does any of this convey what I want to say?—But I have not really laid hands on the emptiness after all.[8] (*D*, 11 October 1929)

The import of this passage evidently spreads far beyond the immediate concerns, which is a good example of why Woolf's writing resists linear, discursive exposition. Words are pools of meaning, with many levels of import and significance that can obtain simultaneous recognition only in the preverbal unconscious of the reading mind. The approach to understanding Woolf's thought must, I feel, lie in such concatenation of passages, a gathering of fragments. With the mirror of complacency broken, nature and humankind are divorced; art, in the form of Mr. Carmichael's poetry, is the fact of life that is set against mystic visions now (*TTL*, 208).

Released from the illusion of reflected beauty and unity, nature is seen as a reasonless and indifferent force; time also, "(for night and day, month and year ran shapelessly together)" (*TTL*, 209). Nature in the novel is like Pascal's desert island: it is what we are thrown into. Attempts to find unity between that emptiness (for nature is empty at heart) and our being are hopeless, resulting only in illusions. Memory, by which, as we have seen, the sense of identity must be formed and sustained, is helpless in stemming the rising "pool of Time":

> What power could now prevent the fertility, the insensibility of nature? Mrs. McNab's dream of a lady, of a child, of a plate of milk soup? It had wavered over the walls like a spot of sunlight and vanished. (*TTL*, 213)

> Here [on the desert island], memory proves itself miserably ineffectual. It could only, by the vain miracle of affective reviviscence, transport us from island to island, from moment to moment, and from place to place. Never, for any moment nor for any place, could it tell us who put us there, nor what we are doing there. (*Circle*, 34)

The language of "Time Passes" reveals an acute struggle in Woolf's thinking: while suffused with the religious sense, it rejects the idea of any external agency, of the supernatural. Despite this, it *does* suggest an informing "spirit"—or, at least, a pattern—that might be described as the non-being from which being arises, and against which being stands out. This otherness is usually misrepresented by mystics and visionaries who seek an escape from the actuality of human being. Without the creative power of human being, nature (or eternity—they seem synonymous here) will prevail. Human being, then, is seen as "rescued" from the dark nothingness of amorphous nature / eternity.

The "singing of the real world," the "voice of the beauty of the world" (*TTL*, 219) (Mrs. Ramsay was described as "the beauty of the world," [61]), goes on unheeded by the sleepers, who might be taken as representing the majority of human beings. Again and again, Woolf emphasizes that apprehension of 'reality' is available only through effort. The voice of beauty is indifferent to those who sleep heedless of it: if they prefer to sleep, "gently then without complaint, or argument, the voice would sing its song" (*TTL*, 220). It is significant that the passage closes with the awakening of the artist, Lily, to whom the song has penetrated.

Once again, thought folds back in on itself when face to face with this metalinguistic 'reality'; it cannot be thought about; the circle cannot be escaped. It is perhaps Woolf's inability to put in *actual* terms what she means by 'reality', beauty, and soul that gives the "philosophy" implicit in the novels its essentially religious character.

CHAPTER EIGHT
TIME

NOW THERE IS NOTHING SO MYSTERIOUS, SO ENIGMATIC, SO WONDERFUL AS TIME. IT IS not only that it is the most difficult of all problems; it is also the most urgent, the one which most frequently confronts us and reminds us of its actual importance, the one which is perpetually experienced not only as a *thought*, but as the very essence of our being. We are not only living *in* time; we are living time; we *are* time.[1]

Woolf's concept of time is essentially Romantic. A sense of transience, of the deficiencies of human life in time, pervades her writing and, with no belief in a supernatural agency, any possibility of transcending the horizon of time must be rooted in actual experience. The most significant feature of the Romantic concept of time is identified by Georges Poulet as a belief in the continued existence of the past. That such a belief was an important part of Woolf's thinking is vaguely implied even as early as *The Voyage Out*: "She was haunted by absurd jumbled ideas— how, if one went back far enough, everything perhaps was intelligible; everything was in common; for the mammoths who pastured in the fields of Richmond High Street had turned into paving stones and boxes full of ribbon and her aunts" (*TVO*, 73). The immanence of the past in the present is felt more definitely later in the novel: "The time of Elizabeth was only distant from the present time by a moment of space compared with the ages which had passed since the water had run between those banks, and the green thickets swarmed there, and the small trees had grown to huge wrinkled trees in solitude" (*TVO*, 323).

Such intimations of the past's persistence in the present lead easily to a belief in the continued existence of some "part" of people's being after death—a belief that Clarissa voices in *Mrs. Dalloway*. The fact of death temporalizes human being; it is that which manifests the horizon of time by which *all* actual being is bounded. Woolf's novels (which she once wrote she would perhaps prefer to call "elegies") testify to a potential in human experience for perceiving a time out of time, for overcoming the limits of actual life through apprehension of a different mode of being altogether.

Her acute sense of life's transience and the search for a way of overcoming it may have arisen from the devastating experiences of her childhood. In an early memoir ("Reminiscences," 1907-8), she wrote, "The effect of death upon those that live is always strange, and often terrible in the havoc it makes with innocent desires" (*MOB*, 31). The "greatest disaster that could happen" was the death of Julia, her mother. The somber world of death and mourning that may be discovered in Leslie Stephen's *Mausoleum Book* is recalled throughout Woolf's fiction. It is interesting to note in the description of Julia Stephen in "Reminiscences" the similarity between mother and daughter's sense of life's ephemerality: "She kept herself marvellously alive to all the changes that went on round her, as though she heard perpetually the ticking of a vast clock and could never forget that some day it would cease for all of us" (*MOB*, 35). Her daughter records that Julia saw those around her as a "vast procession on the march towards death." A namesake of Julia's—Julia Eliot—displays just this sense in *Jacob's Room*: "The tumult of the present seems like an elegy for past youth and past summers, and there rose in her mind a curious sadness, as if time and eternity showed through skirts and waistcoats, and she saw people passing tragically to destruction" (168). Like Woolf, she was poised between making the most of things since we know nothing of the future, and thinking that nothing mattered, as perhaps there is no future.

The deaths that occurred in her early life—particularly that of her mother—were constantly in Woolf's mind: "People never get over their early impressions of death I think. I always feel pursued" (*D*, 5 April 1924). Evidence of this persistence is found, for example, in the striking similarity between a description of Julia's death written in 1924 and another written in 1940:

This is the 29th anniversary of mothers death. I think it happened early on a Sunday morning, & I looked out of the nursery window & saw old Dr Seton walking away with his hands behind his back, as if to say It is finished &

then the doves descending to peck in the road, I suppose, with a fall & descent of infinite peace. (*D*, 5 May 1924)

I leant out of the nursery window the morning she died. It was about six, I suppose. I saw Dr Seton walk away up the street with his head bent and his hands clasped behind his back. I saw the pigeons floating and settling. I got a feeling of calm, sadness, and finality. It was a beautiful blue spring morning, and very still. That brings back the feeling that everything had come to an end. (*MOB*, 84)

The late memoir, "A Sketch of the Past" (from which the latter quotation comes), makes clear that Woolf felt the deaths of her mother and Stella (her half-sister), and later her brother Thoby, in some way revealed to her the *true* lineaments of life:

But at 15 to have that protection removed, to be tumbled out of the family shelter, to see cracks and gashes in that fabric, to be cut by them, to see beyond them—was that good? . . . I would see (after Thoby's death) two great grindstones (as I walked round Gordon Sqe) and myself between them.[2] I would typify a contest between myself and "them"—some invisible giant. I would reason, or fancy, that if life were thus made to rear and kick, it was at any rate, the real thing. Nobody could say I had been fobbed off with an unmeaning slip of the precious matter. So I came to think of life as something of extreme reality. And this, of course, increased my feeling of my own importance. Not in relation to human beings: in relation to the force which had respected me sufficiently to make me feel what was real. (*MOB*, 118).

Allowing for the retrospective modifications of memory, we may say that Woolf's sense of a distinct 'reality' apart from the general reality of everyday life began to develop very early in her life.

In many of the transitional sketches that helped Woolf toward *Jacob's Room*—e.g., "An Unwritten Novel," "Kew Gardens," "The Mark on the Wall" (see *D*, 26 January 1920)—the ghostly atmosphere of that novel is already prevalent, a sense that what is seen is transient, passed away as soon as looked at. *Jacob's Room* is elegaic, incorporating the traditional elements of lonely widows, tolling bells, and country churchyards; echoes of the dead reverberate through the novel, mingling inextricably with the voices of the living. It was in *Jacob's Room* that Woolf felt she had "found out how to begin (at 40) to say something in my own voice". (*D*, 26 July 1922). Although death had been a significant element of her first novel, it does not assume the thematic importance it was to retain in her fiction until *Jacob's Room.*

That novel is, so to speak, "bracketed"; for instance, by the repetition of certain phrases, giving it the appearance of being "scenes from a life": "Then here is another scrap of conversation; the time about eleven in the morning; the scene a studio; and the day Sunday" (126). More than once it is stressed that Jacob is a shadow, blown through the pages of the book like a leaf by the wind. Even in the beginning, on the beach, there is an undefinable note of absence, of loss; a sense that Jacob is already gone when the work opens, that what follows is only an attempt to imagine his life (which is, of course, only imaginary). This note can be heard in Archer's calling for his brother:

> "Ja-cob! Ja-cob!" shouted Archer, lagging on after a second.
> The voice had an extraordinary sadness. Pure from all body, pure from all passion, going out into the world, solitary, unanswered, breaking against rocks—so it sounded. (7)

To call and receive no answer is an intimation of death. Jacob's death is unseen, unknown; all that is known of death is its effect on the living, which was Woolf's habitual focus. At the close of the book, as Bonamy echoes Archer's cry (a bracket), it is the continuing passage of time that dominates.

The sense of the passing of time grows increasingly strong in Woolf's diary from 1920 onward, and with it her search for something apart from time, for moments of timelessness:

> Nowadays I'm often overcome by London; even think of the dead who have walked in the city. Perhaps one might visit <city> the churches. The view of the grey white spires from Hungerford Bridge brings it to me: & yet I can't say what "it" is. (*D*, 8 June 1920)

> Why do I trouble to be so particular with facts? I think it is my sense of the flight of time: so soon Towers Place will be no more; & twigs, & I that write. I feel time racing like a film at the Cinema. I try to stop it. I prod it with my pen. I try to pin it down. (*D*, 22 January 1922)

> I have the sense of the flight of time; & this shores up my emotions. (*D*, 13 June 1923)

In *Mrs. Dalloway* Clarissa expresses her belief in surviving death through the "odd affinities" she has with people and places:

Somehow in the streets of London, on the ebb and flow of things, here, there, she survived, Peter survived, lived in each other, she being part, she was positive, of the trees at home; of the house there, ugly, rambling all to bits and pieces as it was; part of people she had never met; being laid out like a mist between the people she knew best, who lifted her on their branches as she had seen the trees lift the mist, but it spread ever so far, her life, herself. (11-12)

Later in the novel this (Romantic) autochthonous idea is repeated:

But she said, sitting on the bus going up Shaftesbury Avenue, she felt herself everywhere; not "here, here, here"; and she tapped the back of the seat; but everywhere. She waved her hand, going up Shaftesbury Avenue. She was all that. So that to know her, or anyone, one must seek out the people who completed them; even the places. Odd affinities she had with people she had never spoken to, some woman in the street, some man behind a counter— even trees, or barns. It ended in a transcendental theory which, with her horror of death, allowed her to believe, or say that she believed (for all her scepticism), that since our apparitions, the part of us which appears, are so momentary compared with the other, the unseen part of us, which spreads wide, the unseen might survive, be recovered somehow attached to this person or that, or even haunting certain places, after death. Perhaps— perhaps. (*MD*, 168)

As if to illustrate the truth of this theory, there is a remarkable "odd affinity" between Clarissa and Septimus ("She felt somehow very like him—the young man who had killed himself" [*MD*, 204]). His death seems to endorse Clarissa's understanding of the nature of life, something she believes to be distorted and covered over by love and religion: "And the supreme mystery which Kilman might say she had solved, or Peter might say he had solved, but Clarissa didn't believe either of them had the ghost of an idea of solving, was simply this: here was one room; there another. Did religion solve that, or love?" (*MD*, 141). This simple "philosophy of life" is expressive of the divisions between one human being and another. As has been noted many times, there is a profound longing in Woolf's writings that arises largely from the sense of human separateness, and of the failure of relationship to provide anything tangible.

Clarissa's "transcendental theory" suggests that divisions can be overcome, perhaps, by what Woolf sometimes called the soul ("the unseen part of us, which spreads wide"). The word "soul" occurs frequently in the novel, and also in Woolf's diary from about 1922, but in both contexts it is never given any very clear meaning. She uses "soul" to signify the *essence* of a person, and in this signification might be seen a move toward belief in transcendence, the existence of something apart from all modalities (a self). As already seen, however, this essence cannot be approached directly or described:

> But then I should have to speak of the soul, & did I not banish the soul when I began? What happens is, as usual, that I'm going to write about the soul, & life breaks in. . . .
>
> In scribbling this, I am led away from my soul, which interests me nevertheless. My soul peeped out. For it is the soul I fancy that comments on visitors & reports their comments, & sometimes sets up such a to-do in the central departments of my machinery that the whole globe of me dwindles to a button-head. (*D*, 19 February 1923)

Love and religion destroy the "privacy of the soul" in Clarissa's view (*MD*, 140) by their attempt to conclude, to state what the essence of life *is*.

Mrs. Dalloway is explicitly concerned with the experience of time (an early title was *The Hours*) and the role of memory. Life is characterized as a tension between lived time and clock time. Freud, writing about Maury's famous dream of being guillotined (*The Interpretation of Dreams*) says, "It seemed to show that a dream is able to compress into a very short space of time an amount of perceptual matter far greater than the amount of ideational matter that can be dealt with by our waking mind" (131). Woolf's novels reverse this, emphasizing the great discrepancy that exists between the time of the waking mind and that ticked off by clocks.[3] The most fundamental aspect of lived time is tension, which arises from the workings of memory.[4] *Mrs. Dalloway* successfully conveys this form of life, because the act of reading at once involves the reader in the ambiguities of the different characters' experiences of time (as, according to Poulet's "Phenomenology of Reading," a reader's consciousness is invaded by the "consciousness" of a character). J. Hillis Miller has noted that memory often "displaces altogether the real present of the novel and becomes the virtual present of the reader's experience."[5]

The seminal event of Clarissa's refusal of Peter at Bourton reverberates throughout the novel, seeming, to Peter at least, to have defined his life (see above, p. 55). It might be said that in the way shared memories irrupt into the present of the main characters can be seen the possibility of overcoming human separateness. The life of memory is not *actual*; it is an immaterial substance, an access to a timeless world within the world of time.

Clock time threatens an individual's sense of continuity, because it takes no account of the lived experience of time; this threat is actualized in the novel when Clarissa calls out after Peter, as he leaves her house after their reunion: " 'My party! Remember my party tonight!' she cried, having to raise her voice against the roar of the open air, and, overwhelmed by the traffic and the sound of all the clocks striking, her voice crying 'Remember my party to-night!' sounded frail and thin and very far away as Peter Walsh shut the door" (*MD*, 54). If Big Ben strikes clock time, the bell of St. Margaret's seems to sound lived time: it does not coincide with the authoritative strokes of Big Ben, but seems "like something alive." For Peter, the sound contains past, present, and future; it recalls that moment from the past shared by him and Clarissa, which is separated from their "present" by only a moment of space, but also by many of Big Ben's leaden circles. The moment of intimacy has its being in Peter's memory, at one remove, so to speak, from the actual. Peter himself is uncertain of the moment: "But what room? What moment? And why had he been so profoundly happy when the clock was striking?" (*MD*, 56).

The sound of the striking clock contains both his prevailing mood of sadness (at the *memory* of Clarissa's refusal) and his memory of happiness with her. The dislocation of these perspectives unnerves Peter and produces an image of the future that compounds his wretched feelings. To regain his sense of identity, Peter rebels against the inexorable bell that is sounding away the moments of his life: "No! No! he cried. She is not dead! I am not old, he cried, and marched up Whitehall, as if there rolled down to him, vigorous, unending, his future" (*MD*, 56). "The future lies in the hands of young men like that," says Peter as a squadron marches past. He seems to wish to reorganize his past, thinking himself back to how he was thirty years previously, to adapt his memories to his present consciousness in a way that will not represent to him what he feels is his failure. As if to deny the possibility of being anywhere but at the front of a rushing train of time, the human emblems of clock time sweep Peter's dreams and memories away: "On they marched, past him, past everyone, in their steady way, as if one will worked legs and arms uniformly, and life, with its varieties, its irreticences, had been laid under a pavement of monuments and wreaths and drugged into a stiff yet staring corpse by discipline" (*MD*, 57).

The different times must be synthesized: linear, leaden circles, pealing out with inexorable regularity, and the erratic instants of a sudden plunge into the moment. Peter Walsh and Clarissa cannot bear to live linearly, but strive throughout the novel to complete a circle, joining past and present in the hope of achieving unity. The party at the end, which brings the protagonists of the earlier event together once more, does not solve the problem because the characters are no longer those people that came together at Bourton. This "incomplete circle" (J. Hillis Miller) is the form of the novel; it involves the reader by placing him or her in the memories of the characters (and vice versa). For the reader, then, the circle can be completed in that the whole timescale is not in the actual world of time and death, but in the virtual space between reader and text.

The form of the novel anticipates a historic consciousness that is enshrined in T. S. Eliot's quartet of 1935, *Burnt Norton*:

> Time past and time future
> What might have been and what has been
> Point to one end, which is always present.
>
> (44-46)

Such a historic consciousness is most fully expressed in Woolf's last novel *Between the Acts*. For a formal articulation of what the idea implies, we may turn to Cassirer's *Logic of the Humanities*: "History, viewed as spiritual, is in no sense a mere succession of events separating and supplanting each other in time. It is, in the midst of this change, an eternal present. . . . Its "meaning" is in no one of its moments; and yet, in each of them, it is complete and unbroken" (56). The continuous present is created only in the act of reading. For the novel's characters, however, the moment passes, as do all moments.

If the Clarissa-Peter-Richard side of *Mrs. Dalloway* exemplifies the common human experience of time, that other strand of the novel, that relates Septimus Smith's final hours, constructs an image of the actual experience of timelessness. This is a paradox the possibility of which is explained only by the breakdown of the limits "normality" imposes on each individual. Woolf is quite explicit in her diary about the source in her own experience of the contours of Septimus's madness.[6]

Septimus seems to have fallen out of time; he is caught in a perpetual present, a horrific timelessness in which he is no longer sheltered by past and future.[7] The striking clocks of the actual world do not penetrate to Septimus because he experiences himself as beyond time, high above the world where time's "leaden circles" dissolve. It is peculiarly ironic that Septimus should be taken for "help" to the clockwork Bradshaw who gives just three quarters of an hour to his patients in his offices on Harley Street, where the clocks shred and slice the day (*MD*, 113). 99

Septimus's sense of the oneness of the world is a refusal to admit death: if he does not recognize the passage of time, he need not admit death. This, indeed, is the basic tenet of his "new religion"; birds sing to him "from trees in the meadow of life beyond a river where the dead walk, how there is no death" (*MD*, 28). It is in his belief in transcendence that Septimus is allied to Clarissa, the difference between them being that he has lost all touch with the actual. As Clarissa sometimes tends to, Septimus sees himself as wholly essence, as *soul*. It is for this reason that he cannot communicate his visions. They come to him "not in actual words" but in a "language" he cannot read (*MD*, 25). Clarissa, too, feels the pressure of "an inner meaning, almost expressed" (*MD*, 36), but remains rooted in her embodied, time-bound, actual life.

Septimus's death reveals to Clarissa a "thing there was that mattered" (*MD*, 202): as in so many entries in the diary, language halts here. The meaning must be drawn from the similar-

184

ity of expression in those displacements of language found wherever Woolf writes of 'reality' or the soul. Death reveals the "impossibility of reaching the centre" because it manifests the ultimate horizon of time in human life. However much the moment is expanded, the past recreated, or a sense of being outside time achieved, the actual fact of death circumscribes all effort. In death, however, Septimus both retains his integrity and communicates to Clarissa. This communication argues for an abstract 'reality' in which the soul can find rest and continue to exist, but not in the modes of actual life, and not within the scope of language.

In "Impassioned Prose" Woolf asked in conclusion, "whether the prose writer, the novelist, might not capture fuller and finer truths than are now his aim if he ventured into those shadowy regions where De Quincey has been before him" (*GR*, 40). De Quincey's "most perfect passages," she wrote, "are descriptions of states of mind in which, often, time is miraculously prolonged and space miraculously expanded" (*GR*, 39). This could describe many significant passages of Woolf's own novels, which seek to "make of the moment something permanent" (*TTL*, 249). The novels are lyrics, in Cassirer's definition that "by losing itself in the moment, seeking nothing else than to exhaust it of its entire mood and atmosphere [the lyric] thereby invests it with duration and eternity."[8] The effort to escape from the ceaseless flow of future to past that is our present is a common human effort, as Poulet notes: "Each poet, each religion, each philosophy, each time has collaborated in man's attempts to escape out of time" ("Timelessness," 22). Faith in the possibility of such an escape must entail—as it did in the Romantics' case—belief in the continued existence of the past. This Poulet holds to be the "essential belief" of "nearly all the Romanticists":

All our life, and especially all our childhood, with all our perceptions, images and feelings, and whatever ideas we have had, persists in our minds; but as we are living in duration, it is not permitted to us to have anything but rare glimpses, disconnected reminiscences, of this immense treasure stored in a remote place in our soul. ("Timelessness," 11)

Life constantly vanishing into the past (see, for example, *TTL*, 172-73) and the possibility of its recovery is a recurring center in Woolf's thought,[9] a significant mapping of the deep tension in all her thinking between faith and despair:

> And now is life very solid or very shifting? I am haunted by the two contradictions. This has gone on forever: will last forever; goes down to the bottom of the world—this moment I stand on. Also it is transitory, flying, diaphanous. I shall pass like a cloud on the waves. Perhaps it may be that though we change; one flying after another, so quick so quick, yet we are somehow successive, & continuous—we human beings; & show the light through. But what is the light? (*D*, 14 January 1929).

The "light" I understand as synonymous with 'reality', that which is apart from all modalities of being and continuous. It is this timelessness that Lily Briscoe attempts to capture in her painting, through the recreation of her own past as a work of art. Memory and art are explicitly identified with one another by Lily: "That woman . . . made out of that miserable silliness and spite (she and Charles squabbling, sparring, had been silly and spiteful) something . . . which survived, after all these years, complete, so that she dipped into it to re-fashion her memory of him, and it stayed in the mind almost like a work of art"[10] (*TTL*, 248-49). Lily continues by reframing "the old question which traversed the sky of the soul perpetually . . . What is the meaning of life?" The answer she gives to herself illuminates once more the close association between the modes of being of memory and of art:

> The great revelation had never come. The great revelation perhaps never did come. Instead there were little daily miracles, illuminations, matches struck unexpectedly in the dark; here was one. This, that, and the other; herself and Charles Tansley and the breaking wave; Mrs. Ramsay bringing them together; Mrs. Ramsay saying "Life stand still here"; Mrs. Ramsay making of the moment something permanent (as in another sphere Lily herself tried to make of the moment something permanent)—this was of the nature of a revelation. (*TTL*, 249)

Woolf frequently spoke of writers being closer to life, to 'reality', than other artists. Fiction is defined by the creation of a world of time out of time. Novels can achieve a fixing of single moments because they embody a (fictional) present (which may be written as a past) that can be experienced over and over again as a "present" in the act of reading. In this may be seen a correlation between Woolf's 'reality' and her concept of art's ability to overcome time (and hence death).[11]

Identity must have a base; this can be provided by the sense of one's physical being, by a name, by memory, or through relationship with others. Whatever a person's identity, it must exist in and through time; there must be a temporal as well as a spatial aspect to the formation of identity. However, the present is not a unity to be fixed, but the endless flow of future to past. Because past and present can never (as far as actual human identity is concerned) be completely synthesized, an autonomous identity can never form; it proceeds constantly toward death. To locate oneself in time, therefore, requires continuous effort.

The sense that life is a battle against nothingness, that all actions and efforts are merely necessary but futile attempts to disguise life's empty center, is strong in Woolf's thinking. Clock time carries forward a vegetative life controlled by forces that have nothing to do with identity; individual life must be rescued from those forces.[12] This sense is prevalent in *The Waves*, in which the lives of the six characters appear as random moments of organization rescued from unidentified chaos. The import of life being seen as poised over an abyss from which only an accident has momentarily drawn consciousness is that it is not, then, a progression from one moment to the next in order, but has its being in a loop that expands around us all—eternity. The past is always there, ready to irrupt into the present at any moment.

The precariousness of the hold that identity needs to retain on its "present" is illustrated by a moment in Bernard's life:

> And, what is this moment of time, this particular day in which I have found myself caught? The growl of traffic might be any uproar—forest trees or the roar of wild beasts. Time has whizzed back an inch or two on its reel; our short progress has been cancelled. I think also that our bodies are in truth naked. We are only lightly covered with buttoned cloth; and beneath these pavements are shells, bones and silence. (*TW*, 81)

This is not an isolated mood of a single moment but a characteristic expression of an attitude to human being that is found in other of Woolf's novels too. At the reunion dinner, Bernard recalls, "We felt enlarge itself round us the huge blackness of what is outside us, of what we are not" (*TW*, 196-97). It is this radical awareness of being in the face of the possibility of not being that charges Virginia Woolf's fiction with its need for faith and its tendency to despair. "I reflect now that the earth is only a pebble flicked off accidentally from the face of the sun and that there is no life anywhere in the abysses of space" (*TW*, 159). In the face of such perception human history becomes meaningless: "It roars; the lighted strip of history is past and our Kings and Queens; we are gone; our civilization; the Nile; and all life. Our separate drops are dissolved; we are extinct, lost in the abysses of time, in the darkness" (*TW*, 160). Thus Louis voices the brooding perception of the ultimate emptiness of human being that pervades all Woolf's fiction. For meaning, for a center, she looked to a 'reality' that escaped the decadence of human being's spatiotemporal horizons, a 'reality' the *experience* of which she could express, but not the nature. Her faith is in a consciousness of eternity, dissolving the human-made divisions of past, present, and future, a "being" in the mode of nothingness, offered in her art.

The hope for order, for meaning, is not abandoned after *The Waves*. At the party that closes *The Years*, bringing together the different generations, several characters are troubled by that now familiar sense of human separateness. In the face of the chaos to which memory can reduce life (e.g., *TY*, 358), there is still a yearning for conclusiveness: "Millions of things came back to her. Atoms danced apart and massed themselves. But how did they compose what people called a life? . . . Perhaps there's "I" at the middle of it, she thought; a knot; a centre; and again she saw herself sitting at her table drawing on the blotting-paper, digging little holes from which spokes radiated" (*TY*, 395). That image of "I" at the center recurs throughout Woolf's work; in fact, Eleanor's little spoked drawing appears several times, from as early as *Night and Day* when Ralph Denham is embarrassed at Katharine's seeing it. The philosophical implication of the image may be elucidated by reference to Poulet's *Metamorphoses of the Circle* in which he explains that the center's relationship with all the points of the circumference is that of eternity to time. The self-reflexive nature of the circle image fits in well with Woolf's thinking as discussed here. It is the fact of the past's persistence into the present, in memory, that gives Eleanor Pargiter the vague hope of an order to life:

And suddenly it seemed to Eleanor that it had all happened before. So a girl had come in that night in the restaurant: had stood, vibrating, in the door. She knew exactly what he was going to say. . . . As she thought it, he said it. Does everything then come over again a little differently? she thought. If so, is there a pattern; a theme, recurring, like music; half remembered, half foreseen? . . . [in original] a gigantic pattern, momentarily perceptible? . . . But who makes it? Who thinks it? Her mind slipped. She could not finish her thought.[13] (*TY*, 398)

Peggy, too, feels intimations of the possibility of "a state of being, in which there was real laughter, real happiness, and this fractured world was whole; whole, and free" (*TY*, 420).

The Years offers no new ground; a predominant theme is the failure of communication and relationship to establish anything whole or lasting. In many ways the novel merely rehearses what Woolf had already learned. It is clear that the forlorn hope of Eleanor for "another life" (*TY*, 461) is a repetition of the desire to "make of the moment something permanent" in actual life. Such permanence is not in the power of life, the "here and now," but art. Eleanor wishes to "enclose the present moment; to make it stay" by filling it with past, present, and future (*TY*, 462). The effort is doomed to failure, to what Poulet has described as the "shattering return to the misery of the human condition and to the tragedy of the experience of time: in the very instant man catches his prey, experience dupes him, and he knows he is duped. His prey is a shadow. In the instant he catches the instant, the instant passes, for it is instant."[14]

Any hope of *rest* in the actual world now seems entirely mistaken. In the development of her idea of 'reality' and experiences of the soul, Woolf emphasizes the rootedness in actual life of her perceptions. Nevertheless, actual life has seemed hopelessly far removed from 'reality' in the novels. However, in the the last few years of her life, Woolf moved to a more direct expression of her beliefs, achieving in *Between the Acts* a brilliant union of design and substance that holds within it the clearest exposition of her faith in 'reality'.

CHAPTER NINE
THE SINGING OF
THE REAL WORLD

IN HER DIARY FOR 1903, THE TWENTY-ONE YEAR OLD VIRGINIA WOOLF
wrote:

I read some history: it is suddenly all alive, branching forwards & backwards
& connected with every kind of thing that seemed entirely remote before. I
seem to feel Napoleons influence on our quiet evening in the garden for
instance—I think I see for a moment how our minds are all threaded
together—how any live mind today is <conne> of the very same stuff as
Plato's & Euripides. It is only a continuation & development of the same
thing—It is this common mind that binds the whole world together; & all
the world is mind. . . . I feel as though I had grasped the central meaning of the world, & all these poets & historians & philosophers were only
following out paths branching from that centre in which I stand.[1]

There is an almost uncanny prefiguring here of Woolf's concerns
in *Between the Acts*, written over thirty years later. This is a telling
example of the circularity of her thinking; indeed, her last novel
contains several echoes from *The Voyage Out*, from its manuscript drafts (*Melymbrosia*),[2] and from her (as yet unpublished)
1903 diary. At the opening of *Between the Acts*, a quiet evening in
a room with windows open to the garden does feel "Napoleons
influence," and a sense develops throughout the novel of a
"common mind." The image of "I" at the centre, holding in synthesis a circumference of thought and event is paradigmatic in
Woolf's fiction.[3]

Between the Acts seems to me anticipated by all Woolf's
work. The "philosophy" with which we have been concerned is
expressive of a particular view of history, and of human identity
as constituting that history. Although it is not "conclusive," *Between the Acts*' position and Woolf's suicide before its publica-

tion lead us to look for final statements. The work does gather up much of what has been discussed so far, but ultimately presents further questions. The novel's ending is an opening, an opening into silence. Having said that, I would like to read it by way of an ending here, and to read it according to that way of gathering echoes and fragments by which Woolf felt truth might be achieved.

Between the Acts is at once a hall of mirrors and a chamber of echoes; a fully integrated work of art in which the play between individual consciousness and cultural memory is the substance of the book. The classical, linear sequence of time—the prevailing view of history—is superseded in the act of reading, which is a performance of memory and imagination. Woolf often wrote that words by themselves have a deficiency that is overcome by their being joined together.[4] The deficiency of singleness, perhaps, extends deeply into our lives for, she wrote, "only when we put two and two together—two pencil strokes, two written words, two bricks . . . do we overcome dissolution and set up some stake against oblivion."[5]

The last few years of Woolf's life were dominated by the past perhaps even more profoundly than at any other time. More than ever, she was deeply concerned with the relationship between life and art. If, as she suggested, her novels are more properly to be called elegies, then *Between the Acts* is an elegy for herself. At the time she began to compose it she was looking back not only over her own life (to write a memoir and the biography of her old friend Roger Fry), but also to the springs of English literature for her "new criticism."[6] It is in those "hybrid books in which the writer talks to himself about himself for a generation yet to be born"[7]—namely, her diary and the memoir "A Sketch of the Past"—that Woolf is found to write openly and investigatively about her feelings and beliefs over the last few years of her life.

Between the Acts contradicts linear expectations, responding most fruitfully to a reading that is both genetic and archaeological; it invites an erotics rather than a hermeneutics of art.[8] The book is a journey through space-time in which the reader is required to respond to the "infection" of language. Reading *Be-

tween the Acts, Woolf invites us to "put two and two together" and go on doing this; connections must be made not only within the work itself, but reaching back to the beginnings of the author's creativity and into her cultural memory. In *Between the Acts* and the writings contemporary with it, I find the most convincing evidence of the circularity of Woolf's creativity and the need to read her in a way sympathetic to that form.

Between the Acts embodies and arises from the deep concerns of the last few years of Woolf's life, concerns that can be seen to develop from the aesthetic and philosophical matters she engaged with in that middle period of her life that has so far been our primary focus. The work is a palimpsest that must be read from several different perspectives at once; it is densely layered.

It has become almost redundant now to point out that Woolf was aware throughout her life of the pressure of tradition and cultural memory on an individual voice. Long regarded by the "establishment"—particularly in her own country—as an effete soliloquist, Woolf has emerged in the last decade as a writer fully cognizant of her social context.[9] Essential to her work is the tension between "I" and "We," a dynamic interplay between the inner voice and the world of relationships; the one and the many; ontogeny and phylogeny.

Around the time she composed *A Room of One's Own,* a change is discernible in Woolf's perspective. This is not to say a radical change came about in her world-view, but that her angle of vision altered. The pressure of the "common voice" is brought into the foreground. For example, she writes in *A Room* that "masterpieces are not single and solitary births; they are the outcome of many years of thinking in common, of thinking by the body of the people, so that the experience of the mass is behind the single voice" (98). In that same text, she wrote that she was "talking of the common life which is the real life and not of the little separate lives which we lead as individuals."

The shift in her perspective is evident also in *The Years.* Eleanor Pargiter, thinking of the inadequacy of life as it is, is yet enraptured by the possibility of "another life . . . not in dreams; but here and now, in this room, with living people." The importance to Woolf of writing *The Years* and *Three Guineas* cannot be overestimated: the novel and the feminist polemic should, she said, be taken as one book, and in them her very radical feminist politics is evident. In an essay of 1940, "The Learning Tower," she wrote of her younger contemporaries' concern with politics, and yet this "slimy seaweed" she felt was only part of a larger problem,[10] part of the dialectic of a prevailing world-order the very most fundamental structures of which would have to be changed before real changes could take place. The only truly radical politics for Woolf was sexual politics, a change in the patriarchal system of values in which the attitudes of war pervade every aspect of life. The works of the last few years of her life make explicit what had always been implied in earlier works: the tyranny of men in white waistcoats; the mechanic sterility of military pomp and order; the dessicated rationalism of prevailing world-order; a sexual double standard; the arrogance of converters—all these are part of the world of even *The Voyage Out*. In *Three Guineas* she bravely stated her belief; in *Between the Acts* she mythologized it.

Writing *Three Guineas* and *The Years*, although an exhausting and often disheartening task, was important, for Woolf felt, once they were finished, that she had made a stand, stated plainly her case against the world. The sense of being an "Outsider" is prevalent in her subsequent diary entries, but also, paradoxically perhaps so is a growing sense of a collective (feminine) unconscious. This sense finds its most striking embodiment in the women of *Between the Acts*. Most interesting is that change in perspective referred to above, best understood as a shift in focus from "I" to "We":

> But to amuse myself, let me note: why not Poyntzet Hall: a centre: all lit. discussed in connection with real little incongruous living humour; & anything that comes into my head; but "I" rejected: 'We' substituted: to whom at the end there shall be an invocation? "We" . . . the composed of many different things . . . we all life, all art, all waifs & strays—a rambling capricious but somehow unified whole—the present state of my mind? (*D*, 26 April 1938; dots in original)

To identify the strata present in *Between the Acts*, to recognize the play between Woolf's personal history and the history of the race, it is necessary to describe this "present state of my mind;" to enumerate the elements of the matrix from which her last novel arose.

Emerging from Woolf's diary from 1936 onward is a sense of freedom—albeit a hysterical freedom characteristically composed of opposing feelings that, on the one hand, nothing mattered any more because civilization was about to destroy itself, and, on the other, that in the face of this imminent apocalypse things mattered more than ever: "No, I cant get the odd incongruity of feeling intensely & at the same time knowing that there's no importance in that feeling. Or is there, as I sometimes think, more importance than ever?" (*D*, 13 May 1940). She felt that there was no longer anything in life to "contain" her. It has been seen that Woolf believed identity to be founded on a base of some sort: in the last few years of her life securities upon which her identities had rested began to disappear. Lytton Strachey and Roger Fry had died (1932 and 1934); people who had been part of her world began to die—Janet Case (1937), Jack Hills (1937), Ottoline Morrell (1938), Ka Cox (1938). Even if some of these were relatively unimportant to her as friends, such deaths were to Woolf an erosion of her particular world. The death in 1937 of her nephew Julian Thoby Bell may well have seemed to her a cruel repetition of the sudden death of her brother Thoby (in 1906), and also to presage the many deaths the imminent war would bring, mirroring those days before the First World War. In a memoir of Julian, Woolf wrote: ". . . & then I am so composed that nothing is real unless I write it. And again, I know by this time what an odd effect Time has: it does not destroy people—for instance, I still think perhaps more truly than I did, of Roger, of Thoby: but it brushes away the actual personal presence"[11]. It would seem from her diary for 1937 onward that writing was all Woolf could cling to for stability.

Having "done my share, with pen and talk, for the human race," Woolf will not write any more to "please" or to convert. She felt the encircling wall of her audience had disappeared, and so she would write now only for herself. From the silence she felt all round her came another sense, coexisting with her "freedom," of utter meaninglessness:

Whats odd . . . . is the severance that war seems to bring: everything becomes meaningless: cant plan: then there comes too the community feeling: all England thinking the same thing—this horror of war—at the same moment. Never felt it so strong before. Then the lull & one lapses again into private separation—(*D.* Apr. 15, 1939) . . . Boredom. All meaning has run out of everything. . . . Yes, its an empty meaningless world now. . . . And for the 100th time I repeat—any idea is more real than any amount of war misery. And what one's made for. And the only contribution one can make—This little pitter patter of ideas is my whiff of shot in the cause of freedom—so I tell myself, thus bolstering up a figment—a phantom: recovering that sense of something pressing from outside which consolidates the mist, the non-existent. (*D,* 6 Sept. 1939)

Her mood frequently tends to despair; she struggled to find something to push against in order to achieve a sense of identity, but felt often that her world, and so her life, was near its end.

Susan M. Kenney has pointed out that the general tenor of the diary did not find its way into the novel[12]; it is, on the whole, affirmative. Although I would discern a more apocalyptic tone, it is certainly true that in *Between the Acts* we *are* shown "the effort renewed"; again and again everything seems about to grind to a halt and vacancy to prevail, but each time something rescues the scene—a lowing cow, a shower of rain, an old man's brash cry of "Bravo!"— and life lurches on. The novel is a testament of hope created in the face of despair.

Closely allied to Woolf's sense of "freedom" is what, for want of a better term, she called her "spiritual conversion" experienced in 1933 or 1934:

I must cling to my "freedom"—that mysterious hand that was reached out to me about 4 years ago. (*D,* 29 April 1938) . . . still I'm free. This is the actual result of that spiritual conversion (I cant bother to get the right words) in the autumn of 1933—or 4—when I rushed through London, buying, I remember, a great magnifying glass, from sheer ecstasy, near Blackfriars: when I gave the man who played the harp half a crown for talking to me about his life in the Tube station. (*D,* 20 May 1938)

There is nothing to be found in her writings of 1933 or 1934 that refers to a "spiritual conversion." There is, however, an entry in her diary made in the autumn of 1934 that might be read as the record of a moment in which her faith in the power of art to achieve 'reality' came home to her with force. It concerns the funeral of Roger Fry (who had died on 9 September), which took place on "a day as it happened of extraordinary beauty" (*Roger Fry*, 298):

> I had a notion that I could describe the tremendous feeling at R.'s funeral: but of course I cant. I mean the universal feeling: how we all fought with our brains loves & so on; & *must* be vanquished. Then the vanquisher, this outer force became so clear; the indifferent. & we so small fine delicate. A fear then came to me, of death. Of course I shall lie there too before that gate, & slide in; & it frightened me. But why? I mean, I felt the vainness of this perpetual fight, with our brains & loving each other against the other thing: if Roger could die. (*D*, 19 September 1934)
>
> But then, next day, today which is Thursday, one week later, the other thing begins to work—the exalted sense of being above time & death which comes from being again in a writing mood. And this is not an illusion, so far as I can tell. Certainly I have a strong sense that Roger would be all on one's side in this excitement, & that whatever the invisible force does, we thus get outside it. (*D*, 20 September 1934)

From 1937 Woolf's world of friends who had "fought with our brains, loves and so on" seemed to disappear ever faster.[13] Her houses at Mecklenburgh Square and Tavistock Square in London were both bombed, destroying books, letters, and furniture accumulated over many years. Woolf's mood may be judged from the following fragment from a sketch written in late October 1939, headed "London in War":

> Everyone is on business—Their minds are made up. It is extremely sober. The streets are [. . .] lit. They have gone back to the 18th Century. Nature prevails. I suppose badgers & foxes wd. come back if this went on, & owls & nightingales. This is the prelude to barbarism. The city has become merely a congeries of houses lived in by people who work. There is no society. no luxury no splendour no gadding & flitting. All is serious & concentrated. [*It is*] as if the song had stopped—the melody, the unnecessary the voluntary. Odd if this should be the end of town life.[14]

Other details from this period contribute to the sense of ending: for example, in 1936 Violet Dickinson returned to Woolf all the letters she had written her—a strange gift from Woolf's adolescence (see *L*, 3192, 3195). The sense of ending is quite calm, but extremely strong:

> Oh & I thought, as I was dressing, how interesting it would be to describe the approach of age, & the gradual coming of death. As people

describe love. To note every symptom of failure: but why failure? To treat age as an experience that is different from the others; & to detect every one of the gradual stages towards death which is a tremendous experience, & not as unconscious at least in its approaches, as birth is. (*D*, 7 August 1939)

Woolf could, however, still create, could still expand the bounds of the moment by the ordering of chaos that her art achieved in creating its own world. Although the usual view of the end of 1934 and beginning of 1935 is that it was a desolate time for Woolf, I suggest it may have offered her something to fight against, so strengthening in the years that followed her resolve to "squeeze the moment" and continue the effort.[15]

In all the novels there is a sense of yearning, a tending toward the numinous and some revelation of mystery, and this conceptual background often shares the contours of a theology. The conceptual background of *Between the Acts* maps those contours once again. The profoundly personal concept of 'reality' that Woolf had developed in her art and life, and her faith in the possibility of transcendence through art, became the necessary foreground of her thought. What may often have seemed a vaguely articulated, shadowy adumbration was confidently grasped and embodied in *Between the Acts*.

The memoir "A Sketch of the Past," begun at Vanessa Bell's suggestion in 1939, is a fascinatingly rich element of the matrix from which *Between the Acts* arose. "Memory," writes Langer in *Feeling and Form*, "is the great organizer of consciousness" (263). Memory is the organizing principle of "A Sketch," but it is not the memory of a linear chronology. As she proposed to do in her "new criticism," Woolf begins with a memory of an incident and follows it wherever it leads her. The memory at work is a channel to cultural memory, that universal consciousness that informs the novel. Thus, writing of her stepbrother Gerald's indecent fumblings, she says that her instinctive resentment "proves that Virginia Stephen was not born on 25th January 1882, but was born many thousands of years ago; and had from the first to encounter instincts already acquired by thousands of ancestresses in the past" (*MOB*, 69). As we will discover in *Between the Acts*, she is concerned with the "traces" or "scars" that strong emotion leaves: "It is only a question of discovering how we can get ourselves again attached to it, so that we shall be able to live our lives through from the start" (*MOB*, 67). This seems ambiguous, referring both to individual life and the life of the race. In the pageant of *Between the Acts* and the text that surrounds it, just such an attempt at living our lives through from the start is presented, and in the consciousness of Isa and Lucy a sense of return to, or remembering of, the origins of their consciousness.

In *Between the Acts*, and elsewhere, language is seen as an "infection," something part abstract, part physical; a medium in which all human beings are afloat; voices break in on us constantly, whether we will them or not, even in our dreams. *Between the Acts* is deeply concerned with voices in its attempt to render the web of language by and in which consciousness is constituted. "Gathering fragments" when reading this work requires an awareness of the matrix from which it arises, a matrix in which Woolf's circling characteristics of repetition and descriptive homology are fully in play. Language is the medium of connection, linking past and present, "I" and "We." Following Woolf's guide, I would like to explore some of the connections to be made between the novel and the memoir, and, consequently, between art and life.

The heroic Rider (who makes his first appearance in *Night and Day* [e.g., 108]) and the withered tree (which is found, for example, in *The Waves* and *The Years*) are emblems of a longed-for romantic love cut short by death. In *Between the Acts*, Isa chants: "Alone, under a tree, the withered tree that keeps all day murmuring of the sea, and hears the Rider gallop" (125). The source of these emblems is explained in "A Sketch." Writing of her mother Julia's first husband, Herbert Duckworth, Woolf says: "Like all very handsome men who die tragically, he left not so much a character behind him as a legend. Youth and death shed a halo through which it is difficult to see a real face" (*MOB*, 89). To Julia, Herbert was a hero, "and also her husband; and her children's father" (*MOB*, 90). These words are echoed in *Between the Acts* in Isa's "convenient cliché" (19), and Mrs. Manresa regards Giles, Isa's husband, as her "surly hero." Hate and love conflict in Isa, as do impulses toward life and death; she is torn between romantic longing for an ideal represented by Haines, the gentleman-farmer, and the "cliché conveniently provided by fiction" that binds her to the father of her children. The sense of loss and yearning evoked by the memoir also imbues the novel. The connection between novel and memoir is even more interesting when we recall that Herbert was a nickname for Woolf's beloved brother Thoby who, like Duckworth, died tragically young, always to be a hero in his sister's eyes.[16]

Connected with Isa's longing for a lost romantic hero is the withered tree, a version of which is an emblem of death in *The Waves*. In the memoir the meaning is explicit when Woolf writes about the death of her stepsister, Stella, shortly after her marriage to Jack Hills: "And the tree, outside in the dark garden, was to me the emblem, the symbol, of the skeleton agony to which [Stella's] death had reduced him; and us; everything. . . . The leafless tree and Jack's agony—I always see them as if they were one and the same, when I think of that summer" (*MOB*, 121). The tragic death of promising youth had been reenacted for Woolf in 1937 when her nephew, Julian Thoby Bell, was killed in Spain. In that memoir of him referred to above, she wrote of her "legacy of pessimism, which I have decided never to analyze." That legacy is woven into her fiction, and in *Between the Acts* becomes united with an opposition between life and death that is fundamental to her entire oeuvre. The leafless winter tree in summer is a symbol of death in life; it is, essentially, the core of the ancient rituals of death and rebirth that Woolf read about in the works of Jane Ellen Harrison and in J. G. Frazer's *Golden Bough*.[17]

In *A Sketch* Woolf also traces the fundamental polarity in her view of life to childhood experiences. She writes of three "exceptional moments" that often "came to the surface unexpectedly." Briefly, these moments were: a feeling of "hopeless sadness" during a fight with her brother, Thoby; a sense of wholeness on looking at a flower; and horror at hearing her parents mention the suicide of a man who had been staying at St. Ives (*MOB*, 71). Two of these moments find their way into her fiction: Neville, in *The Waves*, is transfixed at hearing of a suicide. The two passages describing the experience are remarkably similar:

I heard about the dead man through the swing-door last night when cook was shoving in and out the dampers. He was found with his throat cut. The apple-tree leaves became fixed in the sky; the moon glared; I was unable to lift my foot up the stair. . . . There were the floating, pale-grey clouds; and the immitigable tree; the implacable tree with its greaved silver bark. (*TW*, 17)

We were waiting at dinner one night, when somehow I overheard my father or my mother say that Mr Valpy had killed himself. The next thing I remember is being in the garden at night and walking on the path by the apple tree. It seemed to me that the apple tree was connected with the horror of Mr Valpy's suicide. I could not pass it. I stood there looking at the grey-green creases of the bark—it was a moonlit night—in a trance of horror. I seemed to be dragged down, hopelessly, into some pit of absolute despair from which I could not escape. My body seemed paralysed. (*MOB*, 71)

The moment of "wholeness" reappears in *Between the Acts*, and again there is a distinct descriptive homology between novel and memoir:

I was looking at the flower bed by the front door; "That is the whole", I said. I was looking at a plant with a spread of leaves; and it seemed suddenly plain that the flower itself was a part of the earth; that a ring enclosed what was the flower; and that was the real flower; part earth; part flower. It was a thought I put away as being likely to be very useful to me later. (*MOB*, 71)

George grubbed. The flower blazed between the angles of the roots. Membrane after membrane was torn. It blazed a soft yellow, a lambent light under a film of velvet; it filled the caverns behind the eyes with light. All that inner darkness became a hall, leaf smelling, earth smelling of yellow light. And the tree was beyond the flower; the grass, the flower and the tree were entire. Down on his knees grubbing he held the flower complete. (*BTA*, 16-17)

In her biography of Roger Fry, Woolf wrote of "moments of vision, when a new force breaks in, and the gropings of the past suddenly seem to have meaning" (*Roger Fry*, 160). The meaning of these moments from her own past now, in 1939, seems clear to her; they represent a "profound difference" between satisfaction and despair: "This difference I think arose from the fact that I was quite unable to deal with the pain of discovering that people hurt each other; that a man I had seen had killed himself. The sense of horror held me powerless. But in the case of the flower I found a reason; and was thus able to deal with the sensation" (*MOB*, 71-72).

All through her life and fiction the possibility of order, of pattern, has been intuited in the midst of uncertainty, the possibility of transcendence of the passage of time. In *Between the Acts*, this possibility is in the foreground of the work: an explicit "private vision" is set against the "scraps, orts, and fragments" of daily life. Woolf, in the last years of her life, asserted what had before been only more tentatively attested to: a 'reality' apart from actual life and yet rooted in it; not mysticism, but a coming to fruition of the potential of imagination to order the world of experience in the forms and modes of art.

It seems likely that the review of Fry's life and work she made to write his biography helped Woolf to reach this new positiveness, for he too had written of a similar perception:

> But if reason must stop short, beyond reason lies reality—if nothing will make him doff his reason, nothing will make him lose his faith. The aesthetic emotion seems to him of supreme importance. But why?—he cannot say. "One can only say that those who experience it feel it to have a peculiar quality of 'reality', which makes it a matter of infinite importance in their lives. Any attempt I might make to explain this would probably land me in the depths of mysticism. On the edge of that gulf I stop." But if he stops it is in the attitude of one who looks forward. We are always left with the sense of something to come. (*Roger Fry*, 229)

That Woolf found a new certainty in her vision in the last few years of her life is borne out once more by her diary:

> I lay awake so calm, so content, as if I'd stepped off the whirling world into a deep blue quiet space, & there open eyed existed, beyond harm; armed against all that can happen. I have never had this feeling before in all my life; but I have had it several times since last summer: when I reached it, in my worst depression, as if I stepped out, throwing aside a cloak, lying in bed, looking at the stars, those nights in Monk's House. (9 April 1937)

As in those records of her summer "retreats" at Rodmell, she has here drawn security from her deepest despair; descending into the depths she finds rest in 'reality'.

During the summer of 1936, she was devastated by the grind of revising *The Years* and *Three Guineas*. Of that time she wrote that she had "never been so near the precipice of my own feeling since 1913—" (*D*, 11 June 1936). It was an "extraordinary summer" in which she felt she had destroyed her writing gift. Thus, she subsequently determined to concentrate on her own private vision, to write for herself: "I wd. like to write a dream story about the top of a mountain. Now why? About lying in the snow; about rings of colour; silence . . . & the solitude. I cant though. But shant I, one of these days, indulge myself in some short releases into that world? Short now for ever. No more long grinds: only sudden intensities" (*D*, 22 June 1937).[18]

Toward the end of her life Woolf planned to write a critical history of English literature that would involve a turning inside-out of the established methods of writing literary history. Rather than a documentary, *Reading at Random* or *Turning the Page* was to be an imaginative recreation of the origins and development of English culture as embodied in its literature. The first chapter ("Anon") and a few pages of the second ("The Reader") are all that we have of this work,[19] but they are enough to see that here again we have an important element of the matrix from which *Between the Acts* was born. Woolf's concern in this critical work is with the voice of the artist, and with the original "song," inspired by the natural world, from which literature, she speculates, developed. She sees "common emotion," a unified source of common belief, as the heart of literature.

Reading at Random is concerned to peel away the layers of influence built up over centuries, to get back to the "common emotion," the voice of Anon. who was "sometimes man; sometimes woman. He is the common voice singing out of doors, He has no house" (382). As in "A Sketch of the Past," Woolf is concerned here with a thinking back to origins. The language of her various creations of this period is often so similar that a line quoted is hard to identify as coming from the memoir, novel, or the history. She speaks, in *Reading at Random*, of "ages of toil and love" lying behind the English people's memory: "This is the world beneath our consciousness, the anonymous world to which we can still return" (385). Isa's chants in *Between the Acts* reveal a buried consciousness of origins, the cultural memory that seems, in the novel, to inhere in literature and in, particularly, the consciousness of women. For example, Isa dreams of walking down a green ride to a wishing-well; "The paths that led to the well and the tree," wrote Woolf in "Anon," "we can no longer see."

"Everybody shared in the emotion of Anon's song and

supplied the story" (382). With the advent of drama the wandering voices of many singers are collected, embodied, and "one man speaks in his own person" (393). Anonymous playwrights retain some of the old "nameless vitality, something drawn from the crowd in the penny seats and not yet dead in ourselves" (398), and it is presumably in an effort to regain this vitality that the "gifted lady . . . wishes to remain anonymous" in *Between the Acts*.

The play eventually gave way to the novel and the special relation between reader and writer. The reader, says Woolf, is brought into being by the personality of the writer shaping his conception. In *Between the Acts*, we might see an attempt to restore the "common emotion," to dissolve the distinction between writer and reader so that everybody will once again take part in the "song." It is interesting to note that in "Anon" Woolf says the reader's importance "can be gauged by the fact that when his attention is distracted, in times of public crisis, the writer exclaims: I can write no more" (428). The figure of the human being lying behind *Between the Acts* is more elusive than in any other of Woolf's works: in 1940 she recorded the death of her writing "I": "It struck me that one curious feeling is, that the writing "I" has vanished. No audience. No echo. Thats part of one's death" (*D*, 9 June 1940).

As always with Woolf, though, there is a contrasting movement. Against the death of her individual writing "I" she placed faith in art as the repository of "common emotion." In *Between the Acts*, "common emotion" seems identified with that female consciousness that perceives pattern in the world. Her embodiment of the feminine principle in *Between the Acts* displays her profound belief in the serious need for the radical alteration of societal structures. "We must compensate the man for the loss of his gun," she wrote in "Thoughts on Peace in an Air-Raid" (1940); "we must give him access to the creative feelings."[20] It is to such "creative feelings" that her last novel seeks to give access, to "common emotion," and the potential for realization of the self in perceiving 'reality.'

This dense web of thought and concern that constitutes the creative matrix of *Between the Acts* brings together Woolf's conscious memory of her own past and the cultural memory that seems to inhere in her unconscious. These gathered frag-ments should be borne in mind while reading the novel.

"If we could see the village as it was before Chaucer's time," wrote Woolf in "Anon" (383), "we should see tracks across the fields joining manor house to hovel, and hovel to church." These tracks (or scars) appear at the beginning of *Be-tween the Acts*: "From an aeroplane, he said, you could still see, plainly marked, the scars made by the Britons; by the Romans; by the Elizabethan manor house; and by the plough, when they ploughed the hill to grow wheat in the Napoleonic wars" (8). The novel links the physical scars on the land with scars in the mind, the imprint of common emotions carried over from one generation to the next. When the pageant is over and the au-dience has left Pointz Hall, it is seen that "the pilgrims had bruised a lane on the grass" (*BTA*, 235). The villagers hanging paper roses in the barn have "taken indelibly the print of some three hundred years of customary behaviour" (*BTA*, 36); the singing "pilgrims" "*wore ruts in the grass*" (*BTA*, 98); and Isa dreams of walking to her death in the waters of the wishing-well "down the ride that leads under the nut tree and the may tree" (*BTA*, 124). Scars in the mind and on the land reveal a continuity of cultural memory and might also be linked to what Woolf her-self felt about her country, as she described it in a letter to Ethel Smyth in January 1941:

> You never shared my passion for that great city [London]. Yet its what, in some odd corner of my dreaming mind, represents Chaucer, Shakespeare, Dickens. Its my only patriotism: save one vision, in Warwickshire one spring when we were driving back from Ireland and I saw a stallion being led, under the may and the beeches, along a grass ride; and I thought that is England. (*L*, 3,678)[21]

Such descriptive homologies occur throughout Woolf's writing, setting up resonances that encourage that gathering of echoes and fragments she said was the way to achieve truth.

Scars in the mind can reach back well beyond personal his-tories. In the course of the June afternoon on which the novel takes place, a facility is revealed in the characters for thinking back imaginatively to a time far beyond their own. Most resonant are the visions Lucy Swithin has of a primeval world of grunting monsters and steaming swamps, which recall the imaginings of Rachel Vinrace and other descriptions from later works.[22] More obscure, but no less telling, are the scars in the mind of Isa, revealed in her enigmatic chanting: Lucy and Isa are driven within themselves by the sterility and arrogance of the men around them and so expand the moments of their own lives by remembering an obscured female consciousness.[23]

Names are also scars in a way, and some of the villagers have names as old as their villages, reinforcing the link between people and land. Women's names, however, are obscured by marriage, as that of the great lady "whose marriage with the local peer had obliterated in his trashy title a name that had been a name when there were brambles and briars where the Church now stood" (*BTA*, 112). In this loss of a name might be seen an image of the male's covering over of the female principle. What cannot be covered over, though, is the secret name, the *nomen numen* in which inheres the very soul of a person.

Between the Acts is concerned with voices; memory, scars, names, and "common emotion" are concerns and functions of language. The novel gives a sense of being afloat on a sea of words. Words and phrases reverberate throughout, slipping in and out of different minds, reflected sometimes by actors, sometimes by the audience. On this particular day, words will not stay still: to Giles Oliver they rise up and become menacing (74) or scornful (174); to William Dodge they become symbolical (88). Words are substantial, rolled and thinned on the childrens' nurses' tongues like sweets (15), or peppering the audience at the pageant "as with a shower of hard little stones" (95). Words evidently cannot be trusted to peg down reality; they are treacherous and shifty, acting differently on the mental substance of each person who hears or utters them. Nevertheless, they are the vehicle of our emotions and in some sense the matter by and in which life moves. The echoes and fragments of *Between the Acts* bind the book together, making of it an enclosed world, a "re-created world."

There is a definite sense in the novel of a voice behind the voices, an unconscious source of the plethora of words. The unconsciousness of artistic creation is a frequently repeated theme of Woolf's writing; in "A Sketch" is found a passage that seems to me to relate this theme significantly to *Between the Acts*:

The lemon-coloured leaves on the elm trees, the round apples glowing red in the orchard and the rustle of the leaves make me pause to think how many other than human forces affect us. While I am writing this, the light changes; an apple becomes a vivid green. I respond—how? and then the little owl [makes] a chattering noise. Another response. St. Ives, to cut short an obscure train of thought, about the other voice or voices and their connection with art, with religion: figuratively, I could snapshot what I mean by fancying myself afloat, [in an element] which is all the time responding to things we have no words for—exposed to some invisible ray: but instead of labouring here to express this, to analyse the third voice, to discover whether "pure delights" are connected with art, or religion: whether I am telling the truth when I see myself perpetually taking the breath of these voices in my sails, and tacking this way and that, in daily life as I yield to them—instead of that, I note only this influence, suspect it to be of great importance, cannot find how to check its power on other people; and so erect a finger here, by way of signalling that here is a vein to work out later. (*MOB*, 115)

It is eloquent that this "third voice" joins art and religion; the "vein," I think, is worked out in the novel, in which the "third voice" seems to exist beyond the perceptions of actual life, connecting consciousness. "Things we have no words for" once again brings to mind the unnameable empty center of Woolf's art.

Isa and William Dodge, together in the greenhouse, hear a simple melody that is to them "another voice, a third voice . . . saying something simple" (*BTA*, 137). Bartholemew Oliver hears the same melody as "another voice speaking" (*BTA*, 139), and it inspires in him a chant that is echoed near the end of the book:

O the winter, will fill the grate with ashes,
And there'll be no glow, no glow on the log.

(*BTA*, 141)

The departure of the bountiful Mrs. Manresa makes Bart once more into a stuffed man, a hollow man: "All were retreating, withdrawing and dispersing; and he was left with the ash grown cold and no glow, no glow on the log" (*BTA*, 236). The "retreating and advancing" that Dodge feels is over for all of them is part of Bart's sense of loss and is incorporated into his song; the swallows fly about the trees "retreating and advancing" (*BTA*, 212), recalling Bart's song of "sister swallow."

Examples of the enormously complex rhyming and rhythming of *Between the Acts* can be found on every page, creating a web of sound in which life is, so to speak, suspended. Language is an infection, spreading among all people, spreading to and from nature; words spill over their context, colliding with each other, infecting thought. When La Trobe's pageant is saved by the noise of the cows, first one lows, "then the whole herd caught the infection" (*BTA*, 166); Bart catches "the infection of the language" of the pageant's eighteenth-century scene (*BTA*, 174). Language is a saving infection, a force to join as well as to divide, and the vessel of "common emotion" as well as that which overlays it.

Language imposes over the confusion and chaos of life an order that is only apparent: as the last scene of the pageant shows, the web of language is in fact a chaos. As long as there are no gaps, no silences, the audience is happy, for silence reveals that "emptiness about the heart of life" that cannot be faced by the crowd. Acquiescence, as "Time Passes" showed, is the easy way out:

> The gramophone, while the scene was removed, gently stated certain facts which everybody knows to be perfectly true. . . .
> The view repeated in its own way what the tune was saying. The sun was sinking; the colours were merging; and the view was saying how after toil men rest from their labours; how coolness comes; reason prevails; and having unharnessed the team from the plough, neighbours dig in cottage gardens and lean over cottage gates.
> The cows, making a step forward, then standing still, were saying the same thing to perfection.
> Folded in this triple melody, the audience sat gazing. (*BTA*, 158-59)

As long as they are distracted from themselves, the audience is happy; very few of them can be at home in solitude; silence brings discomfort. If reality is not distanced, mediated somehow, it cannot be borne. Miss La Trobe's experiment, in which she intends to douche the audience with "present-time reality," fails because what they are exposed to is not framed. It is only when life is presented selectively that anyone notices it; for the most part we live blindly, not seeing what is right before us.[24]

'Reality'—what was called in *To the Lighthouse* "the beauty of the world"—is a momentary experience of that special "self-awareness" that several of Woolf's female characters have shown, when the "eternal passing and flowing" of the actual world is "struck into stability" (*TTL*, 249-50).

The verbal condition of human being is, however, not the whole picture. There is the suggestion in the novel that felt influences pass between people without words. Throughout *Between the Acts* people "hear" when no words have been spoken; silence makes an "unmistakable contribution" to talk (50). Lucy twice gets up—once to show William the house (83), once to return with Bart to the pageant (141)—as if a signal had been given, though nothing was said. Isa, Giles, and William each say "without words" that they are desperately unhappy (205). "Thoughts without words," wonders Bart, the exemplar of reason; "Can that be?" (68). It would seem from the experience of Lucy Swithin and Miss La Trobe that such thoughts can not only be, but are the characteristic mode of discourse of the soul. Beyond words is a timeless medium ("that which is outside of us . . . what we are not" *TW*, 197).

'Reality'; the soul; "that which we are not"—these are a few of the many linguistic displacements Woolf employs to shape round the abstraction that is felt through all her fiction. In her diary she wrote of a "deep blue quiet space" into which she seemed to step, "off the whirling world" (4 April 1937). Lucy Swithin, like Clarissa Dalloway and Mrs. Ramsay before her, is seen early in *Between the Acts* drawn to an impersonal quality felt in the sky:

> There was a fecklessness, a lack of symmetry and order in the clouds, as they thinned and thickened. Was it their own law, or no law, they obeyed? Some were wisps of white hair merely. One, high up, very distant, had hardened to golden alabaster; was made of immortal marble. Beyond that was blue, pure blue, black blue; blue that had never filtered down; that had escaped registration. It never fell as sun, shadow, or rain upon the world, but disregarded the little coloured ball of earth entirely. No flower felt it; no field; no garden. (*BTA*, 30)

We might recall here Woolf's "consciousness of what I call 'reality', a thing I see before me: something abstract; but residing in the downs or in the sky" (*D*, 10 September 1928). This consciousness pervades *Between the Acts*.

For Lucy, time as passage seems irrelevant; she is marking the approach of death. Isa longs to escape to a realm of death where "change is not" (*BTA*, 181). Miss La Trobe sways perpetually between despair and triumph. Only Lucy is at peace, untroubled; only she seems to have found *rest*.

"You don't," says William Dodge to Lucy, "believe in history." History is made by men and divides life into "periods." In her notes for *Reading at Random*, Woolf wrote: "Always follow the genuine scent—the idea of the moment. No 'periods' " (373). Lucy, it will be remembered, "was given to increasing the bounds of the moment" by her mental journeys through time and space. It is the history of *Reading at Random* that *Between the Acts* offers, a psychohistory in which the divisions between one "age" and the next are shown to be merely a matter of appearance (see above, p. 123): "The Victorians," Mrs. Swithin mused. "I don't believe" she said with her odd little smile, "that there ever were such people. Only you and me and William dressed differently" (*BTA*, 203). For Lucy the time of male history—which is primarily a catalog of armed conflicts—does not exist,[25] in the sense of progression from one "period" to the next: "We've only the present." The "present" is lived time that cannot be fixed or named. The import of the pageant is that the audience should not see the various ages passing before them as "real" stages in a process of development along a line, but that the actors merely play different parts while the deep structures of the world remain essentially the same.[26] The effect of the pageant is to cut adrift the audience from the easy identity afforded them by clothes and other external trappings:

> Yet somehow they felt—how could one put it—a little not quite here or there. As if the play had jerked the ball out of the cup; as if what I call myself was still floating unattached, and didn't settle. Not quite themselves, they felt. (*BTA*, 175)

> They were neither one thing nor the other; neither Victorians nor themselves. They were suspended, without being, in limbo. (*BTA*, 207)

The pageant, holding a mirror up to human nature as it quite literally does, tampers with an acquiescent sense of reality by its stirring together of "wandering bodies and floating voices." Real swallows skim over real grass in the scene of the Victorian "age," and someone exclaims in the eighteenth-century scene, "What names for real people!" Our conception of reality is under question, and time is thus dislocated. This is what fiction, and in some sense all art, does. Reading is entering a time and space that is at once apart from and a part of the individual reader's time and space. By the time the pageant, in its "historical" progress, has reached the "present day" the audience finds itself "neither one thing nor the other." Without a spectacle, however, the audience cannot understand what is going on; they do not play their parts in the drama because they are still bound up in their own "period."

Lucy's time is an undivided time; she is not bound by the ticking clock that sounds throughout the novel. The earth is (in all Woolf's novels) the symbol of the elemental changelessness of human being that the "song" expresses,[27] and it is to the female and to children that this consciousness is particularly present, as Woolf's fiction amply demonstrates. Isa's young son, George, is aware of unity in the world, but his moment of vision is shattered by the intrusion of the male, Bart (*BTA*, 16-17). Children are seen as isolated "on a green island," the "drone of the trees" and the "chirp of birds" in their ears; the nursery is "the cradle of our race." Lucy, too, has the song of birds in her ears, that sound Woolf said in "Anon" first inspired people to "sing" and from which literature developed. Lucy is herself frequently likened to a bird.

The pool in *Orlando* was an image of the depths of the mind. In *To the Lighthouse*, the "pool of Time" would eventually cover all; Nancy turned a rock-pool into an entire world. The pool is Woolf's most frequent image of human consciousness, appearing in essays and her diary as well as throughout the fiction. In *Between the Acts*, Lucy sees a world in the lily-pool: "Now the jagged leaf at the corner suggested, by its contours, Europe. There were other leaves. She fluttered her eye over the surface, naming leaves India, Africa, America. Islands of security, glossy and thick" (*BTA*, 239). As the last of the audience leaves, the pageant over, Lucy is found alone by the lily-pool. In this moment of solitude, she expresses her faith: " 'Ourselves,' she murmured. And retrieving some glint of faith from the grey waters, hopefully, without much help from reason, she followed the fish; the speckled, streaked, and blotched; seeing in that vision beauty, power, and glory in ourselves" (*BTA*, 239-40). Her vision is contradicted by her brother's unfeeling reason, but this does not trouble her. That which she apprehends through the efforts of her faith is a universal medium, surrounding all life; in the words of *To the Lighthouse*, Lucy hears the "voice of the beauty of the world." Looking back to Mrs. Ramsay's search for faith (*TTL*, 101), it can be seen now that the vision itself is not new in Woolf's writing; what is new in *Between the Acts* is the directness with which the private vision of faith in transcendent 'reality' is set against the despair of actual life in time.

> Silenced, she returned to her private vision; of beauty which is goodness; the sea on which we float. Mostly impervious, but surely every boat sometimes leaks?
>
> He would carry the torch of reason till it went out in the darkness of the cave. For herself, every morning, kneeling, she protected her vision. Every night she opened the window and looked at leaves against the sky. Then she slept. Then the random ribbons of birds' voices woke her. (*BTA*, 240)

The elements of her faith are these: that life is surrounded by a halo of beauty, a nameless quality inhering in the actual, but not actual and so free of the constraint and decadence of space and time; all beings are afloat on this "sea" of beauty. For the most part all people are impervious to beauty, but sometimes it is glimpsed—as manifest in the novel by the sense of unity the audience sometimes catches in music, the perception of beauty as the actors stand in fading sunlight after the pageant (*BTA*, 228), and the unspoken communications that seem carried by a medium other than words. To live entirely by reason, the logical terms of actual life, is to cast a light into darkness that is merely artificial, never to turn to see the light of 'reality'. Abstract, impersonal beauty resides in the natural world (the uncivilized earth is invariably an emblem of timelessness in the novels), and can be perceived by those who recognize the emptiness at the heart of life.

The 'reality' Woolf felt behind and beyond actual life is the virtual property of her fiction because such creation is free from

the personal, time-bound, death-tending life of its creator to exist on its own terms in the locationless space of art. To come to a
conclusion, to draw a line and give the "solution" to the abstruse
philosophy of Woolf's fiction would be to contradict everything
that fiction implies. However, I have said that in the last years of
her life Woolf approached the perennial questions of her art with
a new boldness.

There is a long passage excised from the final typescript of
Between the Acts that concerns the silence of "the thing that exists when we aren't there" (*D*, 30 October 1926). Perhaps because it has the tone of philosophical speculation, Woolf deleted
the passage, putting in its place the two cryptic sentences that
follow the description of the pictures in the dining-room at
Pointz Hall: "Empty, empty, empty; silent, silent, silent. The
room was a shell, singing of what was before time was; a vase
stood in the heart of the house, alabaster, smooth, cold, holding
the still, distilled essence of emptiness, silence" (*BTA*, 47). Behind these lines might be felt the idea that art can hold within it
the timeless 'reality' that is the background, so to speak, against
which being stands out. Art can "make of the moment something
permanent" because its form transcends the modes of actual life.
Some understanding of the implications of these lines from the
novel might be gained from T. S. Eliot's *Burnt Norton* (1935):

> Words move, music moves
> Only in time; but that which is only living
> Can only die. Words, after speech, reach
> Into the silence. Only by the form, the pattern,
> Can words or music reach
> The stillness, as a Chinese jar still
> Moves perpetually in its stillness.
>
> (137-43)

In her novel Woolf aspires to a poetic communication of concepts she attempted to explain in the deleted passage. That passage seems to me to embody the central concerns of this study of
the novels; it reads as follows:[28]

> There was silence in the dining-room, for lunch delayed. The chairs
> were all drawn up, and the places ready; wine glasses, knives and forks,
> napkins, and in the centre the variegated flowers which Bartlet picked,

mixed and bunched together after a colour scheme of his own. But who observed the dining room? Who noted the silence, the emptiness? What name is to be given to that which notes that a room is empty? This presence certainly requires a name, for without a name what can exist? And how can silence or emptiness be noted by that which has no existence? Yet by what name can that be called which enters rooms when the company is still in the kitchen, or the nursery, or the library; which notes the pictures, then the flowers, and observes, though there itself, the room is empty. The great dictionary which records the names of infinitesimally small insects, has a name for grains of different sand—one is shell, the other rock—has ignored this presence, refusing to attempt to name it. Certainly it is difficult to find a name for that which is in a room, yet the room is empty; for that which perceives pictures, knife and fork, also men and women; and describes them; and not only perceives but partakes of them, and has access to the mind in its darkness. And further goes from mind to mind and surface to surface, and from body to body creating what is not mind or body, not surface or depths, but a common element in which the perishable is preserved, and the separate become one. Does it not by this means create immortality? And yet we who have named other presences equally impalpable—and called them God, for instance, or again The Holy Ghost—have no name but novelist, or poet, or sculptor, or musician, for this greatest of all preservers and creators. But this spirit, this haunter and joiner, who makes one where there are two, three, six or seven, and preserves what without it would perish, is nameless. Nameless it is yet partakes of all things named; it is rhyme and rhythm; is dressing and eating and drinking; is procreation and sensation; is love and hate and passion and adventure; partakes of the dog and the cat; of the bee and the flower and of bodies in coats and skirts.

   This nameless spirit then, who is not "we" nor "I," nor the novelist either; for the novelist, all agree, must tell a story; and there are no stories for this spirit; this spirit is not concerned to follow lovers to the altar, nor to cut chapter from chapter; and write as novelists do "The End" with a flourish; since there is no end; this being, to reduce it to the shortest and simplest word, was present in the dining room at Pointz Hall, for it observed how different the room was empty from what the room was when—as now happened people [entered.] <were about to enter.>

The fictional world is created by an autonomous, impersonal *presence*, but this presence can nowhere actually be located—it is actually absent. The audience in the novel discovers this: "Whom could they make responsible? Whom could they thank for their entertainment? Was there no one?" (*BTA*, 227). By this strange mode of being, the absent presence might be said to create immortality: the world of a novel "is" actually nowhere, and yet locates itself in the world of each reader in the act of reading, thereby becoming a valid part of the actual world. This "something/nothing" shares its mode of being with the ideas of self, or soul, and 'reality'. Thus it might be said that art (in Woolf's sense) *is a product of the soul that gives access to that medium by which all life is surrounded*—'reality.' Writing fiction is creating a world that escapes the spatiotemporal horizons of actual life in the sense described above. Her surer belief in this concept may have contributed to the feeling of freedom noted in the last few years of her life. As her diary reveals, she felt there was no future: her world had disappeared. Like Lucy Swithin, perhaps, she felt "We've only the present"; the continuous present of writing.

Woolf was observing the final chaos from a tiny island of illusory security in which the villagers continued their meaningless doings as the encroaching darkness edged nearer.[29] An apocalyptic feeling is strong in *Between the Acts*: "Only a few great names—Babylon, Nineveh, Clytemnestra, Agamemnon, Troy—floated across the open space. Then the wind rose, and in the rustle of the leaves even the great words became inaudible; and the audience sat staring at the villagers, whose mouths opened, but no sound came" (*BTA*, 164-65). Leaning against a tree, the artist is tormented by her failure to ward off emptiness: "Illusion had failed. 'This is death,' she murmured, 'death' " (*BTA*, 165). Only for instants does the artist have the power of the gods to overcome time: "Ah, but she was not merely a twitcher of individual strings; she was one who seethes wandering bodies and floating voices in a cauldron, and makes rise up from its amorphous mass a recreated world. Her moment was on her—her glory" (*BTA*, 180). Woolf mocks the puppeteer artist in *Between the Acts*, allowing her only a brief triumph in the *giving* of her vision, as Lily Briscoe triumphs in the instant she makes her final brushstroke. "A vision imparted is relief from agony," but "she hadn't made them see" (*BTA*, 117). Art cannot simply *give* the vision; art demands creative participation; in the language of the novel, "hours of kneeling in the early morning" (*BTA*, 239).

Throughout her life and writings Woolf apprehended the 'reality' behind appearances that is the ignored inheritance of all humanity. Her achievement is the creation of a literary form that brings the transcendent into the actual, brings eternity into the world of time in the act of reading. Her diary and novels are full of the records of particular, intense "moments of being" in which 'reality' came closer. In "A Sketch of the Past," for the first time in her life, she wrote in general terms directly of what she believed was the nature of the conceptual "rod" that her writing constantly held to. In the memoir she once again states that her entire life has stood upon a base formed in childhood. Writing was "what is far more necessary than anything else" (*MOB*, 73) because art enshrines the lineaments of 'reality', the form of the "thing itself," timeless and yet inherent in the world of time. This passage is explained by the entire effort of Woolf's life and art, which were inextricably interwoven with each other; it is with this slowly emergent "philosophy," now grasped firmly and become her own, that I have been concerned:

> And I go on to suppose that the shock-receiving capacity is what makes me a writer. . . . it is or will become a revelation of some order; it is a token of some real thing behind appearances; and I make it real by putting it into words. . . . From this I reach what I might call a philosophy; at any rate it is a constant idea of mine; that behind the cotton wool is hidden a pattern; that we—I mean all human beings—are connected with this; that the whole world is a work of art; that we are parts of the work of art. *Hamlet* or a Beethoven quartet is the truth about this vast mass that we call the world. But there is no Shakespeare, there is no Beethoven; certainly and emphatically there is no God; we are the words; we are the music; we are the thing itself. And I see this when I have a shock. (*MOB*, 72)

ABBREVIATIONS

The following abbreviations are used in the text and notes:

AHH	*A Haunted House*
BP	*Books and Portraits*
BTA	*Between the Acts*
CDB	*The Captain's Death Bed & Other Essays*
CR I, II	*The Common Reader*, First Series, Second Series
CW	*Contemporary Writers*
D	*The Diary of Virginia Woolf*
DM	*The Death of the Moth & Other Essays*
GR	*Granite and Rainbow*
JR	*Jacob's Room*
L	*The Letters of Virginia Woolf*
M	*The Moment & Other Essays*
MD	*Mrs. Dalloway*
MOB	*Moments of Being*
ND	*Night and Day*
O	*Orlando*
TTL	*To the Lighthouse*
TVO	*The Voyage Out*
TW	*The Waves*
TY	*The Years*

NOTES

INTRODUCTION

1. *The Diary of Virginia Woolf*, ed. Anne Olivier Bell, 5 vols. (London: Hogarth Press, 1977-84). References to Woolf's diary will be indicated by *D* followed by the date of the entry; in this way entries may be found in any edition of the *Diary*.

2. Leonard Woolf, *An Autobiography*, 2 vols. (Oxford: Oxford University Press, 1980), 93.

3. See, for example, S. P. Rosenbaum, "The Philosophical Realism of Virginia Woolf," in S. P. Rosenbaum, ed., *English Literature and British Philosophy* (Chicago: University of Chicago Press, 1972); Avrom Fleishman, "Woolf and McTaggart," *ELH* 36, 1969: 719-38; Graham Parkes, in an insightful essay on the philosophical implications of Woolf's fiction, suggests that philosophers "(almost all male)" have "failed to touch the heart" of Woolf's "poetic truth" because, "uncomfortable with a woman novelist's having disclosed some profound truths about human existence, they have supposed that if these truths are in any way philosophical, they must be due to the influence of professional philosophers within her range of acquaintance" ("Imagining Reality in *To the Lighthouse*," in *Literature & Philosophy* 6, 1 and 2 [October 1982]: 33).

4. Harvena Richter, *Virginia Woolf: The Inward Voyage* (Princeton: Princeton University Press, 1970), 245. Subsequent references will be made in the text to Richter.

5. Eric Warner, ed., *Virginia Woolf: A Centenary Perspective* (New York: St. Martin's Press, 1984), 158.

6. Ludwig Binswanger, "Freud's Conception of Man in the Light of Anthropology," in *Being-in-the-World, Selected Papers of Ludwig Binswanger* (New York: Basic Books, 1963), 170.

7. M. Merleau-Ponty, "Indirect Language and the Voices of Silence," in *Phenomenology, Language and Sociology* (London: Heinemann, 1974), 123.

8. Georges Poulet, *The Metamorphoses of the Circle* (Baltimore: Johns Hopkins University Press, 1966), 95. Subsequent references will be made in the text to *Circle*.

9. As far as I know, only Graham Parkes (see note 1 above) and Lucio P. Ruotolo in his *Six Existential Heroes: The Politics of Faith* (Cambridge: Harvard University Press, 1973) have drawn attention to the remarkable similarities in the contours of Woolf and Heidegger's thinking about being. As they do, I would stress that there is absolutely no question of "influence" raised here.

10. In her diary for 22 September 1928, Woolf wrote: "We dont belong to any 'class'; we thinkers: might as well be French or German. Yet I am English in some way—"

11. Jeffrey Mehlman, *A Structural Study of Autobiography: Proust, Leiris, Sartre, Levi-Strauss* (Ithaca: Cornell University Press, 1974), 39.

12. Georges Poulet, "Phenomenology of Reading," *New Literary History* 1 (1969):54.

13. Wolfgang Iser, "The Current Situation of Literary Theory: Key Concepts and the Imaginary," in *New Literary History* 11, 1 (Autumn 1979):1-20.

14. Jane P. Tompkins, ed., *Reader-Response Criticism* (Baltimore: Johns Hopkins University Press, 1980), xv.

15. Hume's famous description of the mind is as follows:

[It is] a kind of theatre where several perceptions successively make their appearance; pass, re-pass, glide away and mingle in an infinite variety of postures and situations. There is properly no *simplicity* in it at one time, nor identity in different; whatever natural propension we have to imagine that simplicity and identity . . . They are the successive perceptions only that constitute the mind; nor have we the most distant notion of the place where these scenes are represented or of the materials of which it is composed. (*A Treatise of Human Nature*, vol. 1 [London: J. M. Dent & Sons, 1936]: 239-40).

CHAPTER ONE

1. See Sydney Shoemaker, "Embodiment and Behavior," in Amélie Oksenberg Rorty, ed. *The Identities of Persons* (Berkeley: University of California Press, 1976), 109-37.

2. Descartes begins his project thus:

I shall now close my eyes, stop up my ears, turn away all my senses, even efface from my thought all images of corporeal things, or at least, because this can hardly be done, I shall consider them as being vain and false; and thus communing only with myself, and examining my inner self, I shall try to make myself, little by little, better known and more familiar to myself. (*Discourse on Method and the Meditations*. Trans. F. E. Sutcliffe. [Harmondsworth: Penguin Books, 1979]: 113).

3. To endorse Susan's view, see Virginia Woolf, *The Waves: The Two Holograph Drafts*. Transcribed and edited by J. W. Graham (London: Hogarth Press, 1976), where she says: "It is my self. My self is in my eyes" (503). Subsequent references will be made in the text to Graham.

4. This moment is drawn from an experience Woolf describes in her memoir "A Sketch of the Past" (in *Moments of Being*. Edited with an Introduction and Notes by Jeanne Schulkind [Sussex: University Press, 1976]: 78).

"There was the moment of the puddle in the path; when for no reason I could discover, everything suddenly became unreal; I was suspended; I could not step across the puddle, I tried to touch something . . . the whole world became unreal" [dots in original]. For a full exposition of the implications of this and other correlations between the lived experience of the writer and her fiction, see Roger Poole, *The Unknown Virginia Woolf* (Cambridge: Cambridge University Press, 1978). The question of embodiment—"lived subjective reality"—is comprehensively discussed in this book which opens an avenue of approach to Woolf that has yet to be traveled; see especially chapter 15, "Virginia's Embodiment," to which my chapter must owe a great deal.

CHAPTER TWO

1. Heidegger, in *Being and Time* (Oxford: Basil Blackwell, 1962), writes that the "Self of everyday Dasein is the *they-self*, which we distinguish from the *authentic Self*—that is, from the Self which has been taken hold of in its own way. As they-self, the particular Dasein has been *dispersed* into the 'they,' and must first find itself" (167).

2. Judith Kegan Gardiner, "On Female Identity and Writing By Women" in Elizabeth Abel, ed., *Writing and Sexual Difference* (Chicago: University of Chicago Press, 1982), 185.

3. See "A Sketch of the Past" (*MOB*, 71).

4. John Graham, "The 'Caricature Value' of Parody and Fantasy in *Orlando*," *University of Toronto Quarterly* 30, 4 (July 1961):345.

5. Letter from V. Sackville-West to Woolf, 11 October 1928, in *The Letters of Virginia Woolf*, 6 vols., ed. Nigel Nicolson and Joanne Trautmann (London: Hogarth Press, 1975-80), 3:Appendix. References to Woolf's letters are indicated by *L* followed by the number given in the collected edition.

6. A parallel might be drawn here with Heidegger's complex idea of the "call of conscience" (*Ruf*) that "*discourses solely and constantly in the mode of keeping silent*" as it reveals Self in its authenticity. Those interested in pursuing these similarities between Woolf and Heidegger should refer to paragraphs 54-60 of *Being and Time*.

7. Marguerite Duras. From an interview by Susan Husserl-Kapit in *Signs*, Winter 1975, in Elaine Marks and Isabelle de Courtviron, eds., *New French Feminisms: An Anthology* (Amherst: University of Massachusetts Press, 1980), 175.

8. Xavière Gauthier, "Existe-t-il une écriture de femme?", trans. Marilyn A. August, *New French Feminisms*, 164.

9. Elaine Showalter, "Feminist Criticism in the Wilderness," in Abel, ed. *Writing and Sexual Difference*, 31.

10. Samuel Butler, *The Notebooks of Samuel Butler* (London: Cape,

1912), quoted by Allen McLaurin, *Virginia Woolf: The Echoes Enslaved* (Cambridge: Cambridge University Press, 1973), 8.

11. See Geoffrey Hartman, *Saving the Text: Literature / Derrida / Philosophy* (Baltimore: Johns Hopkins University Press, 1981):

> So naming and the problem of identity cannot be dissociated. So literature and the problem of identity cannot be dissociated. Literature is at once onomatopoeic (name-making) and onomatoclastic (name-breaking). The true name of a writer is not given by his signature, but is spelled out by his entire work. The bad or empty name or nickname may be countered by the melodious or bardic magic of art. (128)

12. In conversation with Georges Duthuit, Samuel Beckett said he felt "that there is nothing to express, nothing with which to express, nothing from which to express, no power to express together with the obligation to express."

CHAPTER THREE

1. See M. Merleau-Ponty, *Phenomenology of Perception*:

> But this is precisely the question: how can the word "I" be put into the plural, how can a general idea of the *I* be formed, how can I speak of an I other than my own, how can I know that there are other *I*s, how can consciousness which, by its nature, and as self-knowledge, is in the mode of the *I*, be grasped in the mode of Thou; and through this, in the world of the "one"? (348)

2. Virginia Woolf, *To the Lighthouse: The Original Holograph Draft*, transcribed and edited by Susan Dick (Toronto: University of Toronto Press, 1982), 295. Subsequent references are to Dick, giving her pagination. Deletions in quotations from manuscript sources throughout the text are indicated by crooked brackets < >.

3. On 25 October 1920, Woolf wrote in her diary, "I dont like time to flap round me." On 28 September 1926, we find: "It is so strange to me that I cannot get it right—the depression, I mean, which does not come from something definite, but from nothing. "Where there is nothing" the phrase came <back> to me, as I sat at the table in the drawing room." It is interesting to look once more at Heidegger. In "What is Metaphysics?" he writes of the experience of anxiety that reveals nothingness:

> Anxiety robs us of speech. Because beings as a whole slip away, so that just the nothing crowds round, in the face of anxiety all utterance of the "is" falls silent. That in the malaise of anxiety we often try to shatter the vacant stillness with compulsive talk only proves the presence of the nothing. That anxiety reveals the nothing man himself immediately demonstrates when anxiety has dissolved. In the lucid vision sustained by fresh rememberance we must say that that in the face of which and for which we were anxious was "really"—nothing. Indeed: the nothing

itself—as such—was there. (*Basic Writings* [London: Routledge & Kegan Paul, 1978]: 103)

Lucio Ruotolo, in *Six Existential Heroes*, remarks, "Heidegger's assertion that man must face nothing in order to be something, and Virginia Woolf's literary treatment of the dilemma she acknowledged in her own life, characterize the ontological reformation that with Schelling and Kierkegaard had begun to transform Western culture" (13).

CHAPTER FOUR

1. In "The Foundation and Manifesto of Futurism," (1908), Marinetti wrote: "We will glorify war—the only true hygiene of the world—militarism, patriotism, the destructive gesture of the anarchist, the beautiful Ideas which kill, and the scorn of woman" (Herschel B. Chipp, ed. *Theories of Modern Art: A Source Book by Artists and Critics* [Berkeley: University of California Press, 1968]: 286).

2. Brian Alderson, "Boy-stew and red-hot slippers," *Times*, 5 May 1978. See also Beverly Ann Schlack, *Continuing Presences: Virginia Woolf's Use of Literary Allusion* (University Park: Pennsylvania State University Press, 1979).

3. Van Gogh wrote from Arles in September 1888 to his brother, Theo: "But I have got back to where I was in Nuenen, when I made a vain attempt to learn music, so much did I already feel the relation between our color and Wagner's music" (Chipp, 38).

4. Chipp, 154-55.

5. Wassily Kandinsky, "Concrete Art" (1938). Chipp, 346-47.

6. See Isabelle Anscombe, *Omega and After: Bloomsbury and the Decorative Arts* (New York: Thames and Hudson, 1982).

7. Richard Shone, *Bloomsbury Portraits: Vanessa Bell, Duncan Grant, and Their Circle* (Oxford: Phaidon Press, 1976), 142.

8. Hugh MacDonald, *Skryabin* (London: Oxford University Press, 1978), 55-56.

9. Chipp, 187-88.

10. Ernst Cassirer, *The Logic of the Humanities* (New Haven: Yale University Press, 1960), 112.

11. Quoted by Paul de Man in *Blindness and Insight* (New York: Oxford University Press, 1971), 128.

12. See, for example, *Mrs. Dalloway*: " 'K . . . R . . . ' said the nurse-maid, and Septimus heard her say "Kay Arr" close to his ear, deeply, softly, like a mellow organ, but with a roughness in her voice like a grasshopper's, which

rasped his spine deliciously and sent running up into his brain waves of sound, which concussing, broke" (25). In *The Waves* the synaesthetic perception of the children seems to suggest that it is only with the development of individual identity that the senses are separated: the cock's crow, to Bernard, is "a spurt of hard, red water in the white tide" (7). The work is, in Harvena Richter's words, "a poetic-encyclopedic reconstruction of the creation and development of man and his mind, moving from his earliest awareness of objects . . . to a perception of the world, death and time" (80).

13. In view of what Quentin Bell says in *Virginia Stephen, 1882-1912* (London: Hogarth Press, 1972), 149, and the following remarks of Woolf's in a letter to Ka Cox (16 May 1913): ". . . the bawling sentimentality [of the *Ring*] which used once to carry me away, and now leaves me sitting perfectly still" (*L*, 668).

14. Virginia Woolf, "Impressions at Bayreuth," in *Books and Portraits* (London: Hogarth Press, 1977), 19.

15. Susanne K. Langer, *Feeling and Form* (London: Routledge & Kegan Paul, 1953), 27. Subsequent references will be made in the text to *Feeling*.

16. See Virginia Woolf, *Melymbrosia. An Early Version of* The Voyage Out, ed. Louise DeSalvo (New York: The New York Public Library, 1982); also, Louise DeSalvo's *Virginia Woolf's First Voyage: A Novel in the Making* (New York: Macmillan Co., 1980).

17. Compare Marcel Proust, *The Captive*, Part Two, trans. C. K. Scott Moncrieff (London: Chatto & Windus, 1929; reprint: 1976).

For instance, this music seemed to me to be something truer than all the books that I knew. Sometimes I thought that this was due to the fact that what we feel in life, not being felt in the form of ideas, its literary (that is to say an intellectual) translation in giving an account of it, explains it, analyses it, but does not recompose it as does music, in which the sounds seem to assume the inflexion of the thing itself, to reproduce that interior and extreme point of our sensation which is the part that gives us that peculiar exhiliration which we recapture from time to time . . . (232).

18. For discussion of this, see Allen McLaurin, *Virginia Woolf: The Echoes Enslaved* (especially chap. 7).

19. Gauguin, in "Notes Synthetiques" (ca. 1888), wrote that painting is "a complete art which sums up all the others and completes them.—Like music, it acts on the soul through the intermediary of the senses: harmonious colors correspond to the harmonies of words" (Chipp, 61).

20. Quoted in Frances Spalding, *Roger Fry: Art and Life* (Berkeley: University of California Press, 1980), 212.

21. *Recent Paintings by Vanessa Bell*, with a Foreword by Virginia Woolf (1930), in S. P. Rosenbaum, ed. *The Bloomsbury Group: A Collection of Memoirs, Commentary and Criticism* (Toronto: University of Toronto Press, 1975), 172.

22. Ibid.

23. The house is full of "unrelated passions," and it seems that Lily must bring order to this chaos. Her first attempts fail because she is too close to her object: her relationship with Mrs. Ramsay is the core of this object, and it is only ten years later, when Lily can hold the object at a distance, that she achieves a form for it.

24. In "Some Questions in Aesthetics," Roger Fry wrote about the unconsciousness of artistic creation and emphasized rhythm in discussing Rembrandt's "Boy at Lessons":

> If for a moment Rembrandt had thought about his picture he was undone; nothing but complete absorption in his vision could sustain the unconscious certainty and freedom of the gesture. Each touch, then, had to be an inspiration or the rhythm would have broken down. (*Transformations; critical and speculative essays on art* [Freeport, N.Y.: Books for Libraries Press, 1968]: 40)

25. Dick, *To the Lighthouse*. See chap. 3, note 2, for bibliographic details. Dick's transcription is sometimes dubious, but I reproduce it without variant readings to avoid confusion.

CHAPTER FIVE

1. J. W. Graham, "Point of View in *The Waves*: Some Services of the Style," *University of Toronto Quarterly* 39, 3 (April 1970): 201-2.

2. The hopelessness of Bernard's endeavor is prefigured in *Orlando*'s last chapter, where the narrator repeatedly admits that life cannot be summed up, e.g.:

> Having asked then of man and of bird and the insects, for fish, men tell us, who have lived in green caves, solitary for years to hear them speak, never, never say, and so perhaps know what life is—having asked them all and grown no wiser, but only older and colder (for did we not pray once in a way to wrap up in a book something so hard, so rare, one could swear it was life's meaning?) back we must go and say straight out to the reader who waits a-tiptoe to hear what life is—alas, we don't know. (244)

3. "Point of View in *The Waves*" (see note 1, above) and "The 'Caricature Value' of Parody and Fantasy in *Orlando*" (see chap. 2, note 5).

4. Iser, "The Current Situation of Literary Theory" (see Introduction, note 10), 17.

5. Ibid., 18

6. Quoted by A. McLaurin (see chap. 2, note 10), 7.

7. Introduction to Charles Dickens, *Bleak House* (Harmondsworth: Penguin Books, 1971), 22.

8. George Steiner, "The Language Animal," in *Extraterritorial: Papers on Literature and the Language Revolution* (London: Faber & Faber, 1972), 72. Subsequent references will be made in the text to *Extraterritorial.*

9. The imagery of the "world seen without a self" almost certainly derives from Woolf's experience of a solar eclipse in 1927. She gives a long description of it in her diary for 30 June 1927. It also forms the substance of an eccentric essay, "The Sun and the Fish." The image of the skeleton of the world is found as early as *The Voyage Out* and appears in nearly all the novels. The following extract from "The Sun and the Fish" demonstrates the enormous scope the eclipse had in Woolf's imagination as she appropriates Christian terminology for cosmic significance:

> So the light turned and heeled over and went out. This was the end. The flesh and blood of the world was dead; only the skeleton was left. It hung beneath us, a frail shell; brown; dead; withered. Then, with some trifling movement, this profound obeisance of the light, this stooping down and abasement of all splendour was over. Lightly, on the other side of the world, up it rose; it sprang up as if the one movement, after a second's tremendous pause, completed the other, and the light which had died here rose again elsewhere. (*CDB*, 215)

10. For example, Yeats's "Among School Children":

> O body swayed to music, O brightening glance,
> How can we know the dancer from the dance?

or Blake's "The Crystal Cabinet":

> I strove to seize the inmost Form
> With ardor fierce and hands of flame,
> But burst the Crystal Cabinet,
> And like a Weeping Babe became—

CHAPTER SIX

1. See S. P. Rosenbaum, "Virginia Woolf and the Intellectual Origins of Bloomsbury," in Elaine K. Ginsberg and Laura Moss Gottlieb, eds., *Virginia Woolf: Centennial Essays* (Troy, N.Y.: Whitston Publishing Co., 1983). Although I think the influences Rosenbaum outlines affected the men of Bloomsbury to a far greater extent than they did Woolf, who reacted against them, his essay provides a useful account of the general intellectual milieu of her contemporaries.

2. Like a nun withdrawing, or a child exploring a tower, she went, upstairs, paused at the window, came to the bathroom. There was the green lino-

leum and a tap dripping. There was an emptiness about the heart of life; an attic room. (*MD*, 35)

3. Only for a moment; but it was enough. It was a sudden revelation, a tinge like a blush which one tried to check and then, as it spread, one yielded to its expansion, and rushed to the farthest verge and there quivered and felt the world come closer, swollen with some astonishing significance, some pressure of rapture, which split its thin skin and gushed and poured with an extraordinary alleviation over the cracks and sores. Then, for that moment, she had seen an illumination; a match burning in a crocus; an inner meaning almost expressed. But the close withdrew; the hard softened. It was over—the moment. (*MD*, 36)

4. Pascal, *Pensées*, trans. A. J. Krailsheimer (Harmondsworth: Penguin Books, 1966; reprint 1978). Subsequent references will be made in the text to *Pensées*.

5. Parkes, in "Imagining Reality in *To the Lighthouse*" (see Introduction, note 1), writes:

In the earliest documents of our culture, the Homeric epics and the fragments of the "presocratic" philosophers, the ancestor of our word "psyche" (the Green *psuchē*) connotes the "world soul"—the *anima mundi*—as much as the soul of the individual. And even Plato, whose thinking has perhaps been the greatest single influence on the Western conception of the psyche, rarely thinks of the human soul apart from its relation to the soul of the universe. Subsequently, the idea that there is a faculty in man that links him at a preconscious level with the world reappears in Kant's reflections upon the transcendental imagination, which in its productive rather than merely reproductive capacity prefigures a priori all experience. (36)

CHAPTER SEVEN

1. In *A Room of One's Own*, 'reality' is said to be found now "in a dusty road, now in a scrap of newspaper" (165). 'Beauty' and 'reality' seem almost synonymous to Woolf, as the following passage suggests: "Then, at a top-floor window, leaning out, looking down, you see beauty itself; or in the corner of an omnibus; or squatted in a ditch—beauty glowing, suddenly expressive, withdrawn the moment after. No one can count on it or seize it or have it wrapped in paper" (*JR*, 14).

2. In *Studies in Human Time* (Baltimore: Johns Hopkins University Press, 1956), Georges Poulet writes this of Montaigne's search for solutions:

Neither God nor nature gives being to thought; they give it only a momentary form. Only one thing remains: never to look for a phantom being outside the human condition, but to accept the situation for what it is, an existence which is not *being*, which is only "flux, shadow, and perpetual variation": "I do not depict being," says Montaigne; "I depict passage." (42-43)

3. In a letter to Paul Engelmann in 1917, Wittgenstein wrote: "And this is how it is: if only you do not try to utter what is unutterable then *nothing* gets lost. But the unutterable will be—unutterably—*contained* in what has been uttered!" (Paul Engelmann, ed., *Letters from Ludwig Wittgenstein* [New York: Horizon Press, 1968], 7).

4. Poulet, *Studies in Human Time*, 45 (my italics); see also Woolf's "Moments of Being": "She saw the very fountain of her being spurting its pure silver drops" (*AHH*, 95).

5. Of this passage, Robert Kiely writes:

The passage sums up better than almost anything else of the period the artist's complex and troubled relation to the natural universe. She is drawn to the real and imagined beauty of nature, to the color and movement that have inspired painters and poets for ages, but she is unable to separate that beauty and rhythmic motion from the random, destructive and ugly shifts that are part of it. She is perfectly capable of reading the literature of the sea, but she cannot read the sea itself and will not, though frequently tempted, pretend that she can. Her struggle for honesty, then, is first of all a struggle with artistic representations that charm and move but do not persuade her. (*Beyond Egotism: The Fiction of James Joyce, Virginia Woolf and D. H. Lawrence* [Cambridge: Harvard University Press, 1980], 43).

6. See Woolf's "On Being Ill" (1930):

It is only the recumbent who know what, after all, Nature is at no pains to conceal—that she in the end will conquer; heat will leave the world; stiff with frost we shall cease to drag ourselves about the fields; ice will lie thick upon factory and engine; the sun will go out. Even so, when the whole earth is sheeted and slippery, some undulation, some irregularity of surface will mark the boundary of an ancient garden, and there, thrusting its head up undaunted in the starlight, the rose will flower, the crocus will burn. But with the hook of life still in us still we must wriggle. We cannot stiffen peaceably into glassy mounds. Even the recumbent spring up at the mere imagination of frost about the toes and stretch out to avail themselves of the universal hope—Heaven, Immortality. Surely, since men have been wishing all these ages, they will have wished something into existence; there will be some green isle for the mind to rest on even if the foot cannot plant itself there. The co-operative imagination of mankind must have drawn some firm outline. (*M*, 16-17)

7. It is interesting to note here the conclusion to a review of H. Fielding Hall's *The Inward Light* that Woolf wrote in 1908.

The continued metaphors in which their philosophy is expressed, taken from the wind and light, waters, chains of bubbles and other sustained forces, solve all personal energy, all irregularity, into one suave stream. It is wise and harmonious, beautifully simple and innocent, but, if religion is, as Mr. Hall defines it, "a way of looking at the world", is this the richest way? Does it require any faith so high as that which believes that it is right to develop your powers to the utmost? (*CW*, 46)

8. See also the holograph draft of *The Waves*: "Her [nature's] effort is to make us acquiescent as she is; ours, to fling off, to get up, to explore, not to be overcome. And I will not fail I said: I will not acquiesce. I will not lose my sense of the enemy" (Graham, 698).

CHAPTER EIGHT

1. Georges Poulet, "Timelessness and Romanticism," *Journal of the History of Ideas* 15, 1 (January 1954):3 Subsequent references will be made in the text to "Timelessness."

2. See also *The Waves*: " 'There is the puddle,' said Rhoda, 'and I cannot cross it. I hear the rush of the great grindstone within an inch of my head. Its wind roars in my face" (113).

3. For example, *Orlando*:

But Time, unfortunately, though it makes animals and vegetables bloom and fade with amazing punctuality, has no such simple effect upon the mind of man. The mind of man, moreover, works with equal strangeness upon the body of time. An hour, once it lodges in the queer element of the human spirit, may be stretched to fifty or a hundred times its clock length; on the other hand, an hour may be accurately represented on the timepiece of the mind by one second. This extraordinary discrepancy between time on the clock and time in the mind is less known than it should be and deserves fuller investigation (91).

4. See Langer, *Feeling and Form*:

Time exists for us because we undergo tensions and their resolutions. Their peculiar building-up, and their ways of breaking or diminishing or merging into longer and greater tensions, make for a vast variety of temporal forms. If we could experience only single, successive organic strains, perhaps subjective time would be one-dimensional like the time ticked off by clocks. But life is always a dense fabric of concurrent tensions, and as each of them is a measure of time, the measurements themselves do not coincide. This causes our temporal experience to fall apart into incommensurate elements which cannot be all conceived together as clear forms. When one is taken as parameter, others become "irrational," out of logical focus, ineffable. (112-13)

5. J. Hillis Miller, "Virginia Woolf's All Souls' Day: The Omniscient Narrator in *Mrs. Dalloway*," in M. Friedman and J. Vickery, eds., *The Shaken Realist: Essays in Honor of F. J. Hoffman* (Baton Rouge: Louisiana State University Press, 1970), 109.

6. See Woolf's diary for 15 October 1923, and note also the following correspondence:

I've had some very curious visions in this room too, lying in bed, mad, & seeing the sunlight quivering like gold water, on the wall. I've heard the voices of the dead here. (*D*, 9 January 1924)

Septimus Warren Smith lying on the sofa in the sitting-room; watching
the watery gold glow and fade with the astonishing sensibility of some
live creature on the roses, on the wall-paper. (*MD*, 152)

7. See *Orlando*:

For what more terrifying revelation can there be than that it is the present
moment? That we survive the shock at all is only possible because the
past shelters us on one side and the future on another. (268)

8. Cassirer, *The Logic of the Humanities*, 84.

9. For example, see "A Sketch of the Past:"

Those moments—in the nursery, on the road to the beach—can still be
more real than the present moment. . . . At times I can go back to St
Ives more completely than I can this morning. I can reach a state where I
seem to be watching things happen as if I were there. That is, I suppose,
that my memory supplies what I had forgotten, so that it seems as if it
were happening independently, though I am really making it happen. In
certain favourable moods, memories—what one has forgotten—come
to the top. Now if this is so, is it not possible—I often wonder—that
things we have felt with great intensity have an existence independent of
our minds; are in fact still in existence? And if so, will it not be possible,
in time, that some device will be invented by which we can tap them? I
see it—the past—as an avenue lying behind; a long ribbon of scenes,
emotions. There at the end of the avenue still, are the garden and the
nursery. Instead of remembering here a scene and there a sound, I shall
fit a plug into the wall; and listen in to the past. I shall turn up August
1890. I feel that strong emotion must leave its trace; and it is only a
question of discovering how we can get ourselves again attached to it, so
that we shall be able to live our lives through from the start. (*MOB*, 67)

10. See above, chap. 3, (p. 54) referring to *D*, 8 August 1928, where
Woolf wrote of her memory of a friend's visit "making a work of art for itself."

11. In her diary on 19 September 1934, Woolf wrote: "But then, next day,
today which is Thursday, one week later, the other thing begins to work—the
exalted sense of being above time & death which comes from being again in a
writing mood."

12. See "A Sketch of the Past":

One must get the feeling of everything approaching and then disappear-
ing, getting large, getting small, passing at different rates of speed past
the little creature; one must get the feeling that made her press on, the
little creature driven on as she was by growth of her legs and arms, driven
without her being able to stop it, or to change it, driven as a plant is
driven up out of the earth, up until the stalk grows, the leaf grows, buds
swell. That is what is indescribable, that is what makes all images too
static, for no sooner has one said this was so, than it was past and altered.
(*MOB*, 79)

13. See Poulet, "Timelessness and Romanticism":

Paramnesia seems to bring forth before our eyes a past which is still real,
still alive. It is as if, abruptly, we were projected into a timeless world or

into a world where time does not flow but stands still. The incredible idea that all the past we thought we had left for ever, continues to stay here, at our very feet, invisible but intact, and in all its forgotten freshness, shoots forth in our minds. . . .

Of course, paramnesia is merely an illusion. It does not bring back the past. It just makes a perception look like a recollection. . . . Generally our memory grows gradually fainter; it tends to disappear. But sometimes association may revivify the past sufficiently to make it flash after a long oblivion into our consciousness; and if those associations are very potent, the flashing may be so intense that it has the vividness of the present. (4)

14. Poulet, *Studies in Human Time*, 85.

CHAPTER NINE

1. This passage is quoted by Brenda Silver in her introduction to *Virginia Woolf's Reading Notebooks* (Princeton, N.J.: Princeton University Press, 1983), 5.

2. See chap. 4, note 16 for bibliographic details.

3. See, for example, "The Moment: Summer's Night," a sketch written as Woolf began composing *Between the Acts*: "But that is the wider circumference of the moment. Here in the centre is a knot of consciousness" (*M*, 4).

4. In "On Not Knowing Greek," Woolf wrote:

For words, when opposed to such a blast of meaning, must give out, must be blown astray, and only by collecting in companies convey the meaning which each one separately is too weak to express. Connecting them in a rapid flight of the mind we know instantly and instinctively what they mean, but could not decant that meaning afresh into any other words. (*CR*I, 48-49)

5. " 'Anon' and 'The Reader': Virginia Woolf's Last Essays," edited, with an Introduction and Commentary by Brenda R. Silver, *Twentieth Century Literature* 25, 3/4 (Fall/Winter 1979):403. Subsequent references will be made in the text.

6. See note 5.

7. See "The Humane Art" (1940): "Instead of letters posterity will have confessions, diaries, notebooks, like M. Gide's—hybrid books in which the writer talks in the dark to himself about himself for a generation yet to be born" (*DM*, 61).

8. "In place of a hermeneutics we need an erotics of art" (Susan Sontag, "Against Interpretation." *A Susan Sontag Reader* [New York: Farrar, Straus, Giroux, 1982]: 104).

9. One critic who has done much to make clear the political nature of Woolf's writing is Jane Marcus; see, for example, "Liberty, Sorority, Misogyny,"

in Carolyn G. Heilbrun and Margaret R. Higonnet, eds., *The Representation of Women in Fiction* (Baltimore: Johns Hopkins University Press, 1983); "No More Horses: Virginia Woolf on Art and Propaganda," *Women's Studies* 4 (1977):265-89; Jane Marcus, ed., *Virginia Woolf: A Feminist Slant* (Lincoln: University of Nebraska Press, 1983); "Quentin's Bogey," *Critical Inquiry* 11, 3 (March 1985):486-97 (note 21 of this article gives a short list of essays on Woolf's politics by other writers).

10. "All books are now rank with the slimy seaweed of politics; mouldy and mildewed." Virginia Woolf to Vanessa Bell, 24 October 1938 (*L*, 3,460).

11. Quoted by Quentin Bell, *Mrs. Woolf, 1912-1941* (London: Hogarth Press, 1972), 255.

12. "Two Endings: Virginia Woolf's Suicide and *Between the Acts*," *University of Toronto Quarterly* 44, 4 (Summer 1975): 265-89.

13. In her diary for 15 September 1934, Woolf wrote about the funeral: "Then Desmond came up: said wdnt it be nice to walk in the garden? 'Oh we stand on a little island' he said. But it has been very lovely I said. For the first time I laid my hand on his shoulder, & said dont die yet. Nor you either he said. We have had wonderful friends, he said."

14. Brenda Silver quotes this in her introduction to " 'Anon' and 'The Reader' " (see note 5 above), note 13, 367.

15. Still I see Lytton's point—my dear old serpent. What a dream life is to be sure—that he should be dead, & I reading him; & trying to make out that we indented ourselves on the world; whereas I sometimes feel its been an illusion—gone so fast, lived so quickly; & nothing to show for it, save these little books. But that makes me dig my feet in, & squeeze the moment. (*D*, 29 June 1939)

16. A fascinating account of the nexus of emotions arising, initially, from Julia's death, and the "legend" of Herbert Duckworth, is given by Mark Spilka in *Virginia Woolf's Quarrel with Grieving* (Lincoln: University of Nebraska Press, 1980).

17. One element of the matrix I am not developing here is the novel's concern with matriarchal mythology and the rituals associated with the Egyptian Isis; see Evelyn Haller, "Isis Unveiled," in Jane Marcus, ed. *Virginia Woolf, A Feminist Slant*.

18. A late short story of Woolf's, "The Symbol," seems related to this entry; see Virginia Woolf, *Complete Shorter Fiction*, ed. Susan Dick (New York: Harcourt Brace Jovanovich, 1986).

19. See note 5, above.

20. The relevance and foresight of Woolf's political thinking is endorsed by the following statement by a woman at the Greenham Common Women's Peace Camp:

I don't see this situation being resolved by parliamentary means . . . maybe if there's enough extra-parliamentary pressure we could do it that way but there's more to it. I don't think disarmament is one little thing that you can achieve without other bits of society changing. You won't achieve disarmament unless you *remove the desire and need for men to fight* . . . I think the future rests on women. (Shushu Al-Sabbagh in Barbara Harford & Sarah Hopkins, eds., *Greenham Common: Women at the Wire* [London: Women's Press 1984]): 24 (my italics; dots in original)

On 11 December 1983, fifty thousand women encircled the USAF Base at Greenham Common in England, reflecting it back on itself with mirrors; perhaps Miss La Trobe inspired this!

21. See also her diary for 22 September 1928: "And I felt this is the heart of England—this wedding in the country: history I felt; Cromwell; The Osbornes; Dorothy's shepherdesses singing: of all of whom Mr & Mrs Jarrad seem more the descendants than I am: as if they represented the unconscious breathing of England."

22. For example:

She was haunted by absurd jumbled ideas—how, if one went back far enough, everything perhaps was intelligible; everything was in common; for the mammoths who pastured in the fields of Richmond High Street had turned into paving stones and boxes full of ribbon, and her aunts. (*TVO*, 73)

Through all the ages—when the pavement was grass, when it was swamp, through the age of tusk and mammoth, through the age of silent sunrise—the battered woman . . . stood singing of love. (*MD*, 90)

See also Gillian Beer's excellent essay "Virginia Woolf and Pre-History," in Eric Warner, ed., *Virginia Woolf: A Centenary Perspective* (New York: St. Martin's Press, 1984). Beer writes that "the idea of origins and the idea of development are problematically connected in that of pre-history. And in the twentieth century the unconscious has often been presented in the guise of the primeval."

23. Compare the following:

"It's the burden of lies" she thought to herself, as she withdrew; "We carry the burden of lies."
Meditating on the burden deposited hundreds of years ago upon the shoulders of all of us, she did not stop to consider the particular case. (*Melymbrosia*, 14; see also *TVO*, 25)

A blankness came over her. Where am I? she asked herself, staring at a heavy frame. What is that? She seemed to be alone in the midst of nothingness; yet must descend, must carry her burden—she raised her arms slightly, as if she were carrying a pitcher, an earthenware pitcher on her head. (*TY*, 44-5)

"How am I burdened with what they drew from the earth; memories; possessions. This is the burden that the past laid on me." (*BTA*, 182)

24. Reading over Roger Fry's *Vision and Design* (London: Chatto & Windus, 1920) when preparing her biography, Woolf must have seen the fol-

lowing passage from Fry's "An Essay in Aesthetics," which explains the effect of framing:

> A somewhat similar effect to that of the cinematograph can be obtained by watching a mirror in which a street scene is reflected. If we look at the street itself we are almost sure to adjust ourselves in some way to its actual existence. We recognize an acquaintance, and wonder why he looks so dejected this morning, or become interested in a new fashion in hats—the moment we do that the spell is broken, we are reacting to life itself in however slight a degree, but, in the mirror, it is easier to abstract ourselves completely, and look upon the changing scene as a whole. It then, at once, takes on the visionary quality, and we become true spectators, not selecting what we will see, but seeing every-thing equally, and thereby we come to notice a number of appearances and relations of appearances, which would have escaped our vision be-fore, owing to that perpetual economising by selection of what impres-sions we will assimilate, which in life we perform by unconscious pro-cesses. The frame of the mirror, then, does to some extent turn the reflected scene from one that belongs to our actual life into one that belongs rather to the imaginative life. (19-20)

Selection was important to Woolf. Writing in her diary of her hopes for what would eventually be *The Waves*, she said:

> Waste, deadness, come from the inclusion of things that dont belong to the moment; this appalling narrative business of the realist: getting on from lunch to dinner: it is false, unreal, merely conventional. Why admit any thing to literature that is not poetry—by which I mean saturated? Is that not my grudge against novel[ist]s—that they select nothing? (*D*, 28 November 1928)

25. "Why leave out the British Army? What's history without the Army, eh?" he mused (*BTA*, 184).

26. Again uncannily, this idea is prefigured on the last page of Woolf's 1903 diary (the holograph manuscript of which is in the Berg Collection of the New York Public Library; apparently it is being edited for publication). She writes there of returning to "that particular act of our drama" which is life in London; although the actors may change, she says, the sameness of the scene lends a "certain continuity" to the whole.

27. For example:

> All passes, all changes, she thought, as she climbed up the little path between the trees. . . . Then, as she watched, light moved and dark moved; light and shadow went traveling over the hills and over the val-leys. A deep murmur sang in her ears—the land itself, singing to itself, a chorus, alone. She lay there listening. She was happy, completely. Time had ceased. (*TY*, 299-300)

28. This passage, marked "silence" in the margin, is from "[*BTA*] Type-script with author's corrections, unsigned, 2 April '38—July 30 '39 (earliest dated draft)" in the Berg Collection. I have cited the transcription from Mitchell A. Leaska, ed., *Pointz Hall* (New York: University Publications, 1983), 61-62, which differs from the typescript only in minor matters of punctuation.

29. See letter to Judith Stephen, 29 May 1940: "We're acting village plays; written by the gardener's wife, and the chauffeur's wife; and acted by the other villagers. Also we're doing this that and the other about an air-raid shelter" (*L*, 3610).

BIBLIOGRAPHY

Abel, Elizabeth, ed. *Writing and Sexual Difference*. Chicago: University of Chicago Press, 1982.

Alexander, Jean. *The Venture of Form in the Novels of Virginia Woolf*. Port Washington, New York: Kennikat Press, 1974.

Anscombe, Isabelle. *Omega and After: Bloomsbury and the Decorative Arts*. New York: Thames and Hudson, 1982.

Auerbach, Erich. *Mimesis: The Representation of Reality in Western Literature*. Berne: A. Francke, 1946. Translated from the German by Willard R. Trask. Princeton: Princeton University Press, 1968.

Bell, Clive. *Art*. London: Chatto, 1914. Reissued, 1920.

Bell, Quentin. *Virginia Woolf: A Biography*. 2 vols. *Virginia Stephen, 1882-1912*. London: Hogarth Press, 1973. *Mrs. Woolf, 1912-1941*. London: Hogarth Press, 1973.

Binswanger, Ludwig. *Being-in the-World, Selected Papers of Ludwig Binswanger*. Translated and with an Introduction to His Existential Psychoanalysis by Jacob Needleman. New York: Basic Books, 1963.

Buber, Martin. *I and Thou*. A New Translation with a Prologue "I and You" and Notes by Walter Kaufman. Edinburgh: T. & T. Clark, 1970.

Butler, Samuel. *Samuel Butler's Notebooks*. Selections edited by Geoffrey Keynes and Brian Hill. London: Cape, 1951.

Cassirer, Ernst. *The Logic of the Humanities*. Translated by C. S. Howe. New Haven: Yale University Press, 1960.

Chipp, Herschel B., ed. *Theories of Modern Art: A Source Book by Artists and Critics*. Berkeley: University of California Press, 1968.

Clements, Patricia, & Isobel Grundy, eds. *Virginia Woolf: New Critical Essays*. Totowa, New Jersey: Barnes & Noble Books, 1983.

Comstock, Margaret. "The Loudspeaker and the Human Voice: Politics and the Form of *The Years*." *Bulletin of the New York Public Library* 80, 2 (Winter 1977):252-75.

DeSalvo, Louise A. *Virginia Woolf's First Voyage: A Novel in the Making*. New York: Macmillan Co., 1980.

———"Sorting Sequencing, and Dating the Drafts of Virginia Woolf's *The Voyage Out*." *Bulletin of the New York Public Library* 82, 3 (Autumn 1979):271-93.

Eliot, T. S. *Four Quartets*. New York: Harcourt Brace Jovanovich, 1971.

Freud, Sigmund. *The Interpretation of Dreams*. [*The Standard Edition of the Complete Works of Sigmund Freud*, Vols. 4 and 5. Edited and translated by James Strachey in collaboration with Anna Freud. London: Hogarth Press and Institute of Psycho-Analysis, 1953-74.] Translated by James Strachey assisted by Alan Tyson; revised by Angela Richards. Harmondsworth: Pelican Books, 1977.

———— *Introductory Lectures on Psychoanalysis.* [*The Standard Edition of the Complete Works of Sigmund Freud*, Vols. 15 and 16.] Translated by James Strachey and Angela Richards. Harmondsworth: Pelican Books, 1973.

Fleishman, Avrom. *The English Historical Novel: Walter Scott to Virginia Woolf.* Baltimore: Johns Hopkins University Press, 1971.

———— *Virginia Woolf: A Critical Reading.* Baltimore: Johns Hopkins University Press, 1975. Reprint 1977.

———— "Woolf and McTaggart," *ELH*, 36 (1969):719-38.

Freedman, Ralph, ed. *Virginia Woolf: Revaluation and Continuity.* Berkeley: University of California Press, 1980.

Fry, Roger. *Vision and Design.* London: Chatto & Windus, 1920. London: Phoenix Library, 1928.

———— *Transformations; critical and speculative essays on art.* London: Chatto & Windus, 1927. Freeport, New York: Books for Libraries Press, 1968.

Ginsberg, Elaine K. and Laura Moss Gottlieb, eds. *Virginia Woolf: Centennial Essays.* Troy, New York: Whitston Publishing Co., 1983.

Gordon, Lyndall. *Virginia Woolf, A Writer's Life.* Oxford: Oxford University Press, 1984.

Graham, John. "The 'Caricature Value' of Paraody and Fantasy in *Orlando.*" *University of Toronto Quarterly* 30, 4 (July 1961):345-65.

———— "Point of View in *The Waves*: Some Services of the Style." *University of Toronto Quarterly* 39, 3 (April 1970):193-211.

Guiguet, Jean. *Virginia Woolf and Her Works.* Translated by Jean Stewart. London: Hogarth Press, 1965. New York: Harcourt Brace Jovanovich, 1976.

Harford, Barbara, and Sarah Hopkins, eds. *Greenham Common: Women at the Wire.* London: Women's Press, 1984.

Harper, Howard. *Between Language and Silence: The Novels of Virginia Woolf.* Baton Rouge: Louisiana State University Press, 1982.

Hartman, Geoffrey. *Saving the Text: Literature/Derrida/Philosophy.* Baltimore: Johns Hopkins University Press, 1981.

Heidegger, Martin. *Being and Time.* Translated by John MacQuarrie and Edward Robinson. Oxford: Basil Blackwell, 1962.

———— *Basic Writings from* Being and Time (*1927*) *to* The Task of Thinking (*1964*). Edited, with a general introduction and introductions to each section by David Farrell Krell. London: Routledge & Kegan Paul, 1978.

Iser, Wolfgang. *The Implied Reader: Patterns of Communication in Prose Fiction from Bunyan to Beckett.* Baltimore: Johns Hopkins University Press, 1974. Reprint, 1978.

———— *The Act of Reading: A Theory of Aesthetic Response.* Baltimore: Johns Hopkins University Press, 1978. Reprint, 1980.

———— "The Current Situation of Literary Theory: Key Concepts and the Imaginary." *New Literary History* 11, 1 (Autumn 1979):1-20.

Kelley, Alice van Buren. *The Novels of Virginia Woolf: Fact and Vision.* Chicago: University of Chicago Press, 1973.

Kenney, Susan M. "Two Endings: Virginia Woolf's Suicide and *Between the Acts.*" *University of Toronto Quarterly* 44, 4 (Summer 1975):265-89.

Kiely, Robert. *Beyond Egotism: The Fiction of James Joyce, Virginia Woolf and D. H. Lawrence.* Cambridge: Harvard University Press, 1980.

Laing, R. D. *The Divided Self.* London: Tavistock Publications, 1960. Harmondsworth: Pelican Books, 1973.

———*Self and Others.* London: Tavistock Publications, 1961. Harmondsworth: Pelican Books, 1976.

——— *The Politics of Experience and the Bird of Paradise.* Harmondsworth: Penguin Books, 1967. Reprint, 1974.

Langer, Susanne K. *Feeling and Form.* London: Routledge & Kegan Paul, 1953.

——— *Philosophy in a New Key: A Study in the Symbolism of Reason, Rite, and Art.* Cambridge: Harvard University Press, 1957.

Leaska, Mitchell A. *The Novels of Virginia Woolf From Beginning to End.* New York: John Jay Press, 1977.

———"Virginia Woolf, the Pargeter: A Reading of *The Years. Bulletin of the New York Public Library* 80, 2 (Winter 1977):172-210.

———"The Death of Rachel Vinrace." *Bulletin of the New York Public Library* 82, 3 (Autumn 1979): 328-38.

Lipking, Joanna. "Looking at the Monuments: Woolf's Satiric Eye." *Bulletin of the New York Public Library* 80, 2 (Winter 1977):141-45.

Macksey, Richard, and Eugenio Donato, eds. *The Structuralist Controversy: The Languages of Criticism and the Sciences of Man.* Baltimore: Johns Hopkins Unversity Press, 1970.

Macdonald, Hugh. *Skryabin.* London: Oxford University Press, 1978.

MacQuarrie, John. *Existentialism.* Harmondsworth: Pelican Books, 1973. Reprint, 1980.

McLaurin, Allen. *Virginia Woolf: The Echoes Enslaved.* Cambridge: Cambridge University Press, 1973.

Marcus, Jane. "*The Years* as Greek Drama, Domestic Novel, and Götterdammerung." *Bulletin of the New York Public Library* 80, 2 (Winter 1977): 276-301.

———"Pargeting 'The Pargiters,' Notes of an Apprentice Plasterer." *Bulletin of the New York Public Library* 80, 3 (Spring 1977):416-35.

———"No More Horses: Virginia Woolf on Art and Propaganda." *Women's Studies* 4 (1977):265-89.

——— ed. *New Feminist Essays on Virginia Woolf.* Lincoln: University of Nebraska Press, 1981.

——— ed. *Virginia Woolf, A Feminist Slant.* Lincoln: University of Nebraska Press, 1983.

———"Quentin's Bogey." *Critical Inquiry* 11, 3 (March 1985):486-97.

Marks, Elaine, and Isabelle de Courtviron, eds. *New French Feminisims: An Anthology.* Amherst: University of Massachusetts Press, 1980.

Mehlman, Jeffrey *A Structural Study of Autobiography: Proust, Leiris, Sartre, Levi-Strauss.* Ithaca: Cornell University Press, 1974.

Merleau-Ponty, M. *Phenomenology of Perception.* Translated by C. Smith. London: Routledge & Kegan Paul, 1962. Reprint, 1974.

———*Phenomenology, Language and Sociology.* London: Heinemann, 1974.

Middleton, Victoria S. "*The Years*: A Deliberate Failure." *Bulletin of the New York Public Library* 80, 2 (Winter 1977):158-71.

Miller, J. Hillis. "Virginia Woolf's All Soul's Day: The Omniscient Narrator in *Mrs Dalloway.*" In M. Friedman and J. Vickery, eds., *The Shaken Realist: Essays in Honor of F. J. Hoffman.* Baton Rouge: Louisiana State University Press, 1970.

————Introduction to Charles Dickens, *Bleak House.* Harmondsworth: Penguin Books, 1971.

Moore, G. E. *Principia Ethica.* Cambridge: Cambridge University Press, 1903. Reprint, 1980.

Naëss, Arnë. *Four Modern Philosophers: Carnap, Wittgenstein, Heidegger, Sartre.* Translated by A. Hannay. Chicago: University of Chicago Press, 1968.

Naremore, James. *The World Without a Self: Virginia Woolf and the Novel.* New Haven: Yale University Press, 1973.

Novak, Jane. *The Razor Edge of Balance: A Study of Virginia Woolf.* Coral Gables: University of Miami Press, 1975.

Parkes, Graham. "Imagining Reality in *To the Lighthouse.*" *Philosophy and Literature* 6, 1 & 2 (Fall 1982):33-44.

Pascal, [Blaise.] *Pensées.* Translated with an Introduction by A. J. Krailsheimer. Harmondsworth: Penguin Books, 1966. Reprint, 1979.

Poole, Roger. *Towards Deep Subjectivity.* New York: Harper & Row, 1972.

————*The Unknown Virginia Woolf.* Cambridge: Cambridge University Press, 1978.

Poulet, Georges. "Timelessness and Romanticism." *Journal of the History of Ideas* 15, 1 (January 1954):3-22.

————*Studies in Human Time.* Translated by E. Coleman. Baltimore: Johns Hopkins University Press, 1956.

————*The Interior Distance.* Translated by Elliott Coleman. Ann Arbor: Michigan University Press, 1964.

————*The Metamorphoses of the Circle.* Translated from the French by Carley Dawson and Elliott Coleman in collaboration with the author. Baltimore: Johns Hopkins University Press, 1966.

————"Phenomenology of Reading." *New Literary History* 1 (1969):53-68.

Richter, Harvena. *Virginia Woolf: The Inward Voyage.* Princeton: Princeton University Press, 1970.

Rorty, Amélie Oksenberg, ed. *The Identities of Persons.* Berkeley: University of California Press, 1976.

Rose, Phyllis. *Woman of Letters: A Life of Virginia Woolf.* New York: Oxford University Press, 1978.

Rosenbaum, S. P., ed. *English Literature and British Philosophy.* Chicago: University of Chicago Press, 1972.

———— ed. *The Bloomsbury Group: A Collection of Memoirs, Commentary and Criticism.* Toronto: University of Toronto Press, 1975.

Ruotolo, Lucio P. *Six Existential Heroes: The Politics of Faith.* Cambridge: Harvard University Press, 1973.

Sartre, Jean-Paul. *Being and Nothingness.* Translated and with an introduction by Hazel E. Barnes. New York: Pocket Books, 1943. Reprint, 1966.

Schlack, Beverly Ann. "Virginia Woolf's Strategy of Scorn in *The Years and Three Guineas.*" *Bulletin of the New York Public Library* 80, 2 (Winter 1977):146-50.

————*Continuing Presences: Virginia Woolf's Use of Literary Allusion.* University Park: Pennsylvania State University Press, 1979.

———— "The Novelist's Voyage from Manuscript to Text: Revisions of Literary Allusions in *The Voyage Out.*" *Bulletin of the New York Public Library* 82, 3 (Autumn 1979):317-27.

Sears, Sallie. "Notes on Sexuality: *The Years* and *Three Guineas.*" *Bulletin of the New York Public Library* 80, 2 (Winter 1977):211-20.

Showalter, Elaine, ed. *A Literature of Their Own: British Woman Novelists from Brontë to Lessing*. Princeton: Princeton University Press, 1977.

———ed. *The New Feminist Criticism, Essays on Women, Literature & Theory*. New York: Pantheon Books, 1985.

Silver, Brenda R. *Virginia Woolf's Reading Notebooks*. Princeton: Princeton University Press, 1983.

Spalding, Frances. *Roger Fry: Art and Life*. Berkeley: University of California Press, 1980.

Spilka, Mark. *Virginia Woolf's Quarrel with Grieving*. Lincoln: University of Nebraska Press, 1980.

Sprague, Claire, ed. *Virginia Woolf: A Collection of Critical Essays*. Englewood Cliffs, New Jersey: Prentice-Hall, 1971.

Steiner, George. *Language and Silence: Essays 1958-1966*. London: Faber & Faber, 1967. Peregrine Books, 1971.

———*Extraterritorial: Papers on Literature and the Language Revolution*. London: Faber & Faber, 1972. Peregrine Books, 1975.

———*Martin Heidegger*, New York: Penguin Books, 1980.

Stephen, Sir Leslie. *The Mausoleum Book*. Oxford: Clarendon Press, 1977.

Stewart, Jack F. "Existence and Symbol in *The Waves*." *Modern Fiction Studies* 18, 3 (Autumn 1972):433-47.

Tompkins, Jane P., ed. *Reader-Response Criticism: From Formalism to Post-Structuralism*. Baltimore: Johns Hopkins University Press, 1980.

Warner, Eric, ed. *Virginia Woolf: A Centenary Perspective*. New York: St. Martin's Press, 1984.

Wittgenstein, Ludwig. *Tractatus Logico-Philosophicus*. Translated by D. F. Pears and B. F. McGuiness with the introduction by Bertrand Russell, F. R. S. London: Routledge & Kegan Paul, 1978. Reprint of original 1921 edition.

Woolf, Leonard, *An Autobiography*. 2 vols. Oxford: Oxford University Press, 1980.

Woolf, Virginia. *The Voyage Out*. London: Duckworth, 1915. London: Hogarth Press, 1975.

———*Night and Day*. London: Duckworth, 1919. London: Hogarth Press, 1977.

———*Monday or Tuesday*. London: Hogarth Press, 1921.

———*Jacob's Room*. London: Hogarth Press, 1922. Reprint, 1976.

———*Mrs. Dalloway*. London: Hogarth Press, 1925. Reprint, 1976.

———*The Common Reader*. First Series. London: Hogarth Press, 1925. Reprint, 1975.

———*To the Lighthouse*. London: Hogarth Press, 1927. Reprint, 1977.

———*A Room of One's Own*. London: Hogarth Press, 1928.

———*Orlando*. London: Hogarth Press, 1928. Reprint, 1978.

———*The Waves*. London: Hogarth Press, 1931. Reprint, 1976.

———*The Common Reader*. Second Series. London: Hogarth Press, 1932. Reprint, 1974.

———*The Years*. London: Hogarth Press, 1937. Reprint, 1979.

———*Three Guineas*. London: Hogarth Press, 1938. Reprint, 1952.

———*Roger Fry*. London: Hogarth Press, 1940. New York: Harcourt Brace Jovanovich, 1976.

———*Between the Acts*. London: Hogarth Press, 1941. Reprint, 1976.

———*The Death of the Moth and Other Essays*. New York: Harcourt Brace Jovanovich, 1942. Reprint, 1976.

——*A Haunted House*. London: Hogarth Press, 1943.

——*The Moment and Other Essays*. New York: Harcourt Brace Jovanovich, 1948. Reprint, 1974.

——*The Captain's Death Bed and Other Essays*. New York: Harcourt Brace Jovanovich, 1950.

——*Granite and Rainbow*. New York: Harcourt Brace Jovanovich, 1958. Reprint, 1975.

——*Contemporary Writers*. London: Hogarth Press, 1965.

——*Mrs. Dalloway's Party: A Short Story Sequence*. Edited by Stella McNichol. London: Hogarth Press, 1973.

——*The Letters of Virginia Woolf*. 6 Vols. Edited by Nigel Nicolson; Joanne Trautman, assistant editor. London: Hogarth Press, 1975-80.

——*Moments of Being*. Unpublished autobiographical writings. Edited with an introduction and notes by Jeanne Schulkind. Sussex: University Press, 1976.

——*The Waves: The Two Holograph Drafts*. Transcribed and edited by J. W. Graham. London: Hogarth Press, 1976.

——*Books and Portraits*. Some further selections from the literary and biographical writings of Virginia Woolf. Edited by Mary Lyon. London: Hogarth Press, 1977.

——*The Diary of Virginia Woolf*. 5 Vols. Edited by Anne Olivier Bell. London: Hogarth Press, 1977-84.

——*The Pargiters: The Novel-essay Portion of "The Years."* Edited with an introduction by Mitchell A. Leaska. London: Hogarth Press, 1978.

——" 'Anon' and 'The Reader': Virginia Woolf's Last Essays." Edited, with an introduction and commentary by Brenda R. Silver. *Twentieth Century Literature* 25, 3 & 4 (Fall/Winter 1979): 356-438.

——*Melymbrosia. An Early Version of "The Voyage Out."* Edited with an introduction by Louise A. DeSalvo. New York: New York Public Library, Astor, Lenox and Tilden Foundations, 1982.

——*To the Lighthouse: The Original Holograph Draft*. Transcribed and edited by Susan Dick. Toronto: University of Toronto Press, 1982.

——*Pointz Hall: The Earlier and Later Typescripts of "Between the Acts."* Edited, with an introduction, annotations, and an afterword by Mitchell A. Leaska. New York: University Publications, 1983.

INDEX